L H M C 1785-1985

The story of the London Hospital Medical College

England's first Medical School

by

Sir John Ellis

MBE MA MD (Cambridge) Hon MD (Uppsala) FRCP

Assistant to the Dean 1947, Sub-Dean 1948-1958, Vice-Dean 1967,
Dean 1968-1981
Senior Lecturer LHMC 1948-1951
Physician to the London Hospital 1951-1981

The College main building in 1985.

CONTENTS

F. REYNOLDS, 15, OLD BROAD S^T. LONDON.

Preface

The London Hospital Medical College, the first complete medical school in England, opened on Thursday 27th October 1785. In the 200 years since then it has produced some 20,000 doctors and dentists. Through its staff and students it has cared for many thousands living in or within reach of the East End of London, and, through its alumni, cared for countless thousands more around the world. Its teachers have made major advances in medicine and dentistry. In addition, and this perhaps is its greatest claim to fame, it has made a unique contribution to the development of medical and dental education in Britain and in those other countries which, in things medical and educational, share a common heritage with us. Yet its story has never been told - which is why the Council of the London Hospital Medical Club deputed me to write this history.

The story falls into three parts. The first covers almost a hundred years, from the foundation in the eighteenth century to 1879. Throughout that period the College remained a private educational institution, able to use the London Hospital but independent of it. Run by the Body of Associated Teachers (who later changed their title to the Medical Council of the London Medical School) it pioneered a new kind of medical education, creating the prototype of what were to become known as the Hospital Medical Schools of London.

In 1879 the Council signed an agreement with the Governors of the London Hospital, merging the two organisations, subject to termination by twelve months notice in writing from either side. The partnership continued for almost seventy years during which the hospital-based vocational training of general practitioners was brought to a peak.

The third period began with the Medical Act which created the National Health Service, incorporated the London Hospital into it, and in 1948 established the school as a College of the University of London. In this period of nearly 40 years up to the Bicentenary of 1985, medical education has had to adapt to the revolution which has been taking place in medicine in these past fifty years, and to social changes of equal magnitude. In the nineteen-fifties the College contended with difficulties of every kind. In the sixties the Dental School was rebuilt and enlarged, and began the reshaping of dental education. In the seventies the medical entry was increased and the academic staffing necessary for the new kind of undergraduate course was built up. The process of providing the equally necessary buildings and facilities began, but was delayed and not completed until the early eighties - while the College also faced the rationalisation of University and Health Service occasioned by medical, social, educational and economic changes.

The changes in medical education for which the College has been re-equipped and restaffed are not yet complete and the rationalisation of the three University Colleges in East London is still (some 17 years after it began) unfinished. In some ways therefore this is not an ideal time at which to write a history of the College - but at almost any time some reason can be advanced for not writing the history of an institution.

The end of the first 100 years of the College called for some kind of publication and indeed there was one. In 1888 there was produced 'by order of the Medical Council' a 'History of the Medical College' and a 'History of the Medical Council, Medical and Surgical Staff and College Board'. The first gives an account of the premises - the original College building of 1785; the new, bigger and resited school of 1854 - and the expansion and modernisation amounting to a total rebuilding, which began in the centenary year of 1885 and was completed by 1887. The second records the management of the school, its relationship with the hospital, and the long, delicate and difficult negotiations which culminated in the union of the two in 1879. Neither, however, describes the courses given in the College or relates its activities to those of other schools.

The second world war followed hard on the 150th Anniversary of the College and coincided with the 200th Aniversary of the Hospital. It was more a time for making history than for writing it but in 1958 the Governors of the London Hospital commissioned the late Dr A E Clark-Kennedy on his retirement to write the history of its first 200 years. He devoted the next five years to the task and his two volumes entitled 'The

London, A Study in the Voluntary Hospital System' tell not only a fascinating story but surely comprise one of the greatest hospital histories ever written. From them a picture of the College emerges but it is seen through hospital eyes. In the early years it is not seen clearly because hospital and College were separate institutions. The hospital records of the London make little reference to the activities of the medical school in contrast to those of other eighteenth century hospitals in which medical schools were gradually created by the hospital governors themselves. At the London the governors did not formally and officially recognise the existence of the school till 1837 by which time it was over 50 years old.

Nearly another fifty years were to pass before hospital and college came together and, as elsewhere in London, were run as one - a process which Archie Clark-Kennedy describes as the relationship of school and hospital being 'regularised and put on a satisfactory footing at last'. In so far as the relationship achieved in 1879 was the same as elsewhere in London and in so far as it was a highly satisfactory one at that time, both descriptions are accurate. Nonetheless it was the independence of the College over the previous century which resulted in its making a unique and very important contribution to the development of medical education.

The history of a teaching hospital necessarily includes descriptions of the place of students, the actions taken to meet their needs, and the roles they have played in the work of the hospital over the years. There is, however, no place in it for more consideration of medical education than that. A history of a medical college, on the other hand, while it must necessarily include a picture of medical care in general and of the hospital with which the college is connected in particular, would be sadly lacking if it did not outline the interaction between the college and the educational thinking of the times or indicate the forces to which it has responded.

This history of LHMC therefore is an account of its staff and students over the past 200 years set against the foreground of medical education in London, the middle distance of medical education in England and the background of medical education in Britain, which has always differed from that in most other countries. Seen in that way certain features stand out. The College was founded to improve medical education not, like most schools in London, to provide students to work the wards. Its students and staff were nonetheless at once involved in maintaining service in a hospital engaged in meeting a more desperate need than almost any other in the country, but even so the betterment of medical education remained the aim of the College for 200 years. Perhaps for that very reason, although it has had it share of those content to keep it as they found it or even to use it for purposes of their own, it has in every generation attracted some who have combined devotion to it with vision and the determination to put the essential timeless trinity of service, education and research on an even better footing.

None such left the College as they found it. Its story is one of constant change in search of an unchanging ideal. Just how that has affected the product is more difficult to tell. Does it account for the fact that in 1958 the Gazette could record over thirty Old Londoners working in missions overseas? Is there some special characteristic which tells the world a man or woman has been at the London ? Can you tell a Londoner anywhere ? Londoners do not commonly exhibit a sense of superiority engendered by a knowledge of what the London Hospital Medical College has contributed to medicine, dentistry or education. But each generation seems to go through life glad to have been at the London and convinced that there is something special, though indefinable about it.

Whatever that something is it undoubtedly began with William Blizard, 'Surgeon, Scientist and Philanthopist', who told students 'let your search be always after truth' and gave the London its motto 'Humani nihil a me alienum puto.' Down the years since then it has captured, motivated and been augmented by innumerable others - like Jonathan Hutchinson, the first Dean, who wished to be remembered as 'a man of hope and forward-looking mind': and Sidney Holland, second Viscount Knutsford, described on the memorial in the front hall of the London as 'a friend of all manner of men'.

Undoubtedly too that same awareness of something special about the London motivates the man responsible for this history of the College being written - John Blandy, Professor of Urology and Chairman of the London Hospital Medical Club who himself wrote that section of the book which brings the College to life in terms of the people - students, their teachers and their patients - whom most Londoners of today have known personally. Others have helped - notably Jonathan Pepler, Archivist to Hospital and College, who simplified the task of studying the records of the

House Committee, the Medical Council of the London Medical School and the College Board; and the College Librarian, P S Hockney, who gathered in histories of most other medical schools in Britain. But the driving force, kindly but relentless, came from John Blandy whose unquenchable enthusiasm and boundless energy (typing endless drafts himself) alone ensured the completion of this book in the spare moments of one year of an all too busy retirement. All errors, of omission and commission, like all the opinions expressed, are mine but the inspiration came from him and those earlier remarkable men and women of the College who made it what it is and in whose footsteps we are proud to tread.

John Ellis
Woodford Green
8 May 1986

This history of LHMC is dedicated to those who are not mentioned in it - the wives and families with whose help so much of what is recorded was achieved, especially Joan Ellis and Anne Blandy.

PART I

THE INDEPENDENT SCHOOL

Chapter 1.

The Foundation

i

The London Hospital Medical College, England's first complete medical school, opened in the Whitechapel Road alongside the London Hospital on Thursday 27th October 1785 - nine years after the American Declaration of Independence, three years after that independence was finally recognised and four years before the fall of the Bastille. Its origins lay in the determination of one man to improve medical education at a time when the need for more and better medical care was desperate.

Enclosures and better methods of farming had much increased the production of food and helped to lower the death rate, but had begun the movement of the rural population into towns. Industry too was moving into the cities as steam became a source of power in manufacture. The coal and iron age was on its way and the industrial revolution about to begin. Disease was rife especially in towns where poverty, malnutrition, overcrowding and primitive living conditions all contributed to infection. Injuries were common. London, consisting of little more than what is now Westminster and the City, contained one tenth of the total population.

Medical knowledge had been growing slowly and the practice of physicians surgeons and apothecaries had been improving ever since the spirit of enquiry had been reawakened in the Renaissance. But despite major advances, like Harvey's discovery of the

Bethnal Green in 1773.

circulation of the blood, and despite more recent developments in the basic sciences, medicine still had little rational basis. It remained 'a system of diagnosis based on history-taking, a system of pathology based on pure theory, and a system of treatment which attempted to counter the theoretical causes of disease and to relieve symptoms ' (1). Physical signs, other than the appearance of the face, excreta, and blood removed by venesection, were totally ignored. Symptoms were all that concerned those with medical qualifications and the untrained and unqualified quacks who greatly outnumbered them. None, save the surgeons, could do much to alter the course of disease and all were equally powerless to prevent it. Yet medical care was much in demand and such help and comfort as could be given was limited by inadequate and unsatisfactory training.

In most of Europe medical education was firmly in the hands of universities, as it had been for five centuries. University degrees ranging from baccalaureates to doctorates conferred licences to practice and teach, under supervision or without restriction. The duration of courses varied from place to place; up to four years for a first degree and six or more for a doctorate. Faculties varied also in the development of university chairs. Paris, for example, at one time had only two: one for 'natural and unnatural things' (anatomy, physiology, hygiene and dietetics) and one for 'things against nature' (pathology and medical subjects) (2). But by the 18th century, most faculties had chairs of anatomy, medicine, surgery and numerous other subjects. Teaching was almost entirely by lectures - usually in Latin. Schools were small in the eighteenth century and in the best of them only some twenty students would enter each year. Hospitals were plentiful but although the continental universities had always had access to hospitals, clinical teaching had been uncommon until the early 1700s when Boerhaave introduced it in Leiden along with the idea of a structured curriculum, beginning with the study of the normal, advancing to the abnormal, and on to clinical studies. Other universities followed, notably Vienna and Edinburgh.

In England the situation was very different. From early times the two universities, Oxford and Cambridge, had offered degrees in Medicine, but the course was mainly in the humanities with officially some practice in dialectics, and included no clinical medicine. Surgery was specifically excluded. From the dissolution of the monasteries in the sixteenth century there were almost no hospitals anywhere until nearly the middle of the eighteenth century, except for two of the old monastic institutions in London (St Bartholomew's and St Thomas's) which had been reopened in response to public pressure in 1547 and 1553 respectively and Bethlem, which had been provided for the care, or at any rate, the custody, of the insane.

Medical practitioners remained firmly divided into three distinct orders, physicians, surgeons and apothecaries, each with different functions and separate preparations under the control of the relevant professional body. Surgeons were trained by apprenticeship to a master surgeon for seven years, usually from the age of fourteen, and licensed by the Company of Surgeons. Apothecaries served an apprenticeship before being licensed by the Society of Apothecaries. A licence to practice as surgeon or apothecary could also be obtained through the Church - a Bishop's licence granted after an oral examination by a physician or surgeon - and anyone who had served in the armed forces in a medical capacity for three years could set up in civilian practice without any examination at all.

A licence to practice as a physician in England could be obtained by passing the examination for licentiate of the Royal College of Physicians of London, admission to which was, by the eighteenth century, virtually restricted to those who had obtained the MD degree of Oxford or Cambridge, or obtained an MD elsewhere which had been incorporated by Oxford or Cambridge. A majority of physicians preferred to study abroad. No specific period of clinical practice was required before taking the LRCP and no great knowledge of clinical medicine was demanded.

So English medical education differed very much from that of other countries. It had developed with little influence from universities or hospitals and was controlled by professional bodies which examined but did not teach, were all situated in London but had nothing to do with each other. At the best a surgeon or an apothecary had years of practical experience under a single master but next to no theoretical teaching, while a physician received (in England) a very theoretical course which had little relevance to medicine followed by a brief experience of clinical practice. Perhaps in consequence English medicine developed particular national characteristics, placing great importance on the care of the individual patient, engaging little in experiment and being generally opposed to it but contributing to knowledge by careful observation of sick people leading to the description and classi-

London in 1751 as depicted by Hogarth.

fication of disease.

During the eighteenth century, however, in England as everywhere else, old ideas began to be challenged in to every aspect of human activity including medicine. Apprentices of surgeons or apothecaries, especially in London and other cities, began to seek more theoretical instruction. Critics of the university preparation of physicians began to campaign for compulsory 'attendance at some public hospital, which ought to be the finishing school of the clinical physician (for) men should not be sent raw into the world, to form their own experience at the hazard of men's lives' (3).In most cities physicians and surgeons began to give lectures, mostly in anatomy, often combining to run a small private tutorial establishment. Then, most important of all, people in England, moved by the growing need of the poor for medical care and perhaps a little anxious as to what might happen if their desperate needs were not met, began to found hospitals.

ii

In London the Westminster Hospital was founded in Petty France in 1720, Guy's was opened in 1724 in conjunction with and next door to St Thomas's, which was then in Southwark and had recently been rebuilt by public subscription, St Bartholomew's was rebuilt by public subscription in 1730, St George's opened at Hyde Park Corner in 1733, the London Hospital in the City in 1740 and the Middlesex near its present site in 1745. Hospitals were founded in most other cities. Addenbrooke's Hospital was opened in Cambridge in 1766 and the Radcliffe Infirmary in Oxford in 1770.

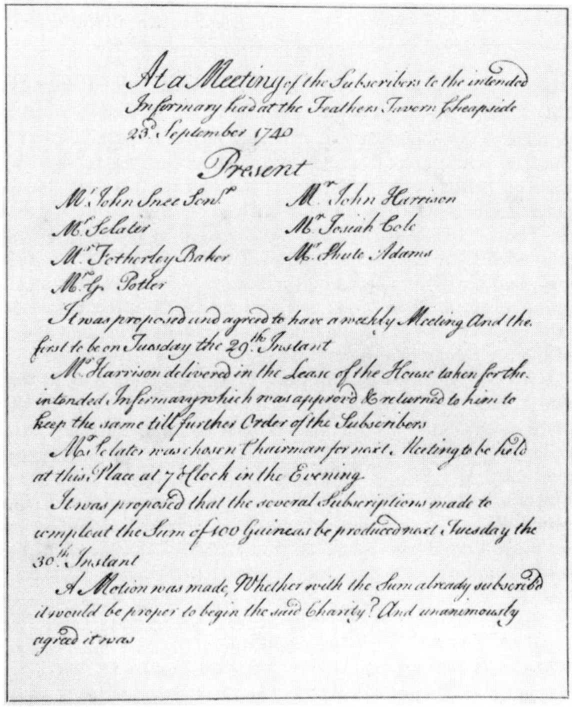

At a Meeting of the Subscribers to the intended Infirmary had at the Feathers Tavern Cheapside 23d September 1740

Present

Mr John Snee Senr — Mr John Harrison
Mr Sclater — Mr Josiah Cole
Mr Fotherley Baker — Mr Shute Adams
Mr G. Potter

It was proposed and agreed to have a weekly Meeting And the first to be on Tuesday the 29th Instant

Mr Harrison delivered in the Lease of the House taken for the intended Infirmary which was approved & returned to him to keep the same till further Order of the Subscribers

Mr Sclater was chosen Chairman for next Meeting to be held at this Place at 7 o'Clock in the Evening

It was proposed that the several Subscriptions made to compleat the Sum of 100 Guineas be produced next Tuesday the 30th Instant

A Motion was made, Whether with the Sum already subscribed it would be proper to begin the said Charity? And unanimously agreed it was

The birth of the London Hospital.

Each hospital, whether founded by an individual or a group, was established as a Charity to provide help for as many of the sick poor as possible and was wholly dependent on voluntary subscriptions and endowments. The Governors of each Charity, many of whom paid their annual subscriptions so as to secure hospital admission for their work-people were mainly and often exclusively laymen. They ran the hospital through a House Committee which decided what kinds of conditions should be treated. Most of the hospitals were small but expanded rapidly. There were for example 30 beds in the London Hospital's first building in Featherstone Street in the City, separated from the Honourable Artillery Company by a small but convenient burial ground. Within a year it was moved to Prescott Street in the shadow of the Tower of

An artist's impression of the new hospital to be built in Whitechapel; painted by William Bellers in 1752, engraved by Chatelain and Toms.

London and before long had 100 beds, and almost at once the Governors made plans to erect a purpose-built hospital outside the city. When this opened in Whitechapel in 1758 its 160 beds were quickly filled without transferring the patients from the old building.

The pattern of staffing was everywhere the same. The House Committee employed as many people to act as nurses and porters as they could afford, none of whom had any training. They also employed an apothecary who was resident and responsible for conducting minor medical or surgical treatments under the direction of a very small number of visiting physicians and surgeons, who were elected by ballot amongst all the governors. Neither physicians nor surgeons received any payment for their hospital work but surgeons might be allowed to bring an apprentice and in most hospitals surgeons, and later physicians, were allowed a few dressing pupils to attend them for upwards of a year, and a limited number of other pupils were allowed to walk the wards. Apprentices paid a lump sum to their master on signing their indentures. Dressing pupils paid a fee to the surgeon. Those who walked the wards paid a fee to the hospital. Luke Coleridge (later to go into practice near Exeter where he died aged 24) joined the London Hospital on 5th October 1784. His younger brother, the poet Samuel Taylor Coleridge, used to visit him.

'Every Saturday I could make or obtain leave, to the London Hospital trudged I. O bliss, if I was permitted to hold the plasters or to attend to the dressings. I became wild to be apprenticed to a surgeon' (4).

Thus the new hospitals quickly added an extra dimension to English medical education as would-be physicians, surgeons and apothecaries sought to augment their practical experience in them and get what teaching they could from the staff. The governors of the charities however were none too keen on the teaching which might well distract the staff from the care of patients and, as much of it would be on anatomy, could lead to problems in regard to dissection. House Committees therefore were naturally interested in students but not in medical education. They permitted lecturing in the hospitals only with reluctance and careful reservations. So formal medical teaching, by lectures and demonstration of dissection, continued to develop mainly outside the new hospitals in the homes of physicians or surgeons or in houses taken for the purpose and run as private schools. The best known of these was started in Great Windmill Street by John Hunter in 1768. Anatomy was also taught in the Hall of the Barber-Surgeons Company, and after they parted company, in Surgeons' Hall.

So in mid-eighteenth century London, the London of Hogarth, in a world full as always of wars and rumours of wars, but seething with new ideas, in a country excited by religious revival, new agricultural policies and the utilisation of steam, the student of medicine could find new opportunities but no medical school. To get the best of what was available each had to complete his university course or his apprenticeship, spend a relatively short period in hospital, and attend such lectures in other places as he could afford.

iii

One such student was William Blizard, born at Barns Elms in Surrey in 1743, fourth of the five children of an auctioneer (5). He was apprenticed to a surgeon and apothecary in Mortlake and then became assistant to a surgeon in Crutched Friars. He also attended lectures on Chemistry by William Saunders at Guy's, on Surgery by Percivall Pott at St Bartholomew's, on Anatomy by John Hunter at St George's, and spent a year as a dressing pupil at the London attached to Henry Thompson, the first surgeon in England successfully to perform an amputation at the hip. He passed the examinations of the Corporation of Surgeons in 1772.

Blizard was a tall man with clear-cut features, a strong personality, and great energy: a man of integrity with firm religious convictions. By all accounts he was always kind and considerate of individuals, especially those in trouble and must have found surgery a strain in the absence of any anaesthetics. Yet he is recorded as being discriminating and decided in his clinical judgement and as an operator 'remarkably cool and determined, never losing his presence of mind' (6). He seems quickly to have built up a large and successful practice and he remained an active surgeon up to the age of 84. He was innovative, though not fascinated by technical or scientific advances, and he was driven by a highly developed and never-satisfied social conscience.

Sir William Blizard, FRS, PRCS aged 61 by John Opie, engraved by Reynolds.

Philanthropist, reformer, and initially, something of a rebel, he was concerned with everything that had to do with the betterment of mankind. He also wrote poetry - or at any rate, verse - but there any resemblance to a dreamer ended. His approach to reform was essentially practical, like his surgery: not much discussion, quick but discriminating decisions, and cool determined action.

As a newly qualified surgeon there was not much Blizard could do about many of the things that concerned him: the need for infant schools, sunday schools, care of chimney-sweeps, prison reform, and some kind of police force. But he wrote articles, always forceful, under the pseudonym 'Curtius' for the Middlesex Chronicle of Liberty, and joined the London Military Foot Association - a group of gentlemen volunteers who drilled in Fishmongers' Hall preparing themselves to combat crime and civil disobedience. Medicine, however, was another matter. He gained an appointment at the Magdalen Hospital, established in the London's old building in Prescott Street, joined forces with a Dr McLaurin to run a medical tutorial school in Thames Street and later on in his own home in Mark Lane, and became a Governor of the London Hospital. As a member of the House Committee and as a visitor he delved into every aspect of hospital life, frequently criticising and constantly making suggestions, on the food and drink, on ventilation, on the reading of prayers, on showing respect for the dead.

When Henry Thompson, his old master, died in 1780, leaving a vacancy for a surgeon at the London there could not have been many governors who did not know William Blizard. On the day of the election 516 governors balloted, and 107 noblemen, Members of Parliament and Ladies voted by proxy. Blizard was elected by a majority of 212 (7). He was 37. The American War of Independence was in full swing and the colony already had three medical schools - the College of Philadelphia, King's College in New York, and William and Mary College.

There is no evidence that any of Blizard's colleagues whom he joined on the staff of the London were particularly interested in teaching. The senior surgeon, Richard Grindall FRS was by then in his late sixties. He was reputed to be an excellent surgeon, a great oddity but a perfect gentlemen in his appearance and manner, never seen by any accident but in a well-powdered wig, silk stockings and silver buckles. It was written of him

> *'No surgeon better loved himself,*
> *He loved old rum and brandy*
> *As much as misers do their wealth*
> *Or children, sugar candy' (5).*

Of George Neale, the second surgeon, nothing is known except that he was appointed to the London in 1753 and was 60 when Blizard joined the staff.

The senior physician, Thomas Dickson FRS was then in his late fifties. As might be expected of a physician born in Dumfries and educated at Edinburgh and Leiden, he was, as the monument to him in St Mary's Whitechapel declared: 'a man of singular probity, loyalty and humanity, kind to his relations, beloved by all who knew him, learned and skilled in his profession, unfee'd by the poor, he lived to do good and died a Christian believer.'

Obviously a nice man, and apparently a very good Greek scholar, but not one to found a medical school; though the only person to be admitted LRCP on the same day with him in 1765 - John Morgan - went straight home to America and helped to found the medical school of the College of Philadelphia (8). If Thomas Dickson had been equally keen, England might have had a medical school before her colony. As it was, he died in 1784, a year before the London school opened. He was replaced by John Cooke (also a graduate of Leiden and Edinburgh) after an election notable for the amount of ballot-rigging by his opponent who, like himself, had been a preacher before taking up medicine.

Dickson would not anyway have been likely to get much support from the London's second physician - Thomas Healde FRS, MD Cambridge and FRCP, elected to the London in 1770. He was busy. Before election to the London he had been Censor of the College of Physicians, and had given the Goulstonian Lectures and the Harveian Oration. After election he was censor for a second time, was the Croonian Lecturer on four occasions and the Lumleian Lecturer three times. He was also Gresham Professor of Physic, the first to get permission to marry. In view of his remarkable propensity for lecturing it is perhaps not altogether surprising that he died in very reduced circumstances leaving his family to the care of the Royal College who voted them £100 (8).

Blizard's remaining colleague was James Maddocks, appointed physician to the London a few months after Healde in 1770. He was born in Herefordshire and took his MD at Edinburgh in 1762. The only portrait of him shows a slightly built young man, with a bright face and a lively, humorous, rather quizzical expression, his dark hair covered by a neat short powdered wig. His appearance contrasts with that of Blizard but the latter was painted at a much older age. Maddocks, sadly, died in 1786 and there is little recorded of his achievements except for one - he was one of the two founders of the London Hospital Medical College.

iv

The physician who had been to a university which made a feature of clinical teaching in hospital joined forces with the surgeon who had augmented his long years of apprenticeship with lectures in three different hospitals and a year's dressership at the London. The first recorded evidence of their efforts is a paper in 1783 'On the Expediency and Utility of Teaching the several branches of Physic and Surgery at the London Hospital and for erecting theatres for the purpose.'

Dr James Maddocks, co-founder of the College.

It outlined the advantages which would accrue to the hospital if teaching were encouraged and developed. It was signed by both, Maddocks' name first, but perhaps because he was a Doctor of Medicine. It was addressed to the Governors of the London Hospital from whom Blizard had resigned on appointment to the staff, asking them to finance the project which it was thought would cost £600. It was suggested that a public appeal be made and that all who contributed £30 should be made Life Governors of the Hospital. The Governors considered this petition on 5th February 1783 and turned it down, just as governors of other hospitals were to turn down similar petitions on the grounds that whatever funds they could acquire should go to the care of the sick and not to medical education.

They were not, however, unsympathetic to the idea of attracting students. They were in a different position to the Governors of other hospitals, not merely because they had been under the powerful influence of the reforming Blizard for some years, but more importantly because the London Hospital differed from any other by being situated in the countryside. The bold decision to move out from the dirty overcrowded City of London with its total lack of sanitation into purpose-built premises in Whitechapel had brought many advantages but it had one drawback. It was not so easily reached by physicians and surgeons who after their daily visits had to get back, by horse or carriage, to their own patients in the City on whom they depended for most of their income - and it was even more inaccessible to the apprentices and dressing pupils on whom they depended for the rest. The Governors of the London therefore had more reason than others to do something to attract students who, besides helping to attract staff, might themselves help to care for patients. Moreoever unlike any other Governors they had land to spare, having wisely bought far more of the (relatively cheap) countryside of Whitechapel than they could immediately use. So led by the Chairman of the House Committee, Mr Lipstrap, they did what no other Governors could so easily have done even had they seen the need. They offered the use of land, adjoining the hospital on the east side fronting the Whitechapel Road, and gave Blizard and Maddocks permission to build on it provided they could find the money, and that whatever teaching went on in the building cost the hospital nothing, that hospital patients were not used for demonstration purposes and that no students would enter the hospital without permission of the House Committee, and then only through a side gate so as not to clutter up the front hall.

V

Blizard and Maddocks immediately decided to build not a lecture theatre but a complete medical school and to raise the money by an appeal to the public. On 12th August 1783 they published their appeal entitled: 'An address to the friends of the London Hospital and of Medical Learning' Signed James Maddocks MD, William Blizard, Surgeon.

A copy remains in the British Museum - the first and one of the shortest, most explicit and readable of the many Recommendations for the reform of medical education for which this country is now famous.

In brief it states that medicine is important to mankind, that its quality depends on good medical education, that: 'skill in the practice of Physic or

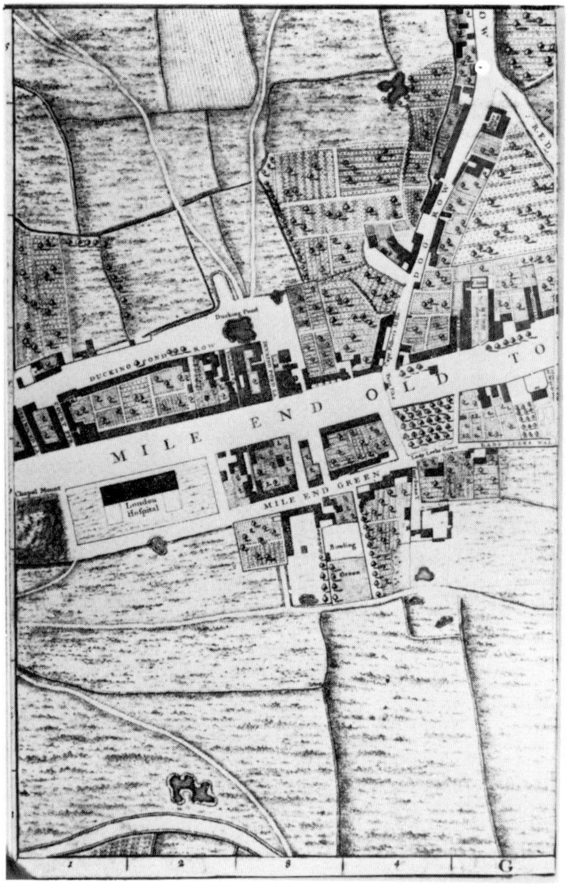

Whitechapel in 1761 from Roque's map of London.

Surgery cannot be acquired without an attendance at an hospital. But that degree of skill which can be acquired from an attendance on hospital practice, without a proper knowledge of principles, as it is the result of mere imitation, must be comparatively very small. It is necessary therefore that principles be studied.

A ſkill in the practice of Phyſic or Surgery cannot be acquired without an attendance at an hoſpital. But that degree of ſkill which can be acquired from an attendance on hoſpital practice, without a proper knowledge of principles, as it is the reſult of mere imitation, muſt be comparatively very ſmall. It is neceſſary therefore that the principles be ſtudied.

From the appeal by Maddocks and Blizard for funds to build the College, 1783.

'But the principles of Physic and Surgery cannot be taught but by means of Lectures publicly read. The experience of learned men from the beginning of Science to the present time, has proved this to be the only true and effective method of instruction. By means of these, the several discoveries that have been made respecting any art or science are properly brought together and preserved and new ones constantly added, which, otherwise, might in time be lost and forgotten.

'But lectures on the principles and practice of Physic and Surgery cannot confidently with the advantage of the student respecting his improvement, be properly given in any other place than the hospital which he attends. If he is obliged to go to distant places to hear lectures, he thereby every day consumes much time, to students extremely precious; and also must neglect his business at the hospital. '

The logic was clear and compelling and remains as true today as when it was written, though since then the experience of learned men has led some, but by no means all, to believe that lectures, publicly read, are not the only effective means of instruction, or at any rate of education.

Those, said Maddocks and Blizard, were some of the reasons why it had been 'judged proper that lectures on the different branches of Physic and Surgery should be read at the London Hospital, the situation of which (then in the green fields of Whitechapel) as being remote from places of dissipation, is uncommonly well calculated for a medical school. '

They went on to outline other reasons, pointing out that teaching raises the standard of care in a hospital, and that students (and their Address must be the earliest in which the apprentices and pupils of medicine are referred to as students) can be of great help to patients.

Interestingly they made no reference to the fact that the kind of school they aimed to create had long existed in many other countries, rightly assuming no doubt that it would not increase the attraction of their appeal to the English public. But they stated they had obtained leave from the Governors of the London Hospital to erect by subscription a building which would be a valuable addition, but no cost, to the Hospital, that work on it was 'in great forwardness' and if the response were good, would open in a month. They added the names of some fifty persons who had already promised a total of £500.

They added one other very practical reason for a medical school - one likely to appeal to the public. They pointed out that humane officers of His Majesty's Navy had given evidence to the Surgeons' Company that: 'in the beginning of the late war (against France and America) numbers of our brave sailors experienced severely or fatally, the effects of the ignorance and unskilfulness of persons too indiscriminately admitted as Surgeons in the Navy.'

They proposed that in order 'as fully as possible to answer the important intention of qualifying young gentlemen for the Service of His Majesty's Navy, and that contracted circumstances may not be a barrier against the pretentions of genius, merit and industry' constantly to allow a certain number of students to attend gratis, provided 'they shall be bona fide either in, or intended for the Service of the Navy. '

The promised £500 was within sight of the original estimate of £600 but that had been merely for a lecture theatre and the 'proper conveniences' of a medical school included also a museum, library and chemical laboratory. The total cost was nearer £2000 and some of the money came out of their own pockets. The School was not of course ready by September 1783.* Building took two more years before England's first complete medical school opened on 27 October 1785. There is no record that at any time in the next 200 years it provided free training for those in, or intended for, service in the Royal Navy. Perhaps no one lacking the necessary funds but with clear pretentions of genius, merit and industry ever came forward with such a career in mind.

vi

Honour and gratitude are due to both Blizard and Maddocks though there is no doubt that Blizard's reforming zeal, vision and determination were the deciding factors. Both took part in the opening ceremony on Thursday 27th October 1785. According to the Gentleman's Magazine and Historical Chronicle this took the form of 'four introductory orations delivered before a splendid auditory: 1. By Dr Harwood on the utility of Physic in General (Busick Harwood

The original building of the medical school alongside the London Hospital in the Whitechapel Road.

* The lecture theatre was completed first and was probably in use by 1783. A silver cup passed on to the London by Viscountess Dawson of Penn bears the inscription: 'To Busick Harwood MD, FRS, with great Deference and regard from the pupils of the London Hospital as an expression (though small and inadequate) of the Gratitude for his exertions in the Cause of Medical Science on every occasion particularly on that of the erection of Theatres there and for his generous labour in giving them a Course of excellent Lectures on Botany, June 2nd 1783 - Amor Unit Plantas.' Busick Harwood came as a student to the London on 14th January 1772 at the age of 27. He had previously gone out to India as a licensed surgeon and apothecary and amassed a small fortune. He gave generously to Blizard's appeal and proposed an approach to the principal people in Calcutta and to British Subjects in East India. He left the London for Cambridge in 1783, took his MB in 1785, later became Downing Professor of Medicine and was knighted in 1806.

the surgeon had by now become physician). 2. By Dr Healde on the first principles of the Science and on the liberal practice of it in opposition to quackeries; of which he opposed the danger. (He like Harwood spoke in Latin). 3. By Dr Maddocks on the particular excellence of the institution of the London Hospital, and 4. By Mr Blizard, Surgeon of the Hospital, who enlarged on the numerous benefits which could not fail to result from the maturity of the present plan; a plan conceived in benevolence, executed in the most eligible (way), and settled, he trusted, on the most solid basis; an illustrious monument to the sensibility and munificence of Englishmen.'

> He congratulated the publick and metropolis, his worthy coadjutors, in carrying on this liberal deſign; the governors of the hoſpital, and human nature at large, on the numerous benefits which could not fail to reſult from the maturity of a ſcheme thus conceived in benevolence, executed the donations of good and ſettled, he truſted on the moſt ſolid baſis, an illuſtrious monument to the ſenſibility and munificence of Engliſhmen.

Excerpt from Blizard's speech at the opening of the College, from the Gentleman's Magazine in 1785.

The same night the event was celebrated by a banquet at the Albion Tavern in Aldersgate Street at which was performed an Ode to the Occasion written by Blizard and set to music by Dr Samuel Arnold, organist to Westminster Abbey. It had previously been rehearsed at the London Tavern by a 'Band of Musick' conducted by Dr Arnold. Blizard, who even in his eighties could reputedly recite the whole of Gray's Elegy, was inclined to mark important events with verses of his own. Unfortunately his poetry lacked the sure swift touch that characterised his surgery. This ode began:

'Hail the return of this auspicious day !
Now let the grateful, gen'rous heart record,
In heartfelt strains, how Providence befriends,
This seat of commerce and benevolence !
In this fam'd city dwells such social love
As smiles alone in climes of liberty'

It ended, some verses later, with the suggestion that the foundation of the College was an example which could be profitably followed elsewhere:

'Britons ever famed for sense,
Famed for sweet benevolence,
With the genuine voice of praise
Noble emulation raise' (8).

Blizard maintained that the opening of the College was the greatest event in his life which apart from his marriage, more than half a century of surgery, Fellowship of the Royal Society, a Knighthood, and two periods as President of the Royal College of Surgeons, was full of excitement. He was born in the year of the Battle of Dettingen - the last time an English King led his troops into action in person, and was two years old when Bonnie Prince Charlie made his unsuccessful bid to regain the throne. As a schoolboy he may have taken Clive's victory at Plassey pretty much as a matter of course, and at the start of his apprenticeship may not have paid much attention to Wolfe's capture of Quebec. The surrender of Cornwallis at Yorktown and subsequent independence of America, the year after he joined the staff of the London, may have seemed matters best forgotten. He certainly took note of the French Revolution and the Napoleonic Wars. He treated survivors of the Battle of the Nile in the London. When the London Military Foot were disbanded, after he had turned out with them in the Gordon riots in 1780 and treated the wounded, he became surgeon to the Honourable Artillery Company for nearly 10 years but when invasion threatened, he left them and the London, and while the emergency lasted became Lieutenant Colonel Blizard in Command of the 6th Regiment of London Local Volunteers. So Trafalgar and Waterloo must have seemed important to him, but not apparently, in the same class as the London Hospital Medical College. He was not one to stand aside from the conflicts of his time or to belittle the importance of great victories or defeats but he was, first and foremost, a reformer.

Today, when medical schools are an accepted though costly necessity, when developed countries are still adding to their number and a medical school ranks with a seat in the United Nations and a National Airline as a manifestation of independent Sovereignty, it is difficult to appreciate how brave and audacious an enterprise it was in 1785 to collect money from the public and build the first School in England. In the context of that time it was a great achievement and Blizard's pleasure in it and his warm gratitude for the public support which made it possible shine through the flowery wording of his Ode. Similarly his desire to improve medical education, his conviction that medical schools were the way to do it, and his confidence in the rightness of his plan for a London Hospital Medical College, ring out clearly in the report of his address on the opening day.

Within a year of the foundation James Maddocks died but Blizard led and nurtured the College for nearly fifty years. It was not his only creation. He founded or helped to found a number of other orgnaisations and institutions which still survive - the Samaritan Society, the Royal College of Surgeons of England, the Anatomical Society, the Horticultural Society, the London Institution in Finsbury Square (a forerunner of the Polytechnic) and the Hunterian Society. To all of them he devoted thought, time, his vast energy and sometimes funds from his far from vast private means. To some of them, or to any one of a number of other interests, he could have devoted himself entirely but nothing, not even the Presidency of the College of Surgeons nor the offer of a Chair at Guy's, diverted him from the continuing care of his Medical College.

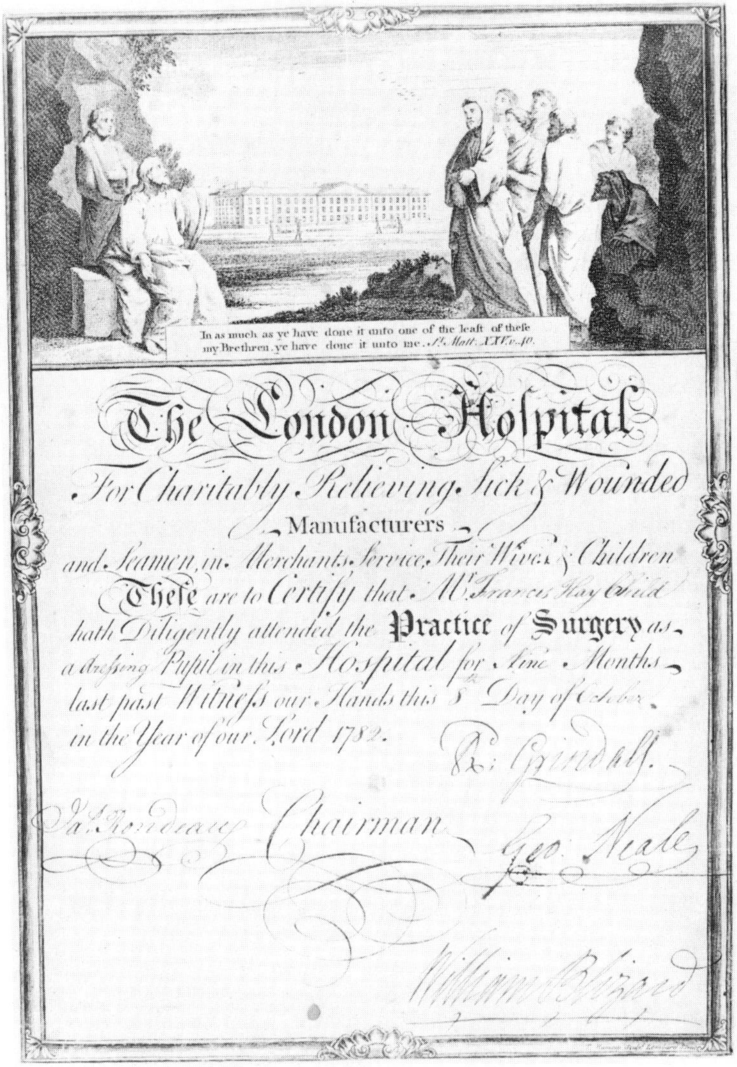
In as much as ye have done it unto one of the leaft of thefe my Brethren, ye have done it unto me. St. Matt. XXV. v. 40.

The London Hospital
For Charitably Relieving Sick & Wounded
Manufacturers
and Seamen in Merchants Service, Their Wives & Children
These are to Certify that Mr. Francis Hay Child
hath Diligently attended the Practice of Surgery as
a dressing Pupil in this Hospital for Nine Months
last past Witness our Hands this 8 Day of October
in the Year of our Lord 1782.
R. Grindall.
Jas. Rondeau Chairman
Geo. Neale
William Blizard

A hospital certificate of 1782, the drawing at the top by Hogarth.

Chapter 2.

The Pioneers 1785-1835

i

The College began as an independent privately owned educational institution but differing from the many other private tutorial establishments of the time in three ways. It was not, as some of them were, founded to make a profit but to improve medical education. Secondly, the improvement sought was defined in a clear statement of objectives, the most important being to provide an opportunity for principles and practice to be learned together. Thirdly facilities for teaching in all subjects were made available next door to the hospital in which clinical experience could be gained and many of the teachers were on the staff of both school and hospital. No other private school could offer the same.

There was however no formal link between school and hospital and throughout the first fifty years they maintained a symbiotic relationship without any kind of open recognition or formal agreement. For almost all that time Blizard remained on the staff of both. He retired at the age of 91 in 1834 and died a year later. In 1837 the Governors of the London Hospital recorded for the first time their formal acknowledgement of the existence of the College.

There is no reference in the minutes of the Governors to the opening of the school in 1785. There is no record of Blizard, or anyone, seeking permission to call the school the London Hospital Medical college. Perhaps it was thought better not to ask lest the answer be in the negative as it might well have been. Not that the London's Governors were particularly opposed to medical education. They were well aware that, from the hospital's point of view, there was much to be said for a medical school alongside the hospital, provided it did not cost them anything. They had made it possible by offering the land on which it was built. But they made sure that the work of their hospital was not impeded in any way by it. The use of patients for teaching had to be carefully controlled and every effort had to be made to ensure that physicians and surgeons on the hospital staff lectured in their own time and not during the hours when they should be tending patients in the hospital to which the Governors had appointed them. As that could be done much more easily by dealing with their own medical officers individually than by entering into formal arrangements with another institution, it was better to avoid public acknowledgement of the school's existence.

During the first fifty years of the school therefore there are no references to it in the records of the hospital. There are references to students who for one reason or another came to the notice of the House Committee usually for some kind of misbehaviour, including the 'borrowing' of hospital equipment, incompetent handling of a clinical procedure such as blood-letting, and once the performance of a post-mortem without official sanction. But there are little or no references to teaching. The school's records over the same period are very scanty. Some legal agreements remain - covering matters such as new staff buying a share in the property or the division of lecture fees. Maybe careful records were kept of meetings dealing with educational policy and the like which have since been lost because when, after nearly 100 years, school and hospital amalgamated, they were of no immediate use or importance. Maybe no minutes were kept. Maybe there were no meetings on such issues.

There were not in fact a large number of important issues to decide. The College could not offer degrees nor a licence to practice any of the three medical professions. There were a limited number of subjects relevant to medicine as a whole and having decided to offer teaching in all of them it was a matter of deciding who was to teach what, and when, and what share of the total receipts for lecture fees each lecturer would receive. The great issue which confronts every new medical school today, what kind of a curriculum is it going to offer, did not arise in 1785.

Eighteenth century students aimed to be either physicians, surgeons or apothecaries. It was possible to become both a surgeon and an apothecary, but impossible for a surgeon to become a physician unless he first renounced, on payment of a fee, his surgical licence. Each student completed only those courses of lectures and that attendance in hospital required by the licensing body of the particular profession he was preparing to enter. Though the requirements differed, all were very undemanding and in terms of medical knowledge and skill were minimal.

The aim of the preparation of a physician was in reality the production of a cultured gentleman, hence the university course (mainly in classics and the humanities), with a sufficient introduction to medicine to allow him to learn more from experience during his professional life-time. No specific period of hospital attachment was required to take the oral examination, in Latin, for the licence to practice in London. It enquired little into medical knowledge and the examination for the licence to practice outside London enquired even less. Neither included reference to anything surgical.

Surgeons were not required to study medicine. In 1785 only a course in Anatomy, another in surgery and a short hospital attachment were needed in addition to the apprenticeship in order to take the viva voce examination of the Company of Surgeons. Up until 1815 nothing more than an apprenticeship was necessary before taking the examination of the Apothecaries Hall. Some surgeon-apothecaries practised as such without an apothecaries' licence.

The requirements for licences have of course to be viewed in the light of the limited medical knowledge of the time. Even so they were patently less demanding than they could and should have been. Reform was urgently needed and had Blizard set out to change the licensing regulations he would no doubt, with his determination to improve medical education, have had some success but it was not in his nature to engage in that kind of reform which required years of battling, through diplomacy and political in-fighting, against numerous conflicting vested interests. He was a man of action, a pragmatist, determined to demonstrate by his own efforts the improvements that could be made within, and despite, the current context of rules and regulations. Just as, no doubt, some surgeons and apothecaries saw their apprentices as something more than a pair of hands to be used until the period of their indentures ran out, and did their best to give them a professional training - and just as some physicians and surgeons aimed to give inspiring and enlightening lectures - so Blizard set out to create an entirely new

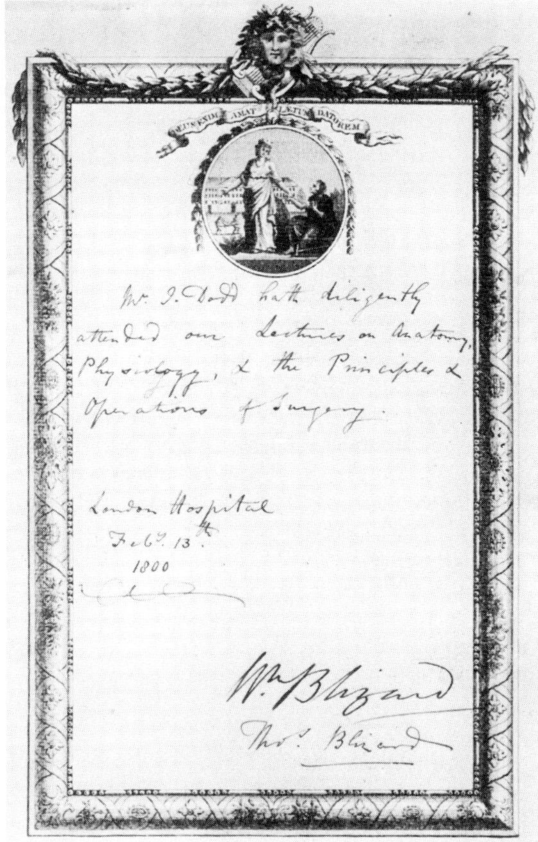

A College Certificate of 1800

educational facility, a complete medical school, in which the best possible clinical training could be combined with the most stimulating lectures possible in all subjects.

ii

The licensing requirements themselves did not in fact prevent any would-be physician, surgeon or apothecary from learning more than the minimum they demanded. Many physicians sought for more clinical experience than was asked of them, often going abroad to get it. Surgical apprentices too sometimes attended lectures in non-required subjects. All, however, faced a financial barrier. Medical education was not cheap in the eighteenth century. In fact it was relatively more expensive in terms of what the English student or his parents had to pay, than at any time since. Lecture fees were appreciable, even in the new medical school at the London where they were paid to the school rather than to the individual teacher who could charge whatever he could get. Walking the wards meant a fee to the hospital in return for which there was no teaching and virtually no chance of any clinical practice. Dressing pupils, like apprentices, paid the individual to whom they were attached and the cost was high. Apothecaries charged least and Physicians most. The latter perhaps had little to teach, for their main stock in trade was wisdom which is not easily taught. But the support of a well-known physician would count for more in later life than any number of certificates of attendance at lectures - and to become a physician offered if not a fortune, at least a chance to climb, though not far, up the social scale. The cost of medical education at the end of the seventeenth century has been estimated at £1000 to become a physician, £120 to become a surgeon and £50 an apothecary (1). By 1785 these costs were much higher - on top of which came board and lodging for five or more years of apprenticeship.

The medical student as envisaged by the public in the late nineteenth century — Bob Sawyer drawn by Phiz from the description by Charles Dickens.

Few of those who entered medicine came from wealthy families. Physicians and surgeons were usually the sons of professional people who, though well off, were not rich. Apothecaries were drawn more often from the families of shop-keepers and craftsmen. Even so medical students 200 years ago and for some time after, were regarded as a distinctly disreputable group, at a time when society as a whole was far from refined. It has been claimed that Dickens in his characterisation of Bob Sawyer and Ben Allen, far from exaggerating, 'was whitewashing over the physical dirtyness, and completely eliminating all allusion to what would have been the first thing to strike an observer, the foul-mouthedness, indecency, callousness and cynicism of the originals'(1). The general courseness is thought greatly to have increased at the time students first began to come together in groups to study anatomy and attend dissections. At the same time, it is claimed, teachers began to exhibit equal courseness in their teaching, in order to gain the attention and favour of their students and 'drive home the meaningless facts of anatomy' (1).

In fairness it should be remembered that being a medical student at the end of the eighteenth century, and after, was not much fun. Apprenticeship, in or out of hospital, to surgeon or apothecary, meant years of long hours of work performing the most menial tasks, frequently under unpleasant conditions, and always at risk of contracting some possibly fatal contagious disease. Lectures had to be fitted in early in the morning or late in the evening. In 1792 Blizard's lectures on Surgery were given at 7.0 pm on Saturday evenings (9). Lectures were seldom intellectually stimulating. For the most part they were dogmatic and the context strictly utilitarian. Whatever the subject there was nothing on the science itself or on the scientific method it exemplified but merely those aspects related to current, or more likely, recent, prescribing habits or surgical practice.

Walking the wards meant little more than the words imply. Attachment to a hospital physician, or being the dressing pupil of a surgeon offered a much greater chance to learn and in the latter case to practise the care of patients, to help with or perform operations. But there was no real attempt to instruct and none at all to incite the student to think for himself or develop his mental processes. The fantastic range of physical signs that must have abounded in every ward went unnoticed by staff and students alike. So far as practical classes were concerned dissecting a corpse snatched from a grave must have been off-putting in the winter and unbearable in the summer. All in all the student's lot was not a happy one, even if in order to help both his own and his master's finances, he lived in the latter's home. He shared little social life with his fellows and there was none of the camaraderie which can be so enjoyable and important a feature of life in a medical school.

Blizard's medical school was intended, by providing an opportunity to learn both principles and practice in the same place at the same time, to create a new environment for medical students in which they could study together, acquire clinical competence and professional attitudes by caring for patients under the supervision of teachers who set high standards, and in which they could be stimulated to learn more than the licensing regulations required of them.

iii

Although he took the trouble to define his objectives before starting the medical school, it is extremely unlikely that Blizard ever called together those who, whether on the staff of the London or not, agreed to join in the school with him, in order to discuss what are now called curriculum planning and teaching or educational methods. In the context of the time the former was impracticable and everything that is known about Blizard suggests that he believed, completely and instinctively, that the way to teach medical students was by example.

By all accounts he was a poor lecturer but revered as a teacher. John Cooke, elected physician to the London in 1784, described him as being 'most happy and appearing to greatest advantage in the wards... the aptness and vivacity of his remarks, and his ready tact in directing the attention of his students to the leading points in the cases under his care, rendered his visits at all times instructive '(6). The description could be applied to so many clinical teachers in more recent times that it is difficult to appreciate how extraordinary and novel such teaching was two hundred years ago.

John Abernethy, Blizard's pupil who was later responsible for developing the medical school at St. Bartholomew's, told vividly how Blizard sought not merely to teach surgery or medicine in a wider sense but to develop the intellects and influence the attitudes of his students.

'My warmest thanks are due to him for the interest he excited in my mind towards those studies and for the excellent advice he gave to direct me in the attainment of knowledge. "Let your search be after truth" he would say, "be eager and constant. Be wary of admitting propositions as facts before you have submitted them to the strictest examination. If after this, you believe them to be true, never disregard or forget one of them. Should you perceive truths to be important, make them the motives of action, let them serve as springs to your conduct. Many persons acknowledge truth with apathy: they assent to it, but it produces no other effect on their minds"' (10).

Such efforts to inspire, guide and uplift were remarkable in the eighteenth century and they were made by an active surgeon who was teaching both surgery and anatomy - especially that very practical functional anatomy on a knowledge of which the speed of surgery depended at a time when there was no anaesthesia. In the educational terminology of today Blizard's teaching was integrated and relevant, but it was by no means limited to vocational training. Apart from the attempt to make students think for themselves, it endeavoured to develop professional attitudes and set high professional standards, as Abernethy also records:

'He contrived by various means to excite a degree of enthusiasm in the minds of his pupils. He displayed to us the beau ideal of the medical character. I cannot tell you splendid and brilliant he made it appear - and then he cautioned us never to tarnish its lustre by anything that wore even the semblance of dishonour. He caused the sentiment of the philanthropic Chreames to be inscribed on the walls of the Hospital Surgery, that we students should have constantly before us an admonition to humanity drawn from a reflection of our own wants: "Homo sum, humani nihil a me alienum puto"'(10).

The quotation from Terence, most commonly translated as 'I am a man and all human calamities come home to me,' has remained the motto of the London Hospital and College ever since.

Abernethy was describing Blizard in his early days but there is nothing to suggest that he ever changed his attitude or that his enthusiasm and zeal ever diminished in the 49 years he inspired and fashioned the school he had started. Five years before his death the Lancet published a letter criticising Headington (a surgeon at the London recently elected President of the College of Surgeons) and Blizard for opposing its editor's campaign to restrict the office of coroner to those with medical qualifications. Thirty-eight students of the London wrote back in protest ending their letter ' We cannot refrain from noticing... the hostile feeling... against the venerable Sir Wm Blizard, and in reply...

we would sincerely wish that every member of our profession may possess the same soundness of mind and intellect still developed in Sir William's character, proving "if this is eve, how great the morn hath been"'. It was perhaps unfortunate that the students put Sir William's age as five years older than he actually was, but they obviously thought he was in good shape and held him in both respect and affection.

Blizard in later years, by William Clift.

His example must have made even more impact than his actual teaching. For many years he did more of the surgical work of the London than anyone else, in addition to his busy and successful private practice. At his last operation, at the age of 84, his hand is reputed to have been as steady as at any time in his life. He was the first to ligate the arteries to an overactive thyroid (applying Hunter's experiments on the antlers of deer) and one of the first to tie the subclavian artery for the then common axillary aneurysm.

In other fields of activity his example was no less striking but more unusual. He founded, served for many years as Treasurer, and helped finance out of his pocket, the Samaritan Society to support patients returning from hospital to destitute homes and to supply them with such necessities as clothes, spectacles and artificial limbs. His determination to leave the field of education better than he found it was shown as much by founding the London Institution in Finsbury Square, not to mention the Anatomical and Horticultural Societies, as by founding the Medical College. The many changes for which he was responsible in the London Hospital, ranging from morning and evening prayers (and weekly services) in every ward to more space between the beds, were evidence of both his firm religious convictions and his pragmatic good sense. He approved of formality and exactness of speech (as witness his reprimanding a student for referring to 'gangrenous intestine' as 'rotten gut'). He was 'punctilious on points of etiquette and exceedingly courteous to younger members of the profession'(6). He was also frequently unpunctual and athough he resigned from the Horticultural Society because he thought its fêtes and public breakfasts out of place in a scientific society, he was much in favour of social gatherings for the staff and students of a hospital. 'No man entered with greater ardour into these functions which engender kind feelings and promote co-operation...the happiness he felt imparting itself to others and often giving a high zest to these convivial occasion', recorded John Cooke (6).

iv

Few students and still fewer staff can have failed to be influenced by Blizard in the first fifty years of the Medical College, not least because at a time when many people were advocating reform in most walks of life, he actually achieved it by his own efforts. It is inconceivable that he did not have the major say in deciding who should join the 'Body of Associated Teachers' who ran the College or that he did not seek people with aims similar to his own. It is difficult to imagine that he would not have rated the ability to demonstrate a high standard of medical care as a more important criterion in choosing a teacher than the ability to teach well. He would have been quick to realise that in the kind of practical school he was creating a second rate physician or surgeon could, if he were a brilliant teacher, easily perpetuate a low standard of practice. It is equally certain that whenever a vacancy occurred on the staff of the London Hospital he would have wanted to see it filled by a member of the school staff, and there is ample evidence that on many occasions this is exactly what happened.

Clark-Kennedy in his history of The London notes that by the end of its first fifty years 'the Medical School had supplied the hospital with many of the distinguished members of its staff' (7). Of the surgeons junior to Blizard no less than four were to become, like himself, Presidents of the College of Surgeons: Richard Headington, John Goldwyer Andrews, James Luke and Thomas Blizard Curling. The last three had all been students at the College, though only one is known to have been a Lecturer in it before appointment to the Hospital. Physicians, however, contributed as much to the development of the school in the first fifty years as the surgeons - some of them in particularly important ways.

John Cooke, who had been appointed physician the year before the College opened and had become a great admirer of Blizard, resigned from the hospital in 1807. He continued in practice however, wrote an important book on nervous diseases, was active in the College of Physicians, became FRS and an active Governor of the London Hospital. In 1816 he became Chairman of the House Committee and remained so until 1822. During that time two portions of the hospital estate were somewhat unwisely sold, including that on which **St Philips Church** (later to be rebuilt as St Augustine's with **St Philips**) was built, but Cooke's support of Blizard ensured a hospital administration sympathetic to the school.

Some physicians of the period are better known for their activities outside the London than in it. One, James Gordon, founded and edited the 'Quarterly Journal of Foreign Medicine and Surgery'. Another was Isaac Buxton, who founded the Royal Hospital for Diseases of the Chest. Another was John Yelloly who played a major part in founding the Medical and Chirurgical Society which became the Royal Society of Medicine. But more important to the development of medical education in the College were two who were appointed physicians to the hospital in 1822.

Archibald Billing, appointed in July 1822, was a graduate of Trinity College Dublin, tall thin and commonly attired in a blue coat, primrose yellow waistcoat and trousers of 'Oxford mixture' (5). He was one of the founders of the Royal Microscopical Society and practised mainly in the theatrical world. According to the Medical Circular (11) his practice was not extensive, 'that is to say his chariot wheels have never been set on fire by the rapidity of their revolutions'. But he was extremely partial 'to horse exercise and may be seen shaking his joints with a jog trot on the back of a sure-footed nag which he treats with

Dr Archibald Billing, FRS, who first organised a system of teaching at the bedside in London.

characteristic benevolence.' This amiable Irishman who published 'First Principles of Medicine' in 1831, became an FRS in 1844 and dedicated his book on 'The Science of Gems, Jewels, Coins and Medals Ancient and Modern' to Queen Victoria in 1867 (and was as fond of music and painting), was the first in London to organise a system of practical teaching at the bedside and to give it full effect by regular clinical lectures. His efforts to foster practical instruction at the London were, records Munks Roll of the Fellows of the Royal College of Physicians, 'indefatigable' (8).

Thomas Davies was born in Carmarthen and came as a student to the London where his uncle was the apothecary. He went into practice in the Mile End Road, got tuberculosis and went to Montpellier for treatment. He recovered and went to Paris where he studied with Laennec who was writing his thesis on the stethoscope at the time. Davies took the MD Paris in 1820 and returned to London where he was the first to lecture on auscultation and the use of the stethoscope. 'On the recommendation of Dr Billing, an additional office was created for him at the London Hospital, that of assistant physician to which he was elected on 5 December 1822 ' (8).

So Blizard's colleagues over the first fifty years of the school included a number as imaginative, creative and energetic as himself.

Dr Thomas Davies who died of pulmonary tuberculosis at the age of 47 after introducing the stethoscope into practice in London.

V

A register of students attending the London has been kept since 1741, first by the hospital and then by the College. It shows that the latter was well attended from the start and that its students came from all over the country. It does not give a precise picture of all they did or exactly what courses each attended. Hospital records confirm, however, that students were attached to each physician as clinical clerks and that each surgeon had six in-patient dressers and additional students in the out-patient departments. Dressers were on duty from 9.0 am to 2 pm and again from 6.0 to 9.0 pm. A tendency to leave the wards 'on the pretext of attending lectures' soon led to the appointment every three months of a senior student as House Surgeon, living in and supported by a few other senior and junior students who lived in on rotation for one week at a time.

Probably in the first twenty or thirty years after the College opened, the majority of students at the London, although they had more variety of teaching available to them, actually took advantage of no more than that taken by students visiting other hospitals. They did however enjoy far better facilities for both learning and teaching and received a different kind of attention. In addition soon after the school opened, before any kind of structured curriculum took shape, a kind of corporate spirit emerged, in response perhaps to the fact that their teachers themselves were joined together in the 'Body of Associated Teachers'. As early as 1792 the Regulations of the Anniversary Dinner of the Gentlemen Educated at the London Hospital were agreed by students and staff. At the first dinner there were nine medical officers (including Blizard), four medically qualified governors of the hospital, nineteen former pupils, twelve present pupils, and one apprentice. The assembled company of 47 drank 19 toasts - in Lisbon, Sherry, Brandy, Punch and Strong Beer. Old Londoners' dinners (out of which arose the London Hospital Medical Club) have been held ever since, except during two world wars, and sometimes twice a year. At the most recent, in the Bicentenary of 1985, fewer toasts were drunk, but over two thousand seven hundred attended from all parts of the world.

The 'atmosphere' of a medical school has a considerable effect on the extent to which, and the ways in which, students respond to the opportunities offered for education and training. Perhaps the most important factor in deciding the atmosphere is the attitude of staff, individually and collectively, to students and their education. Blizard's attitude is well-known and must have influenced that of the Body of Associated Teachers, the very existence of which ensured that teachers felt, as a group as well as individuals, a responsibility to students. Staff-student relationships ceased to be solely that of master and apprentice and included recognition that both were members not only of the same profession but also of the same school.

The atmosphere of the London Hospital Medical College very soon became one to which students might well respond by taking more of the opportunities available than the minimum necessary to obtain a licence. This by itself could in time have led to some students at least beginning to follow a 'curriculum' which included a grounding in the subjects basic to medicine as a whole and a fairly wide clinical experience - a process of internal reform of exactly the kind Blizard had founded the school to achieve. In reality, however, the process was greatly expedited by an external reform with which he was not, so far as is known, in any way connected - the Apothecaries Act of 1815.

The livelihood of Apothecaries, dependent on making

up and selling drugs, was threatened by the large number of untrained and unlicensed competitors. They responded by attempts to seek the right to prescribe as well as dispense, and to make improvements in their training and system of licensure. Help was requested from the Physicians and Surgeons and efforts were made to reform the regulations governing all three professions. More opposition than help resulted, though both the Physicians and Surgeons tightened up their own licensing requirements to some extent. Nonetheless in 1815 the Apothecaries Act was passed extending the legal function of licensed Apothecaries into the care of the sick, leaving the preparation and sale of drugs gradually to become the function of Pharmacists. The Act set up a Register of Apothecaries, entry to which depended on passing examinations after completing a course which included five years apprenticeship, six months attendance in hospital, and lectures on anatomy, physiology, chemistry, materia medica and medicine. Botany and midwifery were added soon after.

The Act led to the eventual evolution of general practitioners and its effects on the pattern of delivery of medical care were far-reaching. Its effects on medical education were more immediate. It made the Apothecaries the most popular branch of the professions, causing the Physicians and Surgeons to tighten up their own training still further, and it greatly increased the number of students needing a period of training in hospital together with lectures in a wide variety of subjects. It did not of course have any immediate impact on how they were taught, but educational methods are usually influenced more by internal reform, such as that which the London Hospital Medical College was achieving, than by the regulations of external bodies.

From 1815 more and more students were wanting just what the College had to offer and even as they did so, Archibald Billing was indefatigably organising 'a system of practical training at the bedside and giving it full effect by regular clinical lectures'. At the same time Thomas Davies began to teach auscultation with the stethoscope and develop, more quickly than in Paris, an entirely new interest in physical signs. As morbid anatomy advanced and more was learned of what went on inside the body, the importance of the outward physical signs of internal disorder grew rapidly. The reform of medical education was firmly interlocked with a revolution in medicine itself. Medical students, not least because they were learning

Apothecaries' Hall.

Barber-Surgeons' Hall.

the new medicine in advance of the main body of practitioners, were soon to become indispensable to charity hospitals seeking to make the new medicine available to the sick poor.

vi

By 1835 and the fiftieth anniversary of the College there had been laid down in it the basis of that general, integrated but clinically orientated, vocational in-service training in hospital for which England, and especially the Hospital Medical Schools of London, were to become renowned. As yet, however, the others were still evolving, students receiving only such teaching as the Governors of the other hospitals permitted, with such facilities as the Governors saw fit to provide. At the Middlesex, the Westminster and St George's evolution had been slow, teaching being permitted only on certain days of the week. At the Middlesex little was demanded anyway because the Great Windmill Street School of the Hunters was close by and there was no call to do more than allow its students to walk the wards or attend as dressing pupils. At the Westminster the staff had repeatedly shown interest but the Governors had been firm, denying their surgeons 'liberty to take any cub, or cubs, or receive any fee or reward for admitting any persons to the practice of the Infirmary, their apprentices excepted' (12). The staff made various efforts to start a school but even in 1834 when they took a house in Dean Street the Governors declined to support it or allow it to be called the Westminster. At St George's a Medical School Committee was allowed consisting of all the Honorary Staff of the Hospital with power to coopt annually up to seven others for the period of one year - and financial management was in the hands of the hospital House Committee (13).

At St Thomas's and Guy's, the United Hospitals next door to each other in Southwark, lectures on some subjects were permitted in one and on other subjects in the other. Not until 1825 was this union (recently revived) dissolved and a separate school emerged at Guy's. At St Bartholomew's John Abernethy, who as a student at the London had so admired Blizard, pressed the Governors relentlessly from the time of his appointment as assistant surgeon in 1787. 'If any man can be named as the founder of the medical school at St Bartholomew's that man is John Abernethy' (14). A lecture theatre was in use on the hospital site in 1795 and a wide range of subjects taught. In 1825 the Governors built a new theatre and generally encouraged more teaching though insisting that the teachers must, except for the lecturer in midwifery, be selected from the Medical Board of the Hospital. Even at this time however the students were left pretty much to themselves. 'No reading room was provided, so the pupils made for themselves a club, and took a small room over a baker's shop where they could sit and read' (15).

Medical schools emerged too in a similar fashion outside London, in Manchester in 1824, in Birmingham in 1825, and then in Sheffield, York, Leeds, Newcastle, Bristol, Liverpool and Exeter. The pattern varied between a private tutorial establishment or a multi-faculty College such as Owens College in Manchester or Queens in Birmingham arranging links with a major hospital in the same city, to the pattern more common in London of hospital governors gradually allowing and even encouraging more teaching within it. As the need of students for attendance in hospital increased so the private tutorial schools began to fade and the hospitals took over.

By 1825 of course the situation was very different to what it had been in 1785. It was becoming clear that the students were not just a means of providing physicians and surgeons with some financial recompense for attending hospital, but themselves an extremely valuable means of providing medical care at no more cost to the hospital than that of maintaining a few facilities for them. It was more important than it had been previously for the hospital authority to control any medical school. Hospitals were glad to respond to the pressure of 'Old Londoners' like Abernethy and build up something of the kind of school that had been created at the London so long as it was not independent. They would have tried to do so, in response to the change taking place in medicine, quite irrespective of whether the London Hospital Medical College existed or not. Whether, if it had not existed, they would have succeeded in the way they did is, however, open to question.

The industrial revolution which was bringing advances of many kinds and wealth to the country as a whole, though leading to appalling overcrowding and poverty in the cities, was also creating a new middle class with a new interest in and concern for education. The need for a university in the capital was felt by many, but pressed first by those who wished to see one free of the religious retrictions on entry which applied to the old ecclesiastic foundations of Oxford and Cambridge. The outcome was the group calling themselves the Proprietors of London University who formed a joint stock company, bought land in Gower Street and in 1826 opened their institution there with courses in various subjects including medicine. Students were quickly attracted from the Great Windmill Street School and arrangements made for them to have clinical experience half a mile away in the Middlesex Hospital. London now had the possibility of a university medical school similar to those which had existed for so long in Scotland and Europe. Had the new London University been granted a charter and gained the right to confer degrees, medical education in London might have taken a very different course.

The granting of a charter, however, met with powerful opposition, not least from medicine in London. There is no record of the views expressed by the London Hospital Medical College but 'The Humble Petition of the Physicians and Surgeons of St Bartholomew's Hospital and of the Lecturers in its Medical School to the Honourable House of Commons against granting a Charter to the London University with the Power of conferring Medical Degrees' was explicit. It ended 'Your Petitioners confidently trust that your honourable House in its wisdom will not sanction the scheme of the Proprietors of the Institution called the London University, which would place the superintendence of Medical Education in the hands of a joint stock association founded and supported by money subscribed in shares which may be bought or sold in the Market like those of other Speculative Undertakings and which from Documents published by the Shareholders themselves it is proved that the London University is devoid of that stability which should be required of any institution soliciting such important and exclusive privileges' (14).

The petition did not mention the effect a university able to confer medical degrees might have on either the petitioners themselves or on St Bartholomew's Hospital, but it had much to say about their medical school. 'In order to afford to the Public every advantage in this Field of Medical Knowledge, the Governors have established within the walls of the Hospital a School in which all the branches of Medicine are taught according to the method which reason and experience have shown to be most efficient, namely by a judicious combination of instruction in the Lecture Rooms with study at the bedside of the Sick.' This statement, which paraphrases so neatly the Appeal of Blizard and Maddocks in 1783 to found their school in Whitechapel, is all the more interesting because, although the Barts school had been organised according to Abernethy's plans, by the time he retired in 1829 it was in fact in a far from satisfactory state. 'Dissension among the teachers had brought the school into disrepute'(14) and the Museums, Library 'and all the other requisites of professional education' had been much below the standard implied by the humble petitioners, and did not really amount to what a medical school might be expected to have. However the petitioners did point out, with great honesty, that the present arrangements on which the various medical schools in London depended for their success, was based on a 'spirit of emulation highly advantageous to the Public.' It is difficult not to feel that what the teachers at St Bartholomew's (later supported by the Hospital) were actually saying was that what Blizard had set out to do, and had achieved at the London, was a much more satisfactory form of medical education than anything a university could provide.

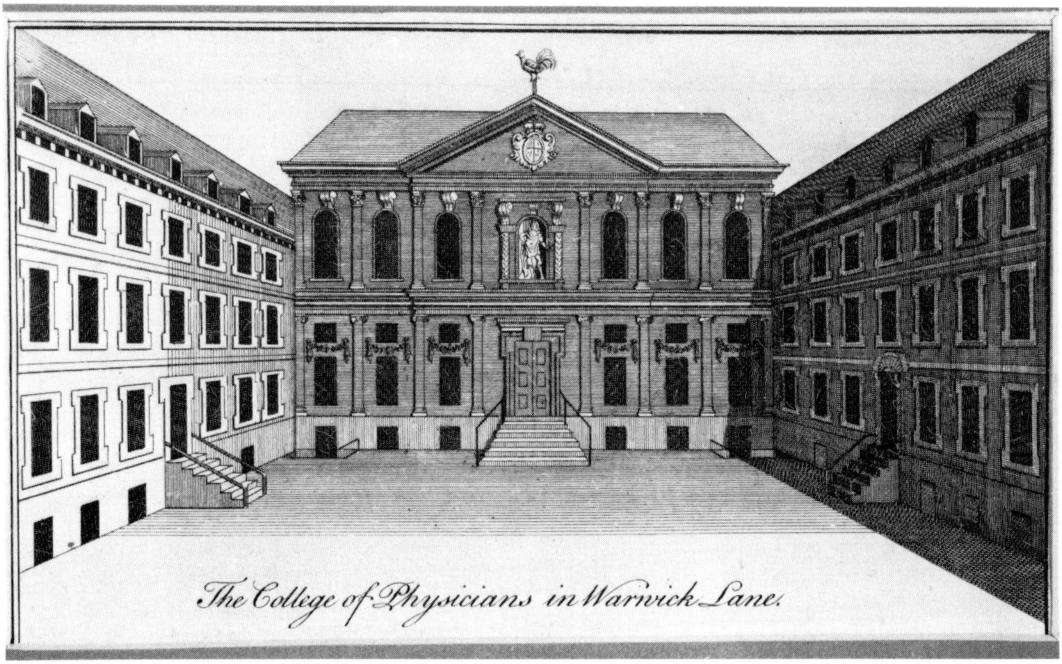

The London University did not get its charter, though the opposition of the medical schools in general and of Barts in particular, may not have accounted for that any more than opposition from other quarters including Oxford and Cambridge. The founding of King's College also introduced a complication. A charter of incorporation was granted to University College as a non degree-giving multifaculty College in 1836, and in the same year a new University of London received a charter, not to teach, but to examine for and grant degrees to anyone in Britain or her territories overseas, and was made responsible to the Home Office. Medical education in London was destined to go forward in the absence of a university and to be based for the next hundred years on Hospital Medical Schools of the kind created at the London in 1785. The new University of London agreed to admit students from the schools to the examinations for its medical degrees.

vii

By the end of its first fifty years, therefore, the London Hospital Medical College had pioneered a new kind of medical school, and of medical education, which were rapidly being copied in other hospitals, and were soon to be adopted by still more. As Blizard had foretold on the opening day, numerous benefits had resulted from the maturation of his plans. But the symbiotic relationship between the College and the London Hospital was not copied elsewhere. Essential though it had been to starting the school and to enabling it to build up a team of like-minded teachers it was not one which could be easily established in the changed circumstances of the second quarter of the nineteenth century. It was not surprising therefore that the Governors of the London felt the need to look at it again.

They were given the opportunity to do so when it was reported to them that the school was causing dissension among the medical staff. The report seems to have come from Goldwyer Andrews, the surgeon, who 'was peremptory in his manner and given to the use of strong language but was a lover of the fine arts and in his mansion at Glanbryden (South Wales) formed a collection of pictures worth £20,000 ' (5). The Governors thereupon set up a Sub-committee to enquire into the medical school the existence of which they had not as yet formally recognised.

The Sub-committee reported in 1834. On the ownership

Mile End turnpike

of the school it admitted the 'scanty information afforded by the hospital records' but expressed its members' conviction that the land on which the school stood belonged to the Hospital though the contents and equipment belonged to the teachers of the school. They had no doubt that the buildings themselves had at one time belonged to Sir William Blizard and were now in the possession of the 'present Managers consisting of a proportion of the Medical Officers of the Hospital who officiate as Lecturers.' For some reason, which they did not give, they regarded this possession as being 'by sufferance' and concluded that the buildings (erected by public subscription) were 'the property of the Corporation' - implying the Governors rather than the Body of Teachers (15).

As to the dissensions the Sub-committee found that 'from time to time, for a considerable number of years past, dissensions and jealousies have unfortunately prevailed.' It had no doubt that these were due to the fact that only a proportion of the hospital staff were involved in the school. It thought it essential that all medical officers of the London Hospital should be included and that this might be achieved either by those not involved buying their way in or alternatively by the Governors purchasing the School and ensuring that the whole medical staff shared in it. They left the Governors to decide what course to take, but recommended that anyway the School should be run by a Medical Board which was in some way responsible to the House Committee of the Hospital which could exert some control, see to it that teaching did not interfere with the teachers' hospital duties, and that there were no lectures at times when students were needed for work in the wards.

The report was discussed at a meeting of the full Court of Governors in 1834 with staff present and students in the gallery (7). Discussion was long and acrimonious and reported in detail in the press. Despite various assertions made by Goldwyer Andrews, such as that the proprietors of the school had made money out of subjects provided for dissection by the students, the main bone of contention was that the school had an undue influence on the election of staff to the hospital. Mr Young, a lay governor who was an MP, claimed there was a 'freehold' in the school controlling staff elections to the hospital and moved that the school be closed down altogether. Others argued that numerous people wholly unconcerned with the school had been appointed to the Hospital. The Chairman of the Committee of Enquiry and the Hospital Treasurer took the view that 'going outside' naturally led to difficulties on occasion but that it would be undesirable to alter the constitution of the Hospital so that noone could be elected to the staff unless he was a member of the School. He moved that no action be taken.

Whitechapel High Street, looking West, in the mid 19th Century.

The chairman of the House Committee gave his view that Hospital and School had grown up together to the common good and that dissensions among the staff did not interfere with their services to the Hospital, which could not do without a School. 'As for the students, he had been chairman of the House Committee for some years, and only occasionally had they "required his attention". Medical students could not be expected to be better disciplined than divinity students in other places (cheers from the Gallery), and he had the greatest satisfaction in stating he could not remember a single instance of neglect towards a patient' (7). He too, no doubt appreciating that there was no easy way by which the independent school could be brought under hospital control, recommended that no action should be taken -and that was agreed.

Not long afterwards the Governors requested their medical officers to hold regular meetings and appoint one of their number as a spokesman with whom the House Committee could communicate and who could advise it of the views of the staff on candidates for vacancies. In 1837 the Governors formally acknowledged the existence of the School, minuting that it had no claim on the General Funds of the Hospital, and that the latter retained its full title to the possession of the land on which the School was built and of the buildings. The School's own property, contents and equipment, was vested in three trustees, the new Chairman of the House Committee, Dr Archibald Billing, and Dr Frederick Cobb, secretary of the Associated Lecturers. The Court of Governors agreed that all vacancies in existing and future departments of the School would be filled up by the existing and future Associated Lecturers together with the principal medical officers of the Hospital. The treasurer of the Hospital was authorised to keep the accounts of the School and to collect subscriptions.

The informal relationship of School and Hospital was replaced by a more formal one but the essential difference between the situation at the London and elsewhere, the freedom of the School to elect its own staff (and indeed its capacity to influence elections to the Staff of the Hospital), remained.

St Mary's Whitechapel about 1840; built in 1329 to replace the original White Chapel, it was rebuilt in 1600, pulled down and rebuilt in 1875, burned down soon after, rebuilt again in 1882 and finally destroyed in the Blitz. The site, a little to the west of the new Mosque in the Whitechapel Road, stands empty today.

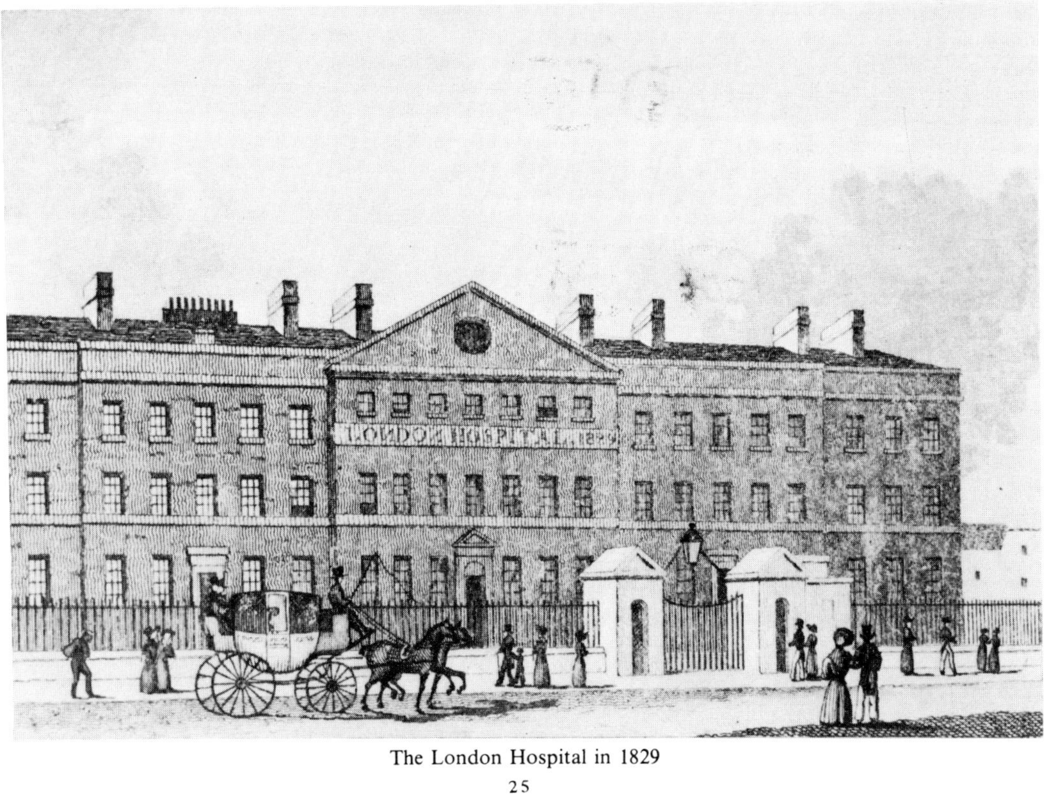

The London Hospital in 1829

Chapter 3.

Consolidation 1835-1879

i

Throughout the second quarter of the nineteenth century the change in medical education interacted with the change brought about in medicine itself by the use of physical signs and their correlation with pathology. Each speeded the other, students acquiring the new knowledge and skills more quickly than older generations out of touch with the hospitals which were the growing points of the new medicine. In them the ability to treat disease, by physical means, increased rapidly and was soon to be further advanced by anaesthesia and antisepsis. At the same time the need for medical care rocketed in response to overcrowding, poverty, the absence of sanitation and the dangerous conditions of work for those lucky enough to have it. In 1785, Whitechapel had been a small village in the countryside between Aldgate and Stratford. By 1825 it was in the midst of a densely populated slum area created by the industrial revolution as rapidly, in the same way and for the same reasons as vast shanty towns have accumulated on the edge of cities in the third world in the 20th century. In East London the slums were accompanied by the rapid growth of industries of all kinds and of the docks to serve them. Elsewhere conditions were less horrific but the hospitals, most of them small, were hard pressed to meet demand and all needed students to help. The 'hungry forties' brought further misery, which the new Poor Law of 1834 and the institution of work-houses augmented rather than relieved.

St Katherine's Dock 1830.

Workhouse Infirmaries, overwhelmed with the destitute and infirm, could do little for the acute sick among the poor who turned in ever-increasing numbers and more and more as emergencies to the Voluntary Hospitals. There, in return for a small charge in some or in others, such as the London, for nothing, they could find not only medical attention but the bed and even the roof which so many of them lacked. To provide that medical attention, however, the hospitals needed unpaid medical staff, not just physicians and surgeons visiting several times a week, but someone on the spot all the time. So students, who in 1785 had been almost as much a nuisance as a help, were by 1825 becoming indispensable to the provision of the more effective medical care which was urgently needed by more and more people. New schools quickly emerged.

The rapid growth of the East End. Wentworth Street, Whitechapel around 1860 by Gustave Doré.

Arrangements between University College and the Middlesex Hospital broke down and in 1835 the Middlesex opened a medical school of its own. So University College built a hospital for its medical students which opened as the North London Infirmary with 130 beds in 1834. In the same year Charing Cross Hospital, which had opened in 1831 with the intention of running a medical school which would contribute to the funds of the hospital, started its school. King's College, which had thought Charing Cross might provide its clinical facilities, found itself with no alternative but to open a hospital of its own. The Governors of the Westminster not surprisingly thought there must be something to be said for medical schools after all and started one in 1840, though it failed in a few years and they had to start again. St Mary's Hospital was founded in 1845 and its school in 1854. Thus by the middle of the nineteenth century, the union of St Thomas's and Guy's having been dissolved in 1825, London had eleven medical schools, eight run by the Boards of Governors of Hospitals, two run by multifaculty colleges, and one by a group of teachers at the London. Private schools outside hospitals had disappeared.

In all the schools, irrespective of how or by whom they were run, the changes in medical education which had begun at the London in its first fifty years, proceeded apace. By 1850 all schools, though they varied much in size, were providing a body of students with a wide range of lectures. The teaching of Anatomy had been improved by the Act of 1832 which facilitated the provision of bodies for dissection and put the 'resurrection men' out of business. All schools offered plentiful opportunities for clinical practice, albeit loosely supervised. The three orders of the profession remained distinct, with separate licensing authorities, but the Physicians and Surgeons had reshaped and tightened up their requirements, and a majority of students were in any case seeking the broad based course required by the Apothecaries.

This combination of changes within the medical schools with changes in the requirements and examinations of the outside bodies, quickly led to the development of something like a general course of 4 or more years duration, all of it obtainable at each school. The system of paying separately for lectures and clinical experience was abandoned and replaced with a composite fee for the whole course (to encourage students to take it in one place) greatly reducing the cost to the student.

By 1850 medical education had become organised, with a structured curriculum beginning with the sciences basic to medicine, on lines which were to last for a hundred years and are still clearly visible today. 'The change from the medical education of 1800 to that of 1850' wrote Newman, 'is astonishing, a change far greater than that between 1850 and 1950, and it all came from within the profession itself, preceding the parliamentary legislation which was to establish the General Medical Council' (1).In most places it was, as he said, 'almost entirely concentrated into the years between 1835 and 1855', but they were building on the changes pioneered at the London from its opening in 1785, and one piece of legislation, the Apothecaries Act of 1815, had contributed to the adoption of them. Moreover the most powerful force shaping the development (as well as the expansion) of medical education in England, and especially in London, between 1825 and 1955, was the need for students to provide care for patients in hospital.

Over London by rail 1860. Doré.

ii

As students took increasing responsibility for diagnosis and initial treatment, aided by untrained nurses, and unsupervised save for the visits of physicians and surgeons and such help as the resident apothecary might be able to give, the burden fell mainly on those attached to surgeons and physicians. Initially they were those who could afford to pay for this privilege. They were not necessarily the best or the most senior though they enjoyed of course the best possible means of learning and acquiring competence.

The larger the hospital and the more it was confronted with emergencies the sooner it had to make some kind of arrangement to ensure that dressers at least were relatively senior and selected for reasons other than their capacity to pay. At the London in 1840 some two-thirds of the 3,339 patients who passed through the 400 beds were emergencies, admitted because of accidents or as 'extra cases' because their lives were in immediate danger. Many of the 10,000 outpatients presented equally acute problems. Action was imperative.

The Governors required the most junior of the surgeons to reside next door to the hospital in No 1 Mount Street. They insisted that three senior students acted as dressers in out-patients in return for free in-patient dresserships, much to the resentment of the surgeons. They then proposed that three posts of house surgeon should be filled by men who had actually passed the MRCS examination. Opposition was immediate, fierce and vociferous. The surgeons claimed that students would lose 'that personal attention to severe cases which alone gives an interest to their situation and constitutes the sole reward for their laborious and for the most part irksome duties' (7) - and that they themselves would lose what little financial recompense they gained from serving the hospital. They claimed they were bound by agreements with students which would not run out till 1845. The students held mass meetings in the College, appealed to the Governors, and published a scathing letter of protest in the Lancet. The Governors nonetheless exerted what the students called their 'despotic power' and two qualified house-surgeons were appointed to supervise the in-patient dressers in return for free board and lodging.

The students did not however cease to give 'personal attention to severe cases'. At the London, and elsewhere as house-surgeons were appointed - a post for a qualified HS holding the MRCS was established at Guy's in 1856 (1) - students continued to take responsibility for the care of patients, though under the supervision of a newly-qualified young man relying mainly on the experience he himself had just had as a student. Dressers were drawn increasingly from the more senior students who had had some experience in out-patients after studying anatomy and the other basic medical subjects. In out-patients and the medical wards, students continued to carry the burden of care without the benefit of qualified junior staff and were to do so for many years to come. In the medical wards however the resident apothecary could be called upon for help.

While the medical school course was gradually becoming organised into one in which students were better equipped to take increasing responsibility for patients, the facilities within the medical schools were

The operating theatre in 1837.

gradually improved between 1825 and 1850. Lecture theatres, libraries and museums were provided. Handbooks were produced giving details of teaching. Wealthy hospitals created large numbers of prizes to attract students and advertised them widely. The London, lacking such resources, took care to emphasise the exceptional opportunities for practical experience it had to offer. In 1843 the Medical Officers at Barts, considering the proposal that the school should be called 'the Medical College of St Bartholomew's Hospital' toyed with the idea of lecturers wearing gowns at their lectures, but the solicitor to the Hospital explained that this was inexpedient at the present time (14).

The House Committee of St Bartholomew's did however fit up houses in Duke St (now Little Britain) for the accommodation of students. The resulting 'Collegiate Establishment', six houses and a College Hall, was opened in October 1843. The catering was provided by the Albion Tavern in Aldersgate Street, the same at which the opening of the the London Hospital Medical College had been celebrated (with Blizard's Ode) in October 1785, and the London

Hospital Medical Club had been founded in May 1838. The name 'Albion' ought to be preserved in some joint London-Barts activity.

James Paget was unanimously elected the first Warden of the St Bartholomew's Collegiate Establishment, which was soon extended. He was required to act as Tutor to the Resident Students (16 at first but soon rising), directing their studies and making himself acquainted with their progress. He was to preside at dinner in Hall and never to absent himself for a whole day or night without giving notice of intention and leaving some competent person in charge (14). Students had to dine every night in Hall unless excused by the Warden and were required to be in College by midnight. Paget kept careful records of his students over a 20 year period. He rated them as having achieved distinguished, considerable, fair or very limited success, failed entirely, left the profession, died within 12 years of starting practice, or died during pupilage. The largest number (507) achieved fair success. Of the 23 who achieved distinguished success one was Jonathan Hutchinson. Of one of the 87 who died within 12 years, Paget wrote 'idle, dissolute, extravagant, vulgar and stupid. He scarcely practised and was chiefly engaged on the turf. He was hung for the murder of a friend.' 41 died as students, clear evidence of the risks inherent in the study or practice of medicine (14).

The Collegiate Establishment must have done much to attract students to Barts, besides providing a model of how in any future combining of the London and St Bartholomew's, the identity of each could profitably be preserved in such a way as to ensure the necessary care and attention to the development of students as individuals. Maybe it accounts for the fact that in 1847 a conference of teachers was held at Barts to consider ways and means of limiting the advertising battle in which the schools were engaged. Six schools were represented and efforts made to draw up a general form of advertisement for all schools, but the effort proved abortive (16). In the expenses of the medical school at St Bartholomew's in 1861, the largest single item was the Scholarship Fund, and the second largest, Advertisement.

Competition between London Schools, or rather hospitals, to attract students was to continue well into the twentieth century, with good and bad consequences. Over the same period the medical faculties of German Universities engaged in equally fierce competition to attract the brightest young men to academic posts, and made little effort to provide for students.

iii

Nowhere was competition for students felt more keenly than at the London. It could offer wonderful clinical experience. Since 1840 the hospital had been extended further, increasing the number of patients who could be treated, though still unable to cope fully with the even more rapidly increasing demand. There was an impressive staff too, in both College and Hospital. There were, of course, some losses. Archibald Billing, for example, who had been so indefatigable in organising clinical teaching, went off in 1847 to do the same as Professor of Medicine at University College Hospital. His 'attached pupils and professional friends' at the London presented him with a magnificent silver tray 'in Testimony of their sense of the benefit conferred upon the profession by the establishment of clinical lectures in London in 1822'. In 1847 too the Body of Associated Lecturers resolved 'that the name of this Society be changed to the Medical Council of the London Hospital School' and included in its membership all the lecturers of one or more years' standing and all the physicians and surgeons of the hospital.

As in the past some of the College lecturers had later been elected to fill vacancies on the Hospital Staff, providing it with some particularly distinguished members. One such was Jonathan Pereira who did so much to advance Pharmacology. He was appointed Lecturer in Chemistry in the College in 1833 and elected assistant physician to the Hospital in 1841.

Jonathan Pereira FRS, "father" of pharmacology.

Pereira had been a pupil at the medical school in Aldersgate Street, a private school competing with St Bartholomew's Hospital.* In 1823 he moved to Barts and qualified LSA the following year. He became dispenser to Barts and to the Aldersgate Street school where he lectured on Materia Medica. He qualified MRCS in 1825 and set up in practice as a surgeon, retaining his teaching appointment in the Aldersgate School after appointment to the London Hospital Medical College in 1833. He 'was a great worker and laboured for about 16 hours a day. He was over 6 feet in height and had an iron constitution' (5). He published his great work 'Elements of Materia Medica' in two parts in 1839-1840 and placed 'the knowledge and use of drugs, which had been chaotic and empirical, on an organised and scientific basis' (8). He also helped to found the City of London Library and Scientific Institution.

In 1836 the Medical Officers at St Bartholomew's invited Pereira to lecture on chemistry there, agreeing that he should continue to teach at the London. He vacated his lectureship at Aldersgate Street when his appointment to Barts was agreed by its House Committee but then the full Court of Governors refused to confirm it and appointed two others as joint lecturers in Chemistry instead (14). The incident shows very clearly the difference between a school run by the Governors of a Hospital and an independent educational institution. The independence of the London Hospital Medical College continued to be of the greatest importance in the appointment of staff.

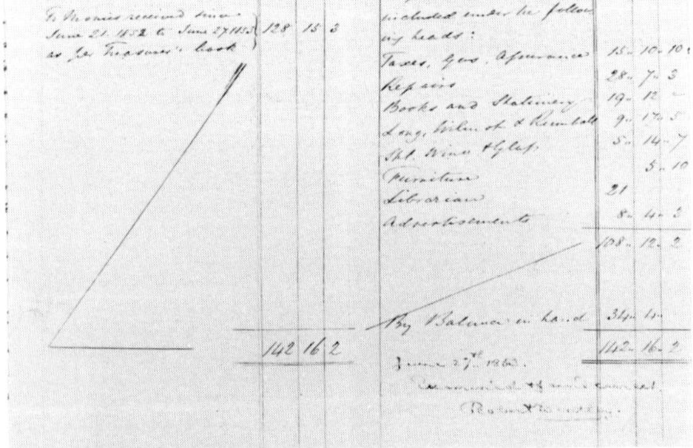
Abstract of Account of ... Treasurer of Museum & Library fund for the year beginning 21st June 1852 to June 27. 1853

Dr		Cr	
To Balance at Audit June 21. 1852	14 0 11	By different items paid as per Treasurer's book, included under the following heads:	
To Monies received from June 21. 1852 to June 27 1853 as per Treasurer's book	128 15 3	Taxes, Gas, Assurance	15 10 10
		Repairs	28 7 3
		Books and Stationery	19 12 –
		Furniture	
		Librarian	21
		Advertisements	8 4 3
			108 12 2
		By Balance in hand	34 4 –
	142 16 2		142 16 2

June 27th 1853.

Accounts of Museum and Library Fund.

*The School was based on the Aldersgate Dispensary.

The school's buildings however were still those that had been opened in 1785 and though providing a full range of the necessary facilities they were now old, compared unfavourably with those put up more recently by hospitals, and prevented any major increase in the size of the intake. New buildings were needed but there was little likelihood of the money being raised by public subscription as had been the case in 1783. In 1851 the Medical Council of the School did the only thing it could, and approached the Hospital Governors with a petition signed by its secretary Thomas Curling, the young surgeon who had already described the connection between burns and duodenal ulceration. The Governors, it said 'need scarcely be reminded that in consequence of the great number of patients admitted into this Hospital, a number exceeding that of any other Hospital in London (with the exception of St Bartholomew's), of the large proportion of surgical cases and accidents, and of the increased number of out-patients, the duties required of the dressers are very onerous.'

A table was supplied showing how much the Governors of each of the other hospitals in London was putting into its school so as to educate and train Gentlemen to qualify them for the more responsible duties of the staff and also to obtain 'the great and important services rendered gratuitously by well-instructed Pupils in the capacities of House-Surgeons and Dressers, which services, without the adjunct of the School, would only be obtained by a heavy outlay of Hospital funds.' The petition sought assistance for the maintenance of the School 'in some degree commensurate with the advantages derived by the Hospital.' The table was in fact one that Curling had obtained from a friend at the Westminster who had compiled it earlier to bring pressure to bear on the Governors there.

The Governors of the London got the message and undertook to provide the School, as soon as funds could be found, 'with increased and improved accommodation'. Two years later, on receiving a legacy of £30,000, the House Committee deemed 'it expedient that the present inconvenient and insufficient buildings used as a medical school should be given up by the Staff for the general purposes of the hospital and their place supplied by one on a larger scale to be erected by the Governors on the South-West corner of the ground within the hospital railings and that such new building be let to the Medical Staff as Tenants at Will'.

The new buildings consisted of two large lecture theatres, two museums, laboratory, library and dissecting room and rooms for lectures. They cost around £10,000 and were described in the press as 'remarkable for the architectural taste displayed and admirable internal arrangements, the most convenient, salubrious and handsome school in the Metropolis.'

The College Bell 1854. Hung in the roof of the new school it was rung to announce the start of lectures. It ceased to be used after the rebuilding of 1887 and was rung for the last time, by students, at 11.00 am on 11 November 1918.

The opening ceremony took place on October 2nd 1854, and the keys of the new School were handed over by the hospital in return for the keys of the old. On the same day began the College's 70th session and W J Little (the same who had gone to Newcastle as a student to study cholera but now senior physician to the London, the first to describe the 'spastic child' and the founder of the Orthopaedic Institution), gave the inaugural address reminding his audience that the College was 'the first example of a complete Medical School in connexion with a Hospital upon the model of the Medical Faculty of an University'.

The fact that the new buildings were leased to the school at a peppercorn rent without any condition for control over it, shows that hospital and school were content to continue as two independent institutions. The legal agreement covering the lease was, however, drawn up between the Governors of the Hospital and the 'Medical and Surgical Officers of the said Hospital', the Governors still taking care to do nothing that might involve them in any continuing obligation to finance the school. Thus the tenants of the building were not precisely the same as the Medical Council which ran the School, presenting a slight problem which was overcome in the simplest possible way. On March 5th 1855 the Medical Council of the London Hospital School met at 23 Finsbury Square with Mr James Luke, Surgeon, in the Chair and resolved: 'that the Medical Council now conducting the affairs of the London Hospital School of Medicine, in order that the future management of its affairs shall accord with the provisions of the deed of agreement made between the Governors of the said Hospital and its Medical and Surgical Officers... hereby relinquishes its functions and concedes its interest... to the said Medical and Surgical Officers, that they may hold the same in trust for the uses of the school.'

Dr William John Little.

This resolution was promptly recorded in the minute book of the Medical Council of the London Hospital School of Medicine. Having done so, exactly the same men sat down again, under the same chairman, but this time as the Medical Officers of the Hospital, and resolved: 'that the Medical and Surgical Officers of the

London Hospital in accepting the Anatomical Museum and other effects conceded to them by the Medical Council lately conducting the affairs of the Medical School, do hereby constitute themselves a Society under the designation of the London Hospital College Council, and bind themselves to the observance of the subjoined laws to which each has individually subscribed his name' and recorded this resolution in the minute book of the Meetings of the Medical Officers of the London Hospital.

The first of the 'fundamental laws' laid down that the Council should consist of the Medical and Surgical Officers and such Lecturers in the Medical School or College as have, or shall have been, such lecturers during two years, and have paid the entrance library fee of five guineas and subscribed to the Rules and Regulations of the Council.'

John Hughlings-Jackson, FRS, MD.

Thus, while the buildings were leased by the hospital staff, the school continued to be run by a Council which included both them and the other teachers. The latter had no direct say in the advice given to the Governors as to who should be appointed to fill vacancies on the hospital staff but, as in the past, those elected were often those who had earlier been appointed to the school; and the presence of College Lecturers in new subjects led to pressure for those subjects to be practised in the hospital. Thus the senior lecturer in midwifery was appointed first as a consulting obstetric physician and eventually given beds. Pathology was another subject to be developed in this way, Andrew Clark being appointed by the College as curator of the museum in 1853 and then becoming assistant physician a year later. Not long after the lectureship in pathology and then in physiology were given to John Hughlings-Jackson, later to become physician to the hospital, and one of the fathers of Neurology.

In 1857, after prolonged pressure and frequent use as a consultant in difficult dental problems, the College Lecturer in Dental Surgery, H J Barrett, was appointed the first Dental Surgeon to the Hospital. Previously patients had received dental treatment from the surgeons or more commonly from students, some of whom on getting the MRCS had, like Barrett himself, specialised in dental surgery. Dentistry was advancing in the early nineteenth century and a Dental School was opened in Baltimore USA in 1839 though not so many years earlier George Washington had sent a bridge with artificial teeth on it to be repaired by a Mr Greenwood in London (the bridge and covering letter are still in the College safe). The Governors of the

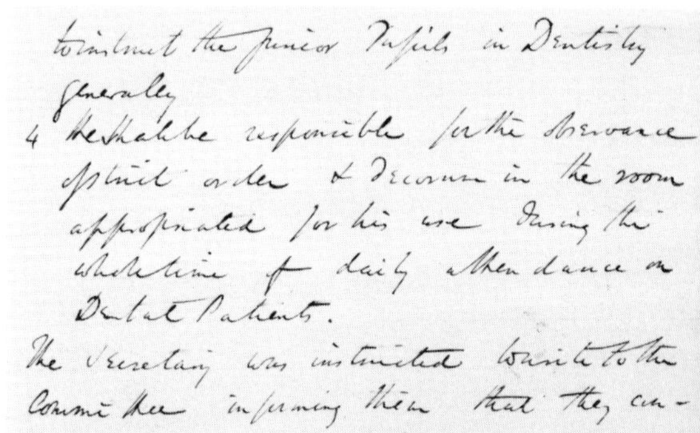

to instruct the junior Pupils in Dentistry generally
4 He shall be responsible for the observance of strict order & decorum in the room appropriated for his use during the whole time of daily attendance on Dental Patients.
The Secretary was instructed to write to the Committee informing them that they considered the scheme proposed would work very imperfectly unless organised under the superintendence of a qualified Dentist who would really impart sound information, and be thus the means of placing this branch of information on a similar footing to other branches of instruction taught in the Institution.

The Medical Council of the School minutes its reactions to the House Committee's proposal to appoint a senior student to oversee the care of dental patients.

London in 1857 however thought that sufficient improvement in the service would be made by arranging for a senior student to attend for an hour a day in the dental room to prevent unseemly haste in extractions by students anxious to get back to their other duties. But the staff pressed the case and Mr Barrett was appointed. Just how much he improved dental care in the hospital is not recorded but his private practice continued to flourish, despite his fondness for sailing, fishing and shooting. When he died in 1901 he left £195,766 5s 4d (£200 of it to the London) but he had also been a member of the Board of the Metropolitan Railway Company (5).

iv

While conditions in the medical schools improved as hospitals competed with each other to attract more students, the attention of Parliament was being drawn to the regulation of medical education. There was no great public concern about the quality of the training available because clearly it had rapidly been improving, but there was anxiety about there being so many different routes to a licence at a time when medicine was increasingly capable of affecting disease. There were no less than nineteen separate licensing bodies in the British Isles, and in addition a licence could still be obtained through the Church or by medical service in the Navy or Army. It was hard for the public to tell those who were licensed from the many practitioners who were not.

The licensing bodies themselves were not very keen on legislation to clarify the situation - but were all strongly opposed to there being one single 'portal of entry' to the profession - as was and is the case in many countries. Fifteen consecutive Bills were rejected before Parliament passed the Medical Act of 1858. This established the 'General Council for Medical Education and Registration', to be responsible for keeping a Register of Licensed Practitioners who had attended courses of a duration laid down by the Council in schools approved by it.

Inevitably something of a compromise, the Act did not really achieve any great simplification of licensing. It made it impossible to become licensed by virtue of service in the Army or Navy, but it actually increased the number of licensing bodies. The Council recognised all the old universities in the British Isles and the degrees of the University of London which remained an examining organisation.As new Universities grew out of Colleges of higher education in the provinces the Council recognised them as licensing bodies also and it continued to recognise all the old professional bodies. Most of these extended the subjects of their diplomas (for example, the College of Physicians of London included surgery and midwifery in the LRCP examinations) but it remained possible to become registered while licensed in only one branch of medicine. Another quarter of a century was to pass before a second Medical Act laid down that registered practitioners must be competent in medicine, surgery and midwifery. Meanwhile the schools produced physicians, a larger number of surgeons, a great many who took the diploma of both the Surgeons and the Apothecaries, and a growing number of dentists licensed by the LDS, for another outcome of the Act of 1858 was the establishment by the College of Surgeons of a diploma of Licentiate of Dental Surgery, the first examinations for which were held in 1860.

The new General Medical Council turned its attention to pre-medical education, laying down the kind of examination that should be passed before entry to medical school. It did not at first have much to say about the medical course, the duration of which was set at four years and stayed at that until 1885. So the coming of the GMC did not bring about any immediate major change in medical education itself. Rather it consolidated and regularised the reforms which had already taken place, confirming a curriculum in which the study of the basic medical sciences preceded entry into the wards. Virtually all teaching continued to be given by practising clinicians but it was obviously necessary that students should not only have a good basis of anatomy, physiology and other subjects before entering the wards but also that they should progress from the least to the most responsible clinical duties as they became more senior. So much more attention had to be paid to the order in which students covered the course and to their performance in each part of it. It was no longer enough for a school to offer wide experience and good teachers. It required an administrative organisation also.

v

At Charing Cross in 1856 it was 'decided on as desirable to nominate a Dean... to conduct the general supervision of the School, in accordance with the decisions of the Managers......................
having under him an efficient person to fulfill all the

clerical and administrative details, and combining therewith the duties of Sub-Registrar or Clerk of the Medical College and Librarian'(13).

Mr Hancock (the Senior Surgeon) 'having consented to undertake the duties of Dean of the Medical College it was deemed desirable that he be appointed to that office.' This administrative policy was only decided upon, however, because the founder of the school and hospital, Dr Golding, had been 'conducting the administrative details' for years with the result that his declining health and strength now necessitated 'some repose from the personal exertions which he had hitherto sustained'. The key to the policy, therefore, was not the Dean, but the 'efficient person to fulfill all the clerical and adminstrative details' - a fact which has all too often been ignored in subsequent times when schools are faced with choosing a Dean.

The London Hospital Medical College however, did not appoint a Dean or any kind of administrator until 1868. The extent of the managerial and administrative burden with which it was then confronted is indicated in the Prospectus of that year. It shows that the emphasis was on clinical practice though there were lectures on all the existing subjects and practical classes in the use of the auriscope, laryngoscope, ophthalmoscope and microscope. Dr Herbert Davies, son of the Davies who had brought the stethoscope to London, still held the class he had been 'accustomed to hold for many years', early in the morning, for 'Practical Auscultation and Percussion'. There was still no rigidly structured curriculum but it was shaped in so far as a student's eligibility to become a clerk, dresser, medical assistant or any other of the numerous positions open to him, depended upon having attended various lectures and served in the more junior posts.

Every student was 'entitled to act as Dresser' for twelve months, during which he worked under all the surgeons in turn, taking his turn too to live in for a week at a time. 'While in the Hospital he sees and attends to all the accidents (amounting on average to 300 weekly) as well as the cases of Surgical disease. When his week is over, he dresses his cases daily and attends the Surgeon under whom he is acting, thus receiving individual and immediate instruction'.

He might also receive assistance from a House-Surgeon - if the latter had time - but he could not have had much because as the Prospectus proudly put it 'the appointment (of house surgeon) as the number of beds possessed by each of the Surgeons is 120, affords an abundant scope for the acquirement of practical experience.'

"Accidents" brought to the London in 1868: from the Hospital's Annual Report.

Fractures	1947
Wounds	3689
Contusions	5023
Sprains	2280
Dislocations	151
Concussions	60
Burns and scalds	750
Hernia	153
Bites of Dogs	214
Retention	233
Haemorrhage	122
Foreign bodies in throat etc	385
Corrosion from acids	0
Thecal Abscess	30
Inflammation	2489
Attempts at suicide	17
Various	216
TOTAL	17759

Students could attend the Physicians on their visits to the general wards and thus qualify for appointment as Ward Clerks, recording in their notebooks the history and progress of cases. From the Ward Clerks three Medical Assistants were selected every three months one for each Physician. Each lived in the hospital for one month out of three 'entirely free of expense' and did the work of a house-physician, aided by a Resident Medical Officer or his deputy in note-taking and in the 'chemical and microscopical observations' made in the room 'specially fitted up' for the purpose.

Two medical wards were set aside expressly for clinical teaching, a practice copied from Guy's where it had been started by Thomas Addison. Patients in these wards were chosen from all those needing admission and selected 'for the systematic illustration of the various diseases of the internal organs'. Each physician had charge of the wards for two months in rotation, gave bedside instructions twice a week and a weekly clinical lecture.

Teaching and still more clinical practice were available in Out-patients, and all students were eligible for appointment as an outpatient dresser, those serving for twelve months becoming eligible for one of six money prizes given by the Governors. The reference to the Maternity Department is equally explicit: 'Six hundred and twenty-two women were attended in labour at their own homes last year. Students can obtain as much practice in this branch as they desire.'

Experience of mental illness was not so easily obtained but students 'desirous of obtaining a practical knowledge of Mental Diseases' could attend Bethnal Green Asylum in the Cambridge Heath Road. Experience of Practical Morbid Anatomy, however, was ensured by requiring all students to act as Post-Mortem Clerks for three months.

CLINICAL LECTURES AND REPORTS,

BY THE

MEDICAL AND SURGICAL STAFF OF THE LONDON HOSPITAL.

CONTENTS OF VOL. I., 1864.

Aneurism of Innominate, &c..by	Dr. Davies.	Gleanings in Medicine...........	Dr. Andrew Clark.
On Leucoderma........................	Mr. Hutchinson.	On Still-birth	Dr. Barnes.
On True Leprosy	Mr. Hutchinson.	Maternity Statistics	Mr Heckford.
On Cerebral Amaurosis	Mr. Hutchinson.	Miscellaneous Cases	Dr. Woodman.
On the Treatment of Polysarcia	Dr. Down.	Notes on the SchleswigCampaign	Mr. Little.
On Hospital Gangrene	Mr. Maunder.	Dislocation of Lower Jaw	Mr. Couper.
On Treatment of Stricture.........	Mr. Maunder.	Treatment of Rheumatic Fever	Dr. Davies.
Cases of Ligature of Arteries......	Mr. Maunder.	Hemiplegia with Loss of Speech	Dr. Jackson.
Fractures of the Vertebræ	Mr. Curling.	Diseases of the Nervous System	Dr. Jackson.
Diseases of the Nervous System	Dr. Jackson.	Extracts from Clinical Lectures	Mr. Hutchinson.
Treatment of Scarlet Fever	Dr. Down.	Cases of Disease of the Heart, &c.	Dr. Ramskill.
On Relapsing Pemphigus	Mr. Hutchinson.	Algesia and Hyperæsthesia	Dr. Ramskill.
On a Case of Hernia.................	Mr. Couper.	Hospital Statistics for 1863......	Dr. Powell.
Surgical Gold Medal Cases	(Various.)		

CONTENTS OF VOL. II., 1865.

Occlusion of Femoral Artery, &c.	by Mr. Adams.	Gunshot Wound of the Thorax	Mr. Maunder.
Report on Colotomy	Mr. Curling.	Fractures into the Elbow, &c., &c.	Mr. Maunder.
Liquid Diffusion	Dr Letheby.	Fracture of Base of Skull.........	Mr. Couper.
On Nitro-Benzole.....................	Dr. Letheby.	Case of Hernia without a Sac ...	Mr. Couper.
On Circumcision in Epilepsy, &c.	Mr. Heckford.	Report on Fifty Cases of Hernia	Dr. Woodman.
Treatment of Hydrothorax.........	Dr. Fraser.	Surgical Gold Medal Cases	(Various.)
Stimulation versus Depletion	Dr. Fraser.	On Hemiplegia	Dr. Jackson.
Cause of Death after Hernia	Mr. Hutchinson.	Extracts from Clinical Lectures	Mr. Hutchinson.
On Lupus and allied Diseases ...	Mr. Hutchinson.	Obstruction of the Bowels	Dr. Davies.
On Inherited Syphilis	Mr. Hutchinson.	Additions to the Museum	Mr. Little.
Tumour of the Scalp	Mr. Hutchinson.	On Simulated Diseases	Dr. Woodman.
Lithotomy with large Stone	Mr. Adams.	Hospital Statistics for 1864	The Registrars.
Blister Treatment of Rheumatism..................	Dr. Davies.		
Use of the Drainage-tube in Diseases of the Knee-joint...	Mr. Curling and Mr. Hutchinson.	And other papers.	

CONTENTS OF VOL. III., 1866.

Case of Ligature of External Iliac	Mr. Adams.	Case of Symmetrical Cancer	Dr. Fraser.
On Spectrum Analysis	Dr. Letheby.	A Case of Gastrotomy	Mr. Curling.
On Cases of Diabetes	Dr. Fraser.	On Marriages of Consanguinity	Dr. Down.
Notes on Special Symptoms	Mr. Hutchinson.	Ethnic Classification of Idiots...	Dr. Down.
On Injections in Cholera	Dr. Little.	On Cerebral Hæmorrhage	Dr. H. Jackson.
On Extravasation of Urine........	Mr. Maunder.	Gold Medal Reports	(Various.)
On some Hernia Cases	Mr. Maunder.	Additions to the Museum	Mr. Little.
On Cases of Stricture	Mr. Maunder.	Cases of Injury to the Spine ...	The Surgeons.
Cases of Acute Synovitis	Mr. Carter.	On Fractures of the Spine	Mr. Hutchinson.
Cure of Abdominal Aneurism ...	Dr. Daly.	On Injuries to Nerve Trunks...	Mr. Hutchinson.
Poisoning by Belladonna	Dr. G. Brown.	On Syphilis (2nd Series)	Mr. Hutchinson.
Poisoning by Belladonna	Dr. Fraser.	Hospital Statistics for 1865	The Registrars.
On Herpes Zoster.....................	Mr. Hutchinson.		
On the Year's Mortality...........	Mr. Tay.	And other Papers.	

That part of the Prospectus which today describes the order of the curriculum consisted, in the 1860s - (and for long afterwards), of a list of 'all the numerous appointments open to students without fee or expense of any kind whatever', adding that some 'are very valuable, far more than the best scholarships or prizes.' There were fifteen different categories of appointments, including the Resident Accoucheur (appointed for six months, free of all expense, and provided with residence and board), an Assistant Dentist, and the Medical and the Surgical Registrars. The Registrars, responsible for medical records and for overseeing students' notes, but with no responsibility to patients, were paid £25 per annum and were qualified. The House-Surgeons and the Resident Medical Officers required a diploma in Surgery or Medicine respectively, the latter being the descendents of the Resident Apothecary of the past.

vi

The management of this emerging curriculum, signing up students for lectures and appointments and constantly selecting them for different posts (appointments were made by the House Committee but recommendations came solely from the Medical Council of the School) must have imposed an enormous burden. But the quality of training received by the average student depended greatly on how well it was done. In addition the staff gave special tutorials to students wishing to take a university degree from London, Oxford, Cambridge or Durham, and it was decided that at the end of each Session (Winter and Summer) every student should be examined in each class he had attended, the results 'being useful both to Teachers and to Pupils and a guide to the bestowal of appointments.' Admissions were running at about 45 new students per year, most taking the whole course but some coming from elsewhere for parts of it, and all arriving at different times. Some came to medical school after whole or part of their apprenticeship. Some came straight from school at 17 or even 16 years of age.

This burden of appointment and signing up was carried by the Medical Council of the School, consisting of some twenty-five lecturers, the senior in each main subject holding 'the chair' but not the title of Professor. Almost every one of them was also a part-time Surgeon or Physician, Assistant Surgeon or Physician, or Dental Surgeon, Obstetrician or the like to the London or some other hospital. The Assistant Surgeons and Physicians at the London had charge of out-patients and usually a few beds, becoming Surgeons or Physicians after seven years or earlier if there were a vacancy and holding that office thereafter for twenty years. Most, by 1868, had a special interest, involving extra clinical duties. These teachers between them taught all the subjects, pre-clinical and clinical, gave all the tutorials, conducted all the school examinations, were responsible for all the patients in the Hospital with the help of six house surgeons and two resident medical officers, and earned their living (apart from what they received from the school) in private practice, travelling around London in the process.

Amazingly, many managed to make significant contributions to medicine. They included Curling of Curling's Ulcer, Little of Little's Disease, Down of Down's Syndrome, Ramskill and Hughlings Jackson of Neurology, Sutton of the Sutton Prize who spent almost all of every day in the wards or post-mortem department, Morell Mackenzie, the physician who became the most famous of laryngologists, Andrew Clark well on his way to being the best known and most sought after physician of his day, and Jonathan Hutchinson. In 1869 they were joined by Tay of Tay-Sachs disease.

These teaching practitioners in addition to all their other activities carried the burden of running the Medical College with all that that involved - planning the curriculum, publishing the prospectus, appointing the students and house officers, maintaining the buildings and facilities, liasing with the Hospital and the outside world, and managing the finances. They had also to cope with those unexpected little problems that arise in every school with monotonous regularity the demonstrator who absents himself, idle students complaining students, students arrested by the police the colleagues who do not want to play their part in the school and the outsiders who do. In reply to a letter from 'the Reverend d'Orsey offering to deliver a lecture on Elocution with or without fee... regretted that no occasion presented itself for the delivery of the lecture.' And always the smaller financial problems: 'Dr — to be informed his son cannot be awarded his medal until he has paid the first instalment of his fees'. And often those differences of attitude between physicians and surgeons which matters such as medals not uncommonly reveal: 'It was decided that the Hospital medal for Medicine should have inscribed on it "For Zeal and Intelligence", and that for Surgery "For Zeal and Humanity"'.

The council met frequently. Its various sub-committees, seldom consisting of more than three members, met somewhere in the College or Hospital, but the Council itself usually met at the home of one of the staff - Finsbury Circus, Russell Square, Cavendish Square. It never met earlier than 8.30 p.m. except in times of great crisis. The Honorary Secretary (usually the most recently appointed member of staff) sent out copies of the agenda and kept the minutes - all of course in long-hand. Successive secretaries wrote a firm but neat, easily legible hand, terse and to the point, and always maintaining courtesy and propriety. Thus Jonathan Hutchinson recording: 'Dr Tidy was appointed for one year to assist Dr Lethaby in Chemical Pathology...Mr Hutchinson reported that at the last meeting of the Library and Museum Committee there

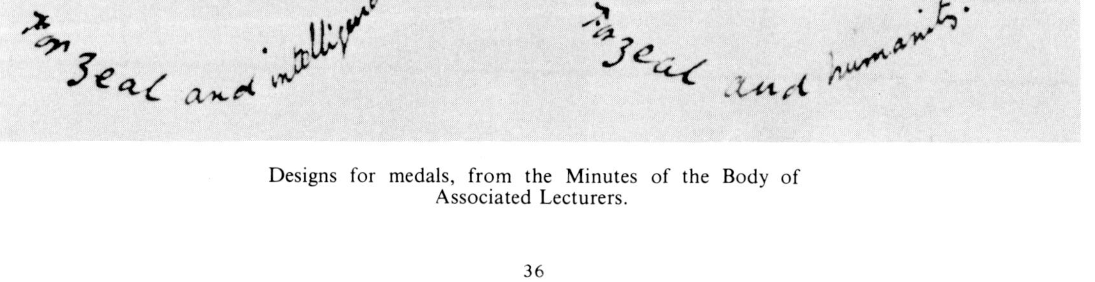

Designs for medals, from the Minutes of the Body of Associated Lecturers.

had been no attendance... and offered to undertake for a time the duties of Hon. Curator with the object of endeavouring to secure the completeness of the catalogue. He was apppointed accordingly.' It is interesting that those who made lasting contributions to the advance of medicine were among the most regular attenders at meetings.

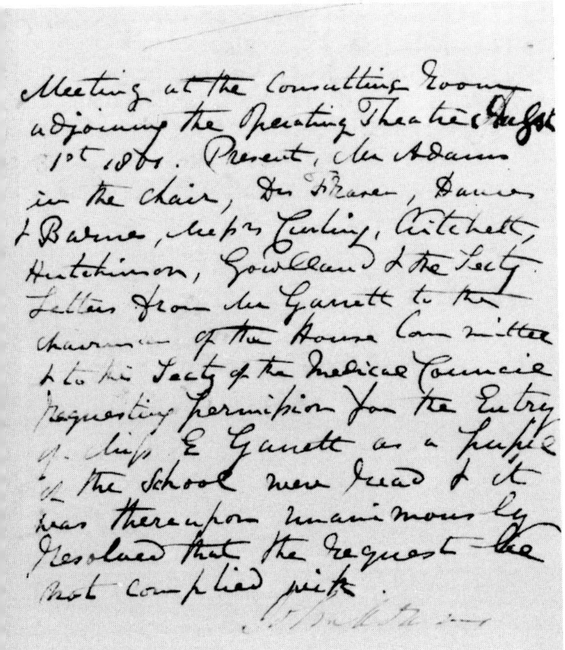

Meeting at the Consulting Room
adjoining the Operating Theatre August
1st 1861. Present, Mr Adams
in the chair, Drs Fraser, Davies
& Barnes, Messrs Curling, Critchett,
Hutchinson, Gowlland & the Secty.
Letters from Mr Garrett to the
chairman of the House Committee
& to the Secty of the Medical Council
requesting permission for the Entry
of Miss E Garrett as a pupil
of the School were read & it
was thereupon unanimously
Resolved that the request be
not complied with

No to Elizabeth Garrett.

School business was of course mixed with hospital affairs. Thus on March 14th 1867 consecutive items were: 'The report of the Library and Museum Committee was read and adopted. The Secretary was requested to communicate with the House Committee on the subject of its recommendations'...A letter from the Secretary (of the Hospital) accompanying a note of thanks to the Medical Staff for their exertions during the epidemic of Cholera was read, and the Secretary was instructed to acknowledge it'. Later in the same minutes 'A letter was read signed by three ladies requesting admission to the College and Hospital as students. It was moved by Dr Down seconded by Mr Curling and carried without dissentient "That the Medical Council of the London Hospital having carefully considered the request made by three ladies to be admitted as students much regrets to be obliged to decline to accede to it."'

In the management of the school the officers of the Council -Chairman (Senior physician or surgeon), Secretary and Treasurer -had the assistance of a Bedell (who lived in the College) and a few porters. Whether or not the administration was all that could be desired, it is impossible not to admire the manner in which such remarkable men devoted themselves to the care of the College. Not infrequently the minutes read 'The meeting adjourned at 12.30 am' - after which the secretary had much writing to do. Nor does it come as any surprise that at a Meeting of the Medical Council held April 29th 1867 at Mr Curling's 'The following resolutions were proposed seriatim by Mr Rivington seconded by other members of the staff and carried'. The first was 'That measures should be adopted to improve the London Hospital Medical College and increase the School.' The second, third, and fourth, related to the registering of students and the signing of schedules. The fifth was 'that the Secretary be called Dean and that if necessary a Sub-Dean be appointed.'

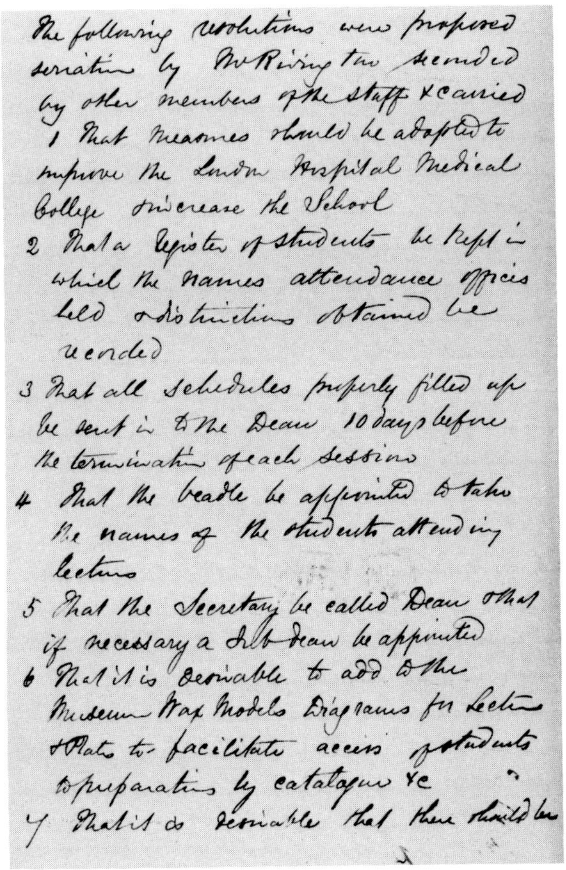

The following resolutions were proposed
seriatim by Mr Rivington seconded
by other members of the staff & carried
1 That measures should be adopted to
improve the London Hospital Medical
College & increase the School
2 That a Register of students be kept in
which the names attendance offices
held & distinctions obtained be
recorded
3 That all schedules properly filled up
be sent in to the Dean 10 days before
the termination of each session
4 That the beadle be appointed to take
the names of the students attending
lectures
5 That the Secretary be called Dean & that
if necessary a Sub-Dean be appointed
6 That it is desirable to add to the
Museum Wax Models Diagrams for Lectures
& Plates to facilitate access of students
to preparations by catalogue &c
7 That it is desirable that there should be

Jonathan Hutchinson, secretary to the Medical Council of the School, minutes resolutions proposed by Walter Rivington.

Thus was appointed the first Dean of the London Hospital Medical College - Jonathan Hutchinson, general surgeon, ophthalmologist, dermatologist, syphilologist, neurologist and secretary of the Medical Council. He took office in 1867 and at the meeting of the Council on October 27th 'Mr Rivington was appointed Vice-Dean and the following duties assigned to that office. The care of all matters relating to the registration of students, their attendance on lectures etc. The arrangements for examinations for prizes etc. The supervision of all matters relating to students' appointments in the Hospital.'

Dean and Vice-Dean were made 'responsible for carrying out the decisions of the Council and entrusted with the maintentance of order and decorum.' It was also determined that the subscription to Lewis' Library should be doubled.

The pattern of Dean and Vice-Dean (or Warden) was common at the time and reflected the need to have one person reponsible for running the school as a whole and another responsible for the care of the students. Apprenticeship outside hospital was ending. Most students spent four years in hospital meeting the differing requirements of differing licensing bodies, and preparing for their differing examinations - a majority working for conjoint or LSA. The quality of training depended increasingly on the satisfactory completion of the scheduled appointments but qualification depended also on passing the increasing number of more testing examinations. This had brought the 'grinders' into business. Some were members of the staff of a school who, acting as guide, philosopher and friend to a group of students, would in effect do their studying for them by talking to them over a glass of ale. Others made a living out of cramming students for examinations. Grinders had the advantage that all who resorted to them had decided 'to do their utmost to ensure success at their examinations' - lecturers and teachers were 'burdened with these men before they had made that decision '(16). The appointment of Vice Deans, Wardens or Tutors was designed to counteract the grinders by providing that care of individual students which the Dean could not give without risking charges of favouritism and the breakdown of discipline.

vii

The London was singularly fortunate in its first Dean and Vice-Dean. Both were dedicated to the improvement of medical education all their lives. Jonathan Hutchinson, later to be Sir Jonathan FRS was, like many who came to the London, a Quaker. Born in Yorkshire in 1820 he did his apprenticeship there, attending courses at the York Medical School (sometimes as the only student) before completing his training at Barts. He was elected Assistant Surgeon to the London in 1859, three years before he took his FRCS. He was appointed lecturer in Surgery to the College in 1862. The 'Spy' Cartoon in Vanity Fair, showing him stooping slightly in his frock coat and high collar, his pince-nez in his hand, and emphasising his long beard and long nose, has made his appearance as familiar as his many and astonishingly wide-ranging contributions which advanced medicine, dermatology, pathology, neurology and ophthalmology as well as surgery.

Sir Jonathan Hutchinson, FRS, PRCS, first Dean of the College.

He was renowned as a teacher, as witness the following tribute from Sir John Byers: 'In 1878, after graduating in medicine I went to the London Hospital where I had the rare good fortune to come under the magic spell and personal inspiration of Jonathan Hutchinson and while no medical school in the United Kingdom had, at that time, an array of more brilliant teachers - Andrew Clark, Hughlings Jackson, Samuel Fenwick, Sutton, James Adams, Morell and Stephen Mackenzie, Couper, Herman, Thomas Barlow and Frederick Treves (as surgical registrar) - it is no disparagement to these most able men to say that Hutchinson was the genius loci who specially attracted outsiders' (17).

Treves described him as having 'the rare gift of making every subject he touched upon interesting and whether he spoke for an hour or two he held the attention of his audience to the end' (18).

Jonathan Hutchinson's contribution to medical education, however, went far beyond providing an example of brilliant teaching and being the London's first Dean. He was responsible for two important advances. One was the development of museums as a means of teaching and learning and the other was postgraduate medical education. He made the museum at the London a model of its kind, persuaded the BMA to mount an exhibition of all things new in the year as part of its annual clinical meeting, and built a museum alongside his home in Park Crescent where he taught at week-ends. Then in 1899 he founded, with Sir William Broadbent and Dr Theodore Williams, the 'Medical Graduates Club and Polyclinic' in Chenies Street.

At the start of the 19th century basic medical education in England had been so inadequate that postgraduate training was important, though it could be obtained only outside the country, mainly in France. By the end of the century basic courses were much improved but medicine was advancing sufficiently quickly to necessitate continuing education as a means of keeping up to date. The West London Hospital began to provide facilities in 1893 but they were limited and poorly taken up. Hutchinson's Polyclinic offered more - lectures, clinical teaching, library and the museum he moved there from Park Crescent. He himself provided periodicals, books and specimens and for some years edited its journal - 'Polyclinic'. Unhappily it depended too much on his personal efforts. When Hutchinson was gone the scheme dried up, wrote Clifford Allbutt in 1921, pointing to the need to provide facilities, staff and organisation for postgraduate medical education. Nonetheless he deserves to be remembered as much for pioneering graduate education in Britain as for his contributions to medical knowledge. His other contribution to the care of medical graduates, the Medical Protection Society, of which he was the first president, continues to flourish.

Walter Rivington: Surgeon and Dean.

The London's first Vice-Dean, Walter Rivington, was born in Highgate, had a brilliant career as a student at the London, was elected to the Staff in 1863 and took the gold medal in the MS the following year. His special clinical field was aural surgery. At one time or another he held all the various lectureships and the chair in Anatomy. He also had nine children and was reported to be one of the best chess players in England. But what concerned him most, and claimed most of his considerable energies throughout his professional life was medical education in general and the London Hospital Medical College in particular. He was the first, though not the last, from the London to win the

Carnegie Prize for medical education, but he soon concentrated his activities on the London itself. He was Vice-Dean for two years, then succeeded Hutchinson as Dean, and throughout his life at the London the minutes of almost every meeting to do with the school include the words 'Mr Rivington proposed', followed by some recommendation for improvement, always well thought through and previously circulated in writing. Not infrequently Mr Rivington appears defending, eventually successfully, but at first alone, a student in trouble or the student body as a whole. For thirty years he was secretary and the moving spirit of the London Hospital Medical Club. Nothing that had to do with the College or its students escaped his notice. It is easy to imagine him writing that piece of the prospectus of 1868-9 which read:

'The health and recreation of Students are not neglected. By kind permission of the House Committee, the Students can play at foot-ball and other games in the field within the Hospital enclosure. There is a foot-ball club. About two years ago one of the Governors built a Fives' Court, on the Eton pattern, for the special use of students.'

Behind Rivington's constant efforts to improve the College and the care of its students lay firm views on medical education derived from the study he made of it in every school in the British Isles, which he wrote up for the Carmichael Prize and published as a book entitled 'The Medical Profession'" in 1879 (16). He concluded that the best, perhaps the only way, by which the teacher can confer lasting benefit is by 'making the student see and feel and reason for himself.' He was also convinced that teaching had a beneficial effect on the standard of hospital care. 'Doing the work of the hospital publicly in the presence of students is the best stimulus to physicians and surgeons to enter thoroughly into the history and nature of their cases'.

The best medical school, he thought, is that 'which adopts a regular system of training in all branches of medical education", but not by organised teaching aimed at covering all subjects in a passive superficial way. He claimed that in the London schools practical physiology 'means cutting up little bits of ordinary tissues and preparing sections for examination under the microscope, and it means looking at specimens supplied by the teacher and listening to a few explanatory comments.' All students and not just a few advanced ones chosen for special instruction, should have the chance given to those at Cambridge, to study the subject more actively and in some depth.

In the clinical subjects nothing should supplant 'painstaking individual training . . . which can only be imparted to groups of 5 or 6 students at the bedside, and in the rooms devoted to the details of clinical work. . .Individual attention to the wants of each student is required.' Tutors, thought Rivington, were needed to supersede the grinders and should be appropriately remunerated for their invaluable functions. Many of Rivington's views were soon applied in practice but today, a century later, many of them are echoed in descriptions of what ought to be, rather than in describing what is.

> Every student should feel that the authorities regarded him with an individual and paternal interest, not unduly prying into his proceedings or subjecting him to any martial discipline, but watching him with that friendly solicitude which would enable them to bring him back to the fold, if unhappily he should be tempted to stray, and afford him such help as he might need to overcome the obstacles to his progress.

Walter Rivington's attitude to students: from his book on "The Medical Profession", 1879.

In other respects if Rivington were to survey the scene today he would be pleased to see his ideas being taken up, even if disappointed that it had taken so long to do so. In 1879 he pointed 'to two circumstances which tend to lower the standards of teaching at the medical schools' in London, especially the smaller ones. The first was the number of schools, which necessitated 11 sets of teachers in the basic medical sciences. 'This diffusion of the teaching function causes a waste and weakness of teaching power and an underpayment of medical professors'. He advocated all the schools joining a Medical Faculty of the University of London which could establish up to three schools of (basic) Medical Science.

The second difficulty in London, in his view, was that all too often teachers were selected from a hospital staff. This not only limited the choice but resulted in too many teachers seeing their lectureship (along with additional hospital appointments, a little private practice, some demonstrating and examining and some insurance work) as a means of earning enough to live on until a large and successful private practice had been built up. 'An iron frame both of mind and body is demanded in this struggle for existence. By concentration alone can excellence be obtained, but the whole system at present in vogue leads to diffusion and loss of strength.'

'No doubt,' wrote Walter Rivington in 1879 (by which time the London School of Medicine for Women had opened in conjunction with the Royal Free Hospital) 'there are immense difficulties in the way of combination of schools: but clearly this is one of the subjects of the future.' The difficulties had been considerably compounded by the time the Todd Report made similar recommendations for similar reasons 89 years later. But he was right in thinking that 'The University of London would become what it ought to become' - a teaching as well as an examining body; and that the State should endow certain professorships for the promotion of science and scientific medicine in the country. Walter was a bit ahead not only of his own but of some in our time too.

The advantages of concentration would be that the lectures would be better worth listening to, the professors would be better paid, and the younger men (the demonstrators) would receive enough to make them devote their whole time to the duties of their office, and would not pay a divided allegiance to hospital and school work, with the chief eye towards the hospital and private practice. All the members of a hospital staff would concentrate their energies on clinical teaching, on medicine, surgery, and pathology, and would receive better remuneration than they do at present. No doubt there are immense difficulties in the way of combination of schools; but clearly this is one of the subjects of the future. At all events let the experiment be tried with regard to botany, comparative anatomy, physics, and inorganic chemistry, which would form the subjects for the preliminary scientific examination. The University of London would gradually become what it ought to become—a teaching as well as an examining body; and the State should endow certain professorships for the promotion of science and scientific medicine in this country.

Rivington pleads for the rationalisation of medical education in London in 1879.

The College ran on under a Dean and Vice Dean for a decade from 1867 to 1876 with the idea emerging that the Deanship should be held by one or other of the senior staff in rotation but that the Vice-Dean's post should be of a more permanent character.

The Deans were, Jonathan Hutchinson (1867-1870), Walter Rivington (1870-1872), Herbert Davies (1872-1873), Andrew Clark (1873-1876). After Rivington, Warren Tay was Vice-Dean from 1870 to 1876.

The decade was, however, one of the most difficult in the history of the College. The increase in the size and workload of the Hospital was enormous. In 1868 it had some 570 beds, admitted over 5000 patients of whom nearly 2600 were emergencies, and cared for 39,000 outpatients, including 3,000 dental patients and 622 women delivered in their own homes. Six years later, with 600 beds, it admitted 5,695 inpatients, more than any other hospital in the country, and tended 46,581 outpatients. Then the number of beds was increased to 800 and in 1877, 6825 inpatients and 47,536 outpatients were treated. Other London teaching hospitals ranged from 150 at UCH to 690 at Guy's. Outside London most were between 200 and 300 with the Royal Infirmary at Edinburgh and Glasgow reaching around 550 (15). It was then agreed at the London to limit the attendance of new patients at each outpatient clinic to 25 and if possible to discharge them again before the end of a month.

As the number of patients increased so did the number of junior posts to be filled by students including posts in the developing special departments: Obstetrics, Dentistry, Skins, Aural, and Ophthalmic. Guy's at this time had some 370 pupils in post at any one time needed for service, not just attached for educational reasons (16). The number of Medical Assistants covering the medical wards at the London was increased almost annually, catching up with the Dressers, and in 1875 it was decided to have 4 House Physicians who had a medical diploma, supported by at first 8, and then 10 Medical Assistants. Students who delivered 100 patients in the District were rewarded with a special Certificate.

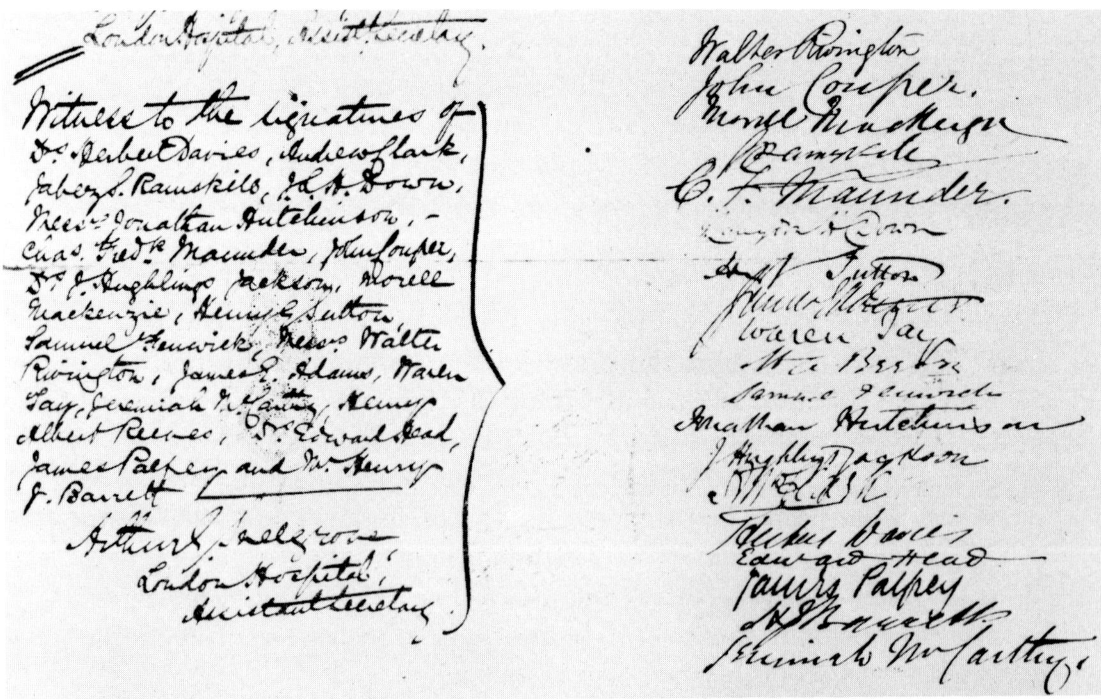
Witness to the signatures of Dr. Herbert Davies, Andrew Clark, Jabez S. Ramskill, J.L.H. Down, Messrs Jonathan Hutchinson, Chas. Fredk Maunder, John Couper, Dr. J. Hughlings Jackson, Morell Mackenzie, Henry G. Sutton, Samuel Fenwick, Messrs Walter Rivington, James E. Adams, Warren Tay, Jeremiah McCarthy, Henry Albert Reeves, Dr. Edward Head, James Palfrey and Mr. Henry J. Barrett

Arthur J. [illegible]
London Hospital,
Assistant Secretary

Walter Rivington
John Couper.
Morell Mackenzie
J. S. Ramskill
C. F. Maunder.
[illegible] H. Down
[illegible] Sutton
[illegible]
Warren Tay
[illegible]
Samuel Fenwick
Jonathan Hutchinson
J. Hughlings Jackson
[illegible]
Herbert Davies
Edward Head
James Palfrey
H. J. Barrett
Jeremiah McCarthy

The College Lecturers agree to the terms of a loan from the Hospital in 1869.

The school had to attract more and more students and to do so had not only to try to ensure good examination results, but above all to improve and extend its facilities. In 1862 improvements were made and paid for by the teachers. In 1869 the Hospital provided £2,000 for enlarging the school buildings, to be paid back by the lecturers over the next 20 years. An additional museum, with a gallery for demonstration purposes, (at the instigation of Jonathan Hutchinson), a further reading room and facilities for microscopy were provided. Then in 1876 the lecturers put up £3,000 for more extensions, in consideration of which they were released from paying back the balance on the loan of seven years earlier.

The need, however, was not only for capital with which to build. Running expenses grew too, and could not easily be met just by raising fees. So in 1871 the House Committee offered a grant of £200 per annum and a Joint Sub-Committee, comprising three Hospital Governors and three members of the School Council, was set up to report on any defects in the working of the College. Inevitably there were plenty. No group of men, increasingly heavily engaged in clinical practice in a constantly expanding hospital and having repeatedly to plan, finance and erect new school buildings, could possibly keep it running at a high level of efficiency with almost no administrative help. It became clear that more revenue was needed but if it were to be provided by the Hospital the Governors, not unnaturally, wanted a say in management and wanted to see a whole-time administrator in post.

Intense negotiations ensued. In 1876 one proposal after another was debated in the House Committee and in the Medical Council, along with Mr Rivington's proposals for curriculum planning and for supervising the clinical work of students. Week after week the lights burned late in Cavendish Square until eventually on Monday, April 10th 1876 at 8.30 o'clock pm at Dr Clark's House, 16 Cavendish Square, the Council agreed that the School should be run by a College Board and a Secretary who should be a medical man, appointed and paid by the Board. The Governors would provide £2,000 per annum for three years and the Board would consist of nine representatives of the House Committee and six of the Council, the Chairman being the Chairman of the House Committee. The Governors undertook to appoint only such members 'as can give sufficient time and attention carefully to consider the special requirements and circumstances of the London Hospital and School - believing that the position of the Hospital has always had a deterrent influence which can only be overcome by the Lecturers, Teachers and other Officers of the College providing greater inducements and opportunities in the London Hospital College than are offered in other Medical Institutions in the Metropolis.'

Subsequently 'it was definitely agreed that the Medical Council should depute its executive functions to the newly instituted Board, meeting only to elect its representatives at this Board' -those elected by ballot for the first twelve months being Rivington, Sutton, Down, Couper, McCarthy and Tidy.

The Council did, however, meet again the following July to discuss the proposed admission of female students on which subject the Chairman, Dr Andrew Clark, drew up the following statement: 'We the undersigned members of the staff having carefully considered the question of the contemplated admission of women to the general practice of the London Hospital are unanimously and strongly of opinion that this measure would prove highly injurious to the interests of the Hospital and would probably lead to the breaking up of the Medical School. The deputation appointed to wait upon the (House) Committee will explain, if desired, the grounds upon which they have been led to this conclusion'.

Subsequently this motion was signed by all the Staff save Dr Fenwick and Dr Hughlings Jackson.

ix

So the system of Dean and Vice-Dean ended. Dr Andrew Clark, the retiring Dean, gave the inaugural address at the opening of the 92nd Session of the College in October 1876. Describing the crucial change in the management of the College he referred to the latter being taken over by the Hospital: 'in virtue of their subsidy to educational work the Governors of it will now have a ruling majority on the new College Board.' He went on to outline the advantages of this arrangement, showing in the process that his reputation as a fluent orator was well merited.

'To its deliberations the medical element will bring its technical knowledge, its educational experience and its high responsibility to the profession; the lay element, its larger leisure, its freedom from the disturbing elements of professional jealousy, and its moral obligations in the interests of the Hospital and the well-being of Society. From their united counsels we expect fresh accessions of administrative strength, unity of plan and action, and a more efficient working of our administrative machine; and lastly, a higher kind and larger measure of educational success.'

Sir Andrew Clark, Bart, FRS, PRCP .

The more efficient working of the administrative machine clearly depended on the appointment of a Secretary and to this the new College Board applied itself at once. In doing so it was influenced by two things. First there was the proposal that Walter Rivington had got through the Council, and the negotiations, that the £2,000 p.a. grant 'be expended on improvements at the school, but not by way of subsidising the members of the Staff and Lecturers' (carried by a majority of 7 to 6). Secondly, the grant had been made on the understanding that if the receipts of the school over each of the three years were greater than over the previous years the difference would be divided between Council and Hospital until the £2,000 was repaid. So the Board had to aim at both enlarging the School so as to satisfy the Hospital and return its money and at improving the quality of the courses so as to satisfy the staff, who thought a beginning should be made by a study of teaching elsewhere including the 'Scotch and English Universities'.

The Sub-committee appointed to draw up the duties of the Secretary put the first as 'ascertaining the methods of teaching, apparatus etc in use in other Hospitals'. He was secondly to keep the Board informed on the attendance of Lecturers and Hospital Staff. He was to see that the Students attended regularly and 'further to exercise such beneficial control as may be practicable over their conduct and occupation after College hours.' He was made responsible for the care of the College and its contents, entrusted with the control of the College Servants (Bedell and porters) and expected generally to assist in developing its resources. Whatever part the lay members (who consisted of Sir Edmund Currie* Chairman of the House Committee, two members of the Buxton family who did so much for the London, Mr Crossman, W J Thompson, the Rev Kitto, the Rev Scott and Commander Davis RN) played in defining this job-description, it must surely have been their business acumen which led to the decision that the Secretary's remuneration (hours of work 10 to 5 'at least') should consist of £300 p a, plus 5% on all students' fees received.

The Sub-Committee was proceeding to consider the appointment, 'when it appeared that Mr Robert Kershaw MRCS who has had considerable experience at the London Hospital and its requirements would be thoroughly qualified for the important and delicate position.' Mr Kershaw, 'who happened to be in the Hospital' was thereupon seen and eventually it was resolved to appoint him. He was allowed to keep but not extend his small local private practice and seems to have set to work with energy and enthusiasm. The teaching of each subject was considered in turn and various changes made, though at times the Board came up against those problems of a medical school to which there is no easy answer. Thus Dr Kershaw reported on his interview with the Lecturer in Botany:

*
Sir Edmund Hay Currie forged the first link between the London Hospital Medical College and Queen Mary College. He had followed his father onto the Governors of the London Hospital and become Chairman of the House Committee. Currie Ward was named after them both. He had served also on the School Board for London before becoming the first Chairman of the new College Board of LMHC in 1876. In 1882 he was made Chairman of the Beaumont Trustees and in that capacity played a leading role in the creation of the Peoples Palace and the technical schools which were to become first the East London Technical College and finally Queen Mary College.

Mr Baker considers that the chief cause of inattention and disturbance is due to the fact that Botany is a subject not required in the majority of examinations- also that the noise is mostly caused by a few students... and second year students are usually the ring-leaders.'

Almost a hundred years earlier Botany had seemed so important to the pupils that they had presented Busick Harwood with a silver cup for giving them a course of lectures in it.

The Board and its several Sub-Committees of lay and medical members applied itself energetically to all aspects of the school, checking on failure rates in examinations, dealing with student discipline, appointing students to posts, and advising the Governors on the suitability of applicants for Hospital Staff vacancies. It insisted on the registrars checking students' clinical notes and reporting on them. It appointed only those who had completed six months clerking and six months dressing as resident accoucheur. Then suddenly in November 1877 Dr Kershaw died, having clearly done much, as the Board put it, to improve the school by his enlightened and conscientious efforts. To make matters worse the Bedell and his assistants had to be summarily dismissed, and the need to extend the buildings yet again was becoming urgent.

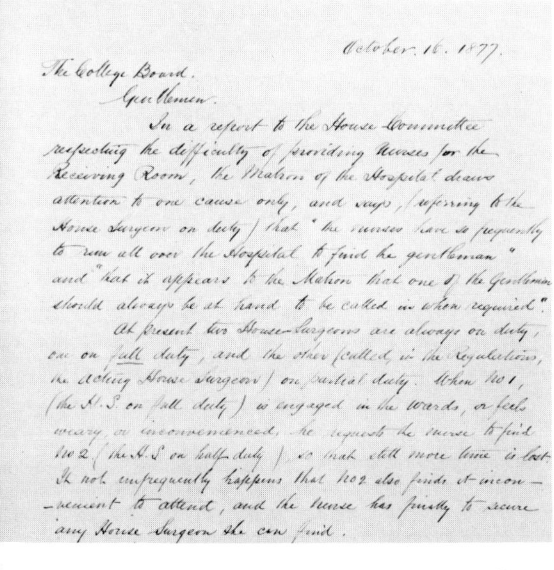

October 16. 1877.

The College Board.

Gentlemen.

In a report to the House Committee respecting the difficulty of providing Nurses for the Receiving Room, the Matron of the Hospital draws attention to one cause only, and says, (referring to the House Surgeon on duty) that "the nurses have so frequently to run all over the Hospital to find the gentleman" and "that it appears to the Matron that one of the Gentlemen should always be at hand to be called in when required".

At present two House-Surgeons are always on duty, one on full duty, and the other (called, in the Regulations, the Acting House Surgeon) on partial duty. When No 1, (the H. S. on full duty) is engaged in the Wards, or feels weary, or inconvenienced, he requests the nurse to find No 2 (the H. S on half-duty) so that still more time is lost. It not unfrequently happens that No 2 also finds it inconvenient to attend, and the nurse has finally to secure any House Surgeon she can find.

A Perennial problem — the post of Receiving Room Officer was created in 1885.

Under such circumstances the Board had to replace the Secretary as quickly as possible - and decided to do so by appointing a Principal who would have a seat on the Board itself. It offered the post to a Dr Norman Chevers MD, FRCS at £300 p.a. and 5% commission on all students' fees. Who proposed him is not clear, but the minutes and subsequent events suggest the Reverend Kitto. Dr Chevers was later to describe himself in the following terms;

'The present incumbent did not seek the appointment which he has the honour to hold. It was offered to him and he was induced with difficulty to accede to the offer. He holds the inspectorial rank of Deputy Surgeon General in Her Majesty's Army; nearly 20 years ago he occupied the office of Inspector-General over the 52 Jails of Bengal for two years in the absence of the permanent incumbent; and for 15 years he was entrusted, under the sole control of the Government, with the post of Principal of the Calcutta Medical College, the number of whose students was raised, under his administration, from 400 to nearly 1500.'

Dr Chevers no doubt felt that the job of Secretary was beneath him and presumably the post of Principal was created in order to attract him. He accepted it and set to work at once. A clerk was soon appointed to assist him. The task of improving the course was continued and changes made to ensure that students were more adequately prepared for each increase in clinical responsibility. The entry of students increased, however, from around 60 in 1877 to 100 in 1878-9. But only 50 came for the full course, the other 50 were 'special' students, graduates of colonial and foreign Medical Colleges, coming for as much of the clinical course as they needed to take an English qualification. Some came from America and Canada and others from Calcutta. Dr Chevers had seized upon the device by which British Universities seek today to make both ends meet, increasing the number of overseas students.

'The service of the Hospital' wrote Dr Chevers in a 'Memorandum by the College Board' printed in May 1879, 'benefits considerably by the work done by these gentlemen, as efficient Dressers and Clinical Clerks, and our Students also benefit by a valuable class of men, who are generally their seniors and who have come from distant lands with an earnest determination to accomplish themselves by acquiring a knowledge of English practice.' Upwards of £500, he added, had been received as fees from Special Students during the last twelve months (and in fact the receipts of the College had enabled the Hospital subsidy to be paid back).

The 'full' students, not surprisingly, would have preferred to forgo the benefit of contact with a valuable class of foreign graduates in return for a better chance of obtaining the coveted clinical appointments. This feeling was, however, not referred to in the Board's Report. This stated that in its desire to 'make their Students gentlemen (worthy to become members of the noble profession which they are about to practice; self-denying men, consulting the interests of their science and of their patients before their own)' the Board had appointed as Principal of the College 'an independent physician, sedulous in cultivating a high tone of feeling among the Students, and in promoting among the Teachers that unity of working, the result of which is success.' As a result 'The Board are happy in being able to declare that almost perfect discipline is maintained among the Students, who are a very industrious and gentlemanly body of young men.'

That the College Board of 1879 could describe the students of the London in such terms is naturally pleasing but in fact the College Board had seen nothing of the Memorandum until it was circulated, and were far from happy with any part of it. The only unity it promoted among the Teachers was one of hostility to Dr Chevers, not least because of his opening statement to the effect that in 1876, before he came, the College was in an unsatisfactory condition, altogether unable to supply the increasing demands of the enlarged Hospital, and mainly because 'the system of administration was extremely defective.'

No doubt there was some truth in most of Dr Chevers' statements, particularly if the College were to be viewed solely as a mechanism for staffing the Hospital. Very obviously the Staff had never seen it in that light, but even if they or anyone else had, the Chevers method of improving the situation was unacceptable and Dr Chevers himself was equally unacceptable as the main means of providing the much needed administrative infrastructure.

X

Even before Dr Chevers had produced his Memorandum the Medical Council of the Medical School had been struggling with the problem of what to do for the best for the College which they still saw as theirs, inherited from their predecessors and held in trust for their successors. The three years of the £2,000 p.a. subsidy from the Hospital were coming to an end. They accepted that a grant from the Hospital would always be needed. They considered it was no more than a fair payment for services rendered (by the students) but that in return for financial help the Hospital should in equal fairness have a say in management. They accepted the concept of the joint lay and professional College Board - but not the 9 lay and 6 professional composition that had been agreed in 1876 - an agreement which they considered to be for three years only. They were determined that College posts should not be filled solely from Hospital Staff and that the executive officer, whether Secretary or Principal, should be restricted to implementing the Board's policy and not in a position to decide it for himself.

Plaque on No 15 Cavendish Square.

Sir Andrew Clark lived next door at No 16 where in 1879 the Medical Council agreed to the merger of College and Hospital.

On top of all that the Council faced the problem that the increase in students made further extension of the College buildings essential. So through the early months of 1879 the Council met repeatedly until late into the night at 16 Cavendish Square, with Andrew Clark in the chair and Dr Thomas Gilbart Smith*, recently appointed Assistant Physician, as Secretary. He was a graduate of Trinity College Dublin and had also studied at Barts and in Paris. He 'kept up considerable style, driving to the Hospital in a stylish Victoria with red painted wheels'.

The Governors of the Hospital and especially the House Committee also met frequently to consider the future of the school. They too wanted a bigger and better school but only so as more easily to meet the needs of a large and still growing hospital. They took the view that by the arrangement of 1876 the Staff had surrendered its right of ownership in and management of the School. After nearly 100 years as an independent educational institution the battle for the future of the College was well and truly joined. Describing it later in a 'History of the Medical Council, Medical and Surgical Staff, and College Board' published by order of the Medical Council, Gilbart Smith wrote:

'The year 1879 witnessed a well fought contest between the House Committee and the Medical Council during which opposing views led to long and intricate negotiations involving conflicting interests, which happily were at length amicably arranged by the Governors and Staff entering into agreement. This established the College Board on a firm and satisfactory basis; safeguards the interests of the Staff and Lecturers as handed down by a long line of predecessors; and gives to either party the right of terminating the arrangement at a year's notice.

'While thus the College Board manages the School on behalf of the Hospital, the Medical Council consisting of the Staff of Lecturers, meets from time to time in accordance with its time-honoured regulations to discuss, and to advise the House Committee upon all matters affecting the joint interests of the Hospital and its Medical and Surgical Staff and to elect its representatives on the College Board; while in the event of a vacancy occurring on the staff of the Hospital, a meeting of the Medical and Surgical Staff is thereupon summoned to instruct the Senior Physician and Senior Surgeon to recommend the candidate selected to the consideration of the House Committee.'

The New College Board was composed of equal numbers, six each, from the House Committee and the Medical Council of the School comprising the Hospital Staff and Lecturers. It was agreed that the Chairman of the House Committee would chair the Board, with a casting vote. Agreements were drawn up covering the earnings of Lecturers. Hospital staff would be appointed to Lectureships only if considered in all ways qualified. Finally it was agreed that the College Board should appoint a Secretary at a fixed salary with the addition of a percentage on the amount divided among the staff and lecturers, that his duties should be definitely prescribed in harmony with the laws of the Council, and that lay and medical Visitors should inspect the College once a week and report to the Board.

The final agreement was drawn up in a legal document and signed on June 4th 1879 by the Hospital Treasurer on behalf of the Governors and by the twenty six members of the College Council. After 94 years of independent existence the London Hospital Medical College amalgamated with the London Hospital, with each retaining the right to terminate the arrangement by giving 12 months notice in writing.

The College Board met later in June to discuss the appointment of visitors. Dr Chevers regarded this as a personal insult but failed to find much support in the Board. A proposal that he should be given three months' notice led to the resignation of three of the lay members and his own resignation was unanimously accepted on October 20th.

Dr Andrew Clark 'in the name of the Council, presented Dr Gilbart Smith with a silver salver in acknowledgement of his indefatigable, able and valuable services throughout the long course of the negotiations ending in the establishment of the new College Board.'

By the end of 1879 the College had been extended yet again, enlarging and improving the dissecting room, adding to the laboratories and providing a special room for practical Physiology and a separate reading room for students taking examinations.

* A granite memorial in the shape of a seat was erected to his memory near Sidmouth. The inscription reads: 'Thomas Gilbart Smith a succourer of many. Thus closed a noble life spent in the service of his fellow men. He never turned his back on duty but faithful to his motto "dare and do" remained undaunted to the end. On this spot at half past nine o'clock after watching the glorious sunset of Aug 3 1904 Thomas Gilbart Smith fell dead from his bicycle. '

xi

So ended the independent phase of the London Hospital Medical College. It had lasted for nearly a hundred years. Its founders had created a school of a kind previously unknown in England. They had then pioneered over the first fifty years a new form of medical education. This had been consolidated and organised during the subsequent half-century and further developed in eleven more schools of a similar kind in London. The new type of medicine had been forwarded thereby - making hospitals dependent upon students and medical schools dependent on hospitals. But England's first 'complete medical school in connection with a hospital upon the model of the medical faculty of a University' (as Little had described the London in 1854) had not become the kind of university medical school which had existed for so long in other countries and which in 1879 were more active than ever.

Some at the London had obviously hoped that it would. There had been no vehement protest from the London against a charter for London University as there had been from Barts and elsewhere. Some years later Walter Rivington, for one, saw clearly the need for a teaching university in London, not least to ensure the kind of research which, in the German universities especially, was doing so much to advance medicine - though he was careful to point out that 'the wisdom of advocating a recourse to the German system as a panacea for our own shortcomings can be doubted'. He did in fact try hard to persuade his colleagues to issue a statement that it would be against the public interest for the Victoria University of Manchester to be allowed to give degrees in medicine - but that was only because he was opposed to adding yet another Licensing Body to the existing long list of those with differing requirements and examinations. Besides, he was convinced that the training which the metropolitan medical schools, retaining their 'independent organisation' but properly related to a university and properly 'distributed (like the work-house infirmaries) with a due regard to the wants of the population' could not be equalled elsewhere. 'By all means let us have a University system and a University Faculty in London, but let us not scatter Universities broadcast over the land, and lose the practical training which is the best feature of medical education' (16).

Rivington's concept of what might be achieved in the provinces may have been limited by the feeling (not uncommon in those who work in it) that the Metropolis reaches standards which other parts cannot reach, but he had a very clear perception of London's weaknesses as well as strengths. The Faculty of Medicine was needed and it did come, but not for another 20 years from the time at which he was writing. By the time the University of London was reconstituted at the turn of the century, the London Medical Schools had become as dependent on hospitals as the hospitals were on the schools. After the union of College and Hospital at the London in 1879 the medical schools of University College and Kings College still remained parts of independent educational institutions, but not long after 1900, and the reconstitution of the University, the two Colleges both turned their medical schools over to the hospitals which they themselves had founded. Medical education in London, because of the direction it took in 1785, because for so long there was no university, and because of the coincidental ever-growing need for medical care in Voluntary Hospitals, became firmly based on the Hospital Medical Schools and remained so till nearly the middle of the twentieth century. Nor, as it turned out, was this unique pattern of medical education anything other than excellent over the whole of that long period.

The pattern of training in London was based on the principle of students entering the wards as informed apprentices and therafter learning by participation in medical care under supervision. It was perfectly tailored to prepare practitioners for the medicine of the late nineteenth and early twentieth centuries, a medicine which consisted of 'a system of diagnosis based on the elucidation of physical signs, a system of pathology based on purely physical science (morbid anatomy, bacteriology and the beginnings of chemistry), and a system of treatment which attempted to counteract the physical causes of disease' (1). What went on in hospital mirrored precisely what went on in medicine outside, and all that could be done outside could be learned inside. By 1879 the aim of medical schools had become, and after 1886 was required to be, the production of fully trained safe general practitioners; and the training given in the London schools was probably the best in the world. It contrasted sharply and favourably with that obtainable in the university-based research-orientated schools best exemplified in Germany. It had many advantages over that provided separately by university and hospital authorities as in France and to a lesser extent in Scotland and the English provincial schools.

The London pattern depended for its success on the closest possible collaboration between school and hospital to ensure not only the right mixture of patients and the right number and kind of teachers but also the right facilities. During its independent phase the London Hospital Medical College had always had access to an ample supply of patients. Its original buildings had been erected by means of a public subscription. They had been replaced at the hospital's expense and added to by the teachers themselves, and the hospital had stepped in to meet the rising cost of administration. The school because of its independence had not only been free to select its teachers but in a position to get many of them appointed to the hospital. The results were remarkably successful. Of the twenty-six lecturers and members of the hospital staff who signed the agreement to unite with the Hospital in 1879, five were Fellows of the Royal Society, three had been or were to become President of the Royal College of Surgeons and two became President of the Royal College of Physicians, though one, Thomas Barlow, was to return to his alma mater University College before doing so. The names of no less than five are still to be found in every textbook of medicine.

There were distinctive features about the students also. One example serves to indicate a type of student commonly attracted to the London at this time and personifies how some reacted to its established tradition. Thomas Barnardo came to train as a medical missionary and, while still a student, started first his school and then his Childrens' Homes. He was not the first, or the last of his kind, but remains perhaps the best known of the many who were like him.

The Homes Barnardo founded as a student are still at work today.

So the first phase (of independent educational institution) ended, and the second phase (of Hospital Medical School) began, with the College having the advantage of the biggest hospital in the country, a team of exceptional teachers, and a student body including many with unusually strong motivation. It had one further asset which was perhaps even more important - the peculiar, perhaps unique, quality of the relationship between school and hospital which derived from the school's long initial period of independence.

A glance at the 'well-fought contest' of 1879 reveals with sharp clarity the 'conflicting interests' of a hospital desperately needing clerks and dressers and a school striving to offer the best education and training. Closer study of the account of those interminable meetings in Cavendish Square reveals something else - the extent to which the school ('as distinguished from the buildings') existed as a living entity in the minds of its staff. True they saw it as a means of remuneration but they undoubtedly saw it as much more than that, an educational institution handed down to them 'by a long line of predecessors' and held by them in trust for the future.

It is equally clear that those lay representatives of the Hospital engaged in the contest of 1879 also came to see the College in the same light. In consequence the agreement reached was very different from the proposals originally made by the Hospital and included all that was sought by the Council of the College in order to safeguard education. In the end it was not a take-over. It was an agreement (terminable by a year's notice on either side) between two bodies, with common interests but differing though interwoven aims, and with respect for each other.

PART II

THE HOSPITAL SCHOOL

Chapter 4.

The Fortunate School

i

During the period 1879-1948, medicine advanced steadily, even rapidly after the turn of the century. Progress however was a matter of improvement and extension on lines already laid down. There was no revolution in medicine such as that which had taken place in the middle of the 19th century or that which was to occur in the middle of the 20th.

Asepsis and anaesthesia (ether, chloroform and nitrous oxide) made surgery more successful. Pathology, Bacteriology and the basic sciences led to an increased understanding of disease processes but medical treatment progressed more slowly. Compassion, comfort and loving care remained the physician's most effective weapons, including the comfort that comes from being given a precise diagnosis even if it is no more than the name of a disease. Little comfort and not much care, however, were available for mental disorders of any kind. Concern was for organic disease and signs drew more interest than symptoms.

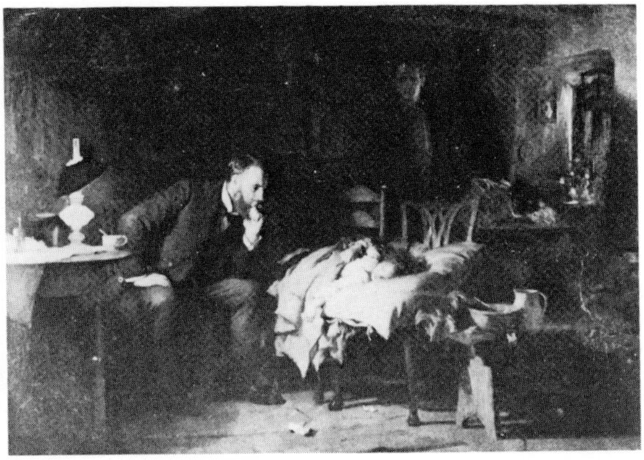

The Doctor, by Luke Fildes 1891

Throughout the whole period, too, the need for medical care continued unabated. The incidence of trauma was maintained by accidents in the home, at work and on the streets. The building of sewers and other public health measures prevented major epidemics of cholera and typhoid but acute virulent infective disease took its constant toll of infants, children and those in the prime of life, especially the many facing poverty, bad housing and malnutrition. Not till the second world war did the majority of the population begin, despite rationing, to enjoy a reasonably nutritious diet. Not till after it did the country contain large numbers of old people.

In 1886 a further change in the medical licensing laws confirmed the pattern of health care delivery as a large number of generalists and a smaller number of, at first broadly based, specialists. The General Medical Council as constituted in 1858 had not done much to enable the public to know who was properly trained and who was not - and the profession were unhappy with their lack of representation on the Council. Efforts to improve the situation were continuing but were constantly thwarted by one vested interest or another, until after some twenty unsuccessful Bills and a Royal Commission, a new Medical Act was passed in 1886. It allowed for representation of the profession on the Council and laid down:

'that the standards of proficiency required from candidates at the qualifying examination shall be such as to guarantee the possession of the knowledge and skill requisite for the efficient practice of medicine, surgery and midwifery.'

From then on all medical schools had one single clear purpose -the preparation of fully trained general practitioners.

General Practitioners provided care, mostly surgical of course, in their 'surgeries' or in the homes of their patients. Physicians and surgeons too, becoming progressively more easily able to travel long distances, treated the better off at home or in nursing homes. Big hospitals began to maintain a staff of trained nurses available on call to move into a home anywhere, in return for payment to the Charity.

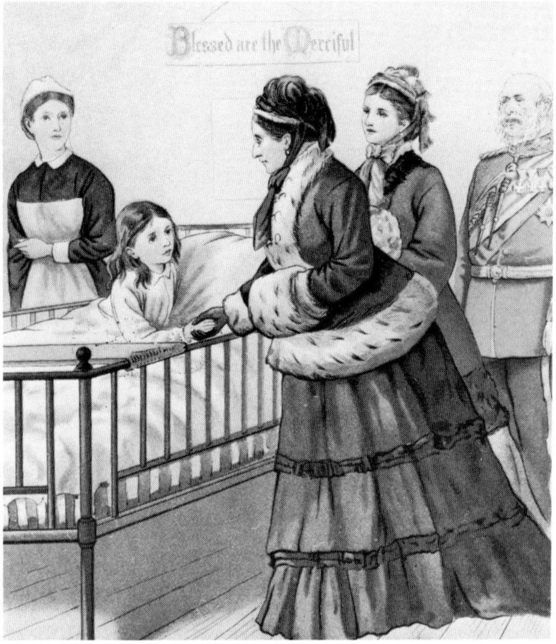

Queen Victoria visits the London: the text above the bed contrasts with the No Smoking notices of today.

For much of the period from the 1880s to the 1940s home or a nursing home were the safest places in which to be ill, but hospitals remained the major and often the only source of help for the poor. After 1911, National Health Insurance made general practitioner care available to working men, but for the thousands of men, women and children crowded in slums, admission to hospital offered the only hope of survival when serious illness or injury struck. The state began to provide fever hospitals, sanatoria for those with tuberculosis and institutions for the mentally ill. Workhouse infirmaries improved slowly. The first attempt to provide general hospitals funded by local rates began in Birmingham in 1913, was held up by the Great War, but was successfully completed after it. Municipal hospitals followed in most big cities and were made the responsibility of city councils in 1930. None of these developments however could keep the demand on the voluntary hospitals down to a level they could easily meet.

From 1879 to 1948 the London Hospital continued to face a rising need for its services, coming almost entirely from the population around it. It continued to grow, upwards and outwards as fast as money could be found for more wards and more accommodation for nurses, reaching 900 beds soon after the turn of the century. After that the struggle for growth continued, not for more beds, but to provide the space and facilities (theatres, laboratories and departments of many kinds) on which diagnosis and treatment came increasingly to depend.

Queen Victoria arriving at the London

The spectrum of disease within a hospital continued to mirror precisely that outside, making it the perfect situation in which to acquire, in the five year course laid down tby the GMC in 1885, the knowledge and skill needed by the fully trained safe general practitioner which every student had to become. The GMC listed the subjects and all licensing bodies were required to examine them all, the Colleges of Physicians and Surgeons forming the Conjoint Board for the purpose. The last remaining vestiges of the old apprenticeships to individual doctors went when the GMC, under pressure from the schools, forbade the attachment of students to general practitioners, but within the hospital schools apprenticeship to hospital firms remained the essential learning situation.

Right up to the end of the second world war students learned by participating in the care of the sick, as a clerk, dresser or assistant of some kind attached to one or two physicians or surgeons, aided by a qualified house officer and perhaps a 'First Assistant' or registrar. The English hospital provided an ideal basis for this system of training because unlike those of other countries, it was subdivided into as many small autonomous clinical units as it had permanent, though part-time, senior medical staff.

Students came to the wards after a vocationally orientated introduction to the sciences basic to medicine, and then, as informed apprentices, shared in the work of a firm, and were an essential part of the functioning machine. They carried considerable responsibility, though with gradually increasing supervision and steadily increasing support from an expanding force of better trained nurses. They shared the enormous burden of daily - often twice daily - dressing of wounds, and a vast quantity of minor surgery, performed in wards and out-patients. Right up to 1948 they dealt with acutely ill young people suffering from florid organic disease, relatively easily diagnosed and much of it due to infection which in the absence of antibiotics frequently necessitated the letting out of pus. Along with the acquisition of manual skills they built up that knowledge of people, and of how they react to adversity, which comes best (perhaps only) from actually participating in the care of large numbers of them. They were taught little or no psychiatry but they learned about people.

The statue of William Booth in Mile End Waste commemorates his founding of the Salvation Army there in 1865. From then till now the London and its students have shared in the care of the thousands of men and women succoured in the "Army's" Hostels in and around the Whitechapel Road.

Up to 1900 'preclinical' instruction came only from practising clinicians holding posts of lecturer in anatomy, physiology or pathology prior to or at the same time as a clinical hospital appointment. Then as the basic medical sciences advanced specialist appointments were made in them, leading to whole-time academic posts of Professor, Reader or Lecturer when the University of London was reconstituted as a federal university able not only to hold examinations, but to foster teaching and research in the various colleges (including the medical schools) incorporated in it.

Soon after, efforts were made to introduce senior whole-time paid clinical appointments. Considerable anxiety was felt that Britain, though increasingly well served by well trained doctors, was lagging behind in the advancement of medicine, the frontiers of which were being more rapidly pushed back in countries like Germany, where University Medical Schools provided ample opportunities for research in professorial clinical units. In 1913 the Haldane Commission recommended the establishment of whole-time clinical units in British teaching hospitals, and funds were provided by the Board of Education. The first world war intervened but after it a number of hospitals, including the London, started such units in Medicine and Surgery, financed by a new body called the University Grants Committee, which required the directors of units to be professors.

The purpose of these professorial units was to forward research, to train a cadre of academic clinicians, and to introduce students to the scientific method of thought and a more critical approach to clinical practice. It was not intended that professors should teach the whole of their subject to all the students: this task the part-time staff were admirably equipped to perform and prepared to do for nothing, their recompense being that today's students would become tomorrow's general practitioners and refer to their old teachers the private patients through whom they earned their living.

The introduction of small numbers of whole-time teachers reflected the increasing sophistication of medicine, as did the proliferation of laboratories, anaesthetic rooms, arrangements for sterilisation, and in time Xray departments. All made medical care more effective and more expensive, less easily given in the home and more dependent on purpose-built premises - though in fact those provided were more often than not very old premises converted to a new use. Each step forward was one step nearer to the eventual break-down of the system; the capacity of voluntary hospitals (even though aided by municipal general hospitals) to provide hospital care for the poor and the increasing numbers of not so poor now requiring it; the capacity of students to acquire all the knowledge and skill requisite for the efficient practice of medicine, surgery and midwifery; the capacity of doctors to give good care, even if possessed of the relevant knowledge and skill, unless also equipped to think critically for themselves.

Even in the nineteen-thirties, however, the system continued to function and medicine remained in balance. Doctors were well-prepared (especially by the practical training in the hospital medical schools) to provide most of what medicine had to offer and the pattern of health care delivery allowed them to make it available to a majority of the people - certainly to the rich and the very poor, though much less easily to those in between. Probably no other country had a form of medical education better suited to the medicine of the time and undoubtedly no medical school in Britain was better placed to give it than the London Hospital Medical College between 1879 and 1948.

Munro Scott, Paymaster R.N.,
Warden of the College 1880-1910.

ii

The College's first advantage was of course the size of the London Hospital and the nature of its work, the exceptionally high proportion of accidents and emergencies and the extraordinary range of disease consequent on its proximity to the vast Port of London bringing people from all over the world, very many of whom came as immigrants and refugees to settle, or at least squat, in the already overcrowded East End. A second advantage was the quality of the nursing which, as unsatisfactory as in most hospitals until the 1850s was raised (not without great trials and tribulations at first) to a level unsurpassed anywhere by Eva Lückes who came as Matron in 1879 and died still in post in 1919.

A third advantage was the preparedness of the Hospital Governors to support the school despite the immense difficulties of maintaining and constantly extending and modernising the hospital. The College Board, drawn equally from the school and the hospital governors and chaired by the Chairman of the Hospital House Committee, took its duties very seriously. Its first action in 1880 was to advertise for a lay Warden. From ten applicants it chose Munro Scott, an ex-Paymaster RN. As executive officer in charge of students, he maintained his particular Naval brand of discipline for 30 years. Not until his retirement in 1910 did the College return to Deans.

From 1879 to the outbreak of the Second World War in 1939 all but the few whole-time members of staff continued to earn their living in private practice. Back in the 1870s 'Mr Rivington proposed and the Council unanimously agreed to petition the Hospital that physicians and surgeons be paid', but the Hospital had no money. Payment for teaching became progressively less as the years went by, finally becoming a token honorarium. Yet always individuals came forward to take on those extra tasks which are as important to the well-being of a medical school as teaching, care of patients and research - committees, sub-committees, management of the library, curatorship of the Museum (in which the mantle of Jonathan Hutchinson fell eventually on Donald Hunter) and all the innumerable activities associated with students and the Clubs Union. More important still, every year some carried the burden of serving on the College Board.

This small compact group dealt, year in year out, with every aspect of the school, from the details of the curriculum to the planning of the future, all the problems of keeping pace with constantly changing circumstances, all the complaints about students and all the complaints by students. 1885 - 'Resolved, House Officers to have certificate of proficiency in anaesthetics; Secretary to enquire which surgeon willing to give instruction...Reported no surgeon willing'. June 1866 Mr Fred Hewitt appointed as teacher of anaesthetics... Mr —, student, refused leave of absence during take-in week... The Board finds no evidence that the Warden acted in an arbitrary and unjust manner...Dr — to be informed there will be no refund of fees -his son's failure in the MRCS examination being caused entirely by lack of application and not by want of ability...The three month course in practical surgery to include operations on dead subjects, to be provided at the Hospital's expense.'

Over the years the nature of the problems changed but never the quantity. Sometimes, but not often, the student body put forward suggestions for changes in the course or additions to it. More often their problems centred on anxiety that one particular group might be receiving preferential treatment in clinical appointments or the allocation of house posts. In all these issues, big and small, the lay members of the Board shared, bringing their experience of other worlds but acquiring the most detailed knowledge of College and Hospital. As Sir Andrew Clark had forecast the Board combined the 'medical' elements - technical knowledge, educational experience and responsibility to the profession, with the 'lay' elements - moral obligations in the interests of the Hospital and the well being of Society.

Marlborough R Pryor, Governor of the Hospital, joined the College Board in 1880.

The College owes a great debt of gratitude to those who have provided it with a 'lay element' from 1876 to now. In all that time it has never lacked, not even for a month, the voice of the lay public in its affairs. It can boast of a record of service and loyalty from one particular family which it is unlikely that any other school can equal. Mr Marlborough R Pryor joined the College Board in February 1880. He was succeeded by his son Col R Marlborough Pryor who served on it till he became Chairman of the Council of Governors of the College in 1948, in which position he was succeeded by Mr Matthew Pryor, who remains Chairman today -106 years of service from three members of one family.

The Medical Council of the College continued to watch over the academic affairs and development of the school but it became at first equally and later primarily concerned with hospital matters. From the 1800s to the 1930s medical education was in any case in a settled state, and there was no fundamental change in medicine to which it had to adapt. Apart from issues such as the appointment of whole time teachers in basic medical sciences, pathology, and then in the clinical field, medical education remained a relatively cheap by-product of medical care and followed in the wake of hospital organisation. But it needed buildings, and certain facilities for students and teaching in the hospital itself.

In 1882, three years after the union of College and Hospital, a spacious structure, named the London Hospital Students Club, standing upon ground allotted by the Governors 'was built so that students and others occupied in the Hospital and College should be able to obtain a comfortable meal at a reasonable cost and with little loss of time.' Three years later, in 1885, the College Board celebrated the Centenary of the College, not as the Bicentenary is being celebrated by an appeal for a new library, but by an appeal to the Hospital Governors for a loan to extend the College in such a way as virtually to rebuild it.

Despite the desperate need to provide a new nurses home to attract more nurses, the Governors agreed, spurred on no doubt by the new Library and Museum Block opened at Barts in 1879. The home and the new College were built at the same time, the latter costing some £15,000 and rented to the College Board for £150 p.a. The architect was Roland Plumb and the cornerstone was laid by Mr Thompson, Chairman of the College Board and House Committee on March 9th 1886. The College remained in action in what was left

The new College, built with a loan from the Hospital, and opened in 1887. (Illustrated London News).

of the old buildings as the new were built around them. The library was accommodated in a ward. In the absence of heating it was cold in the old dissecting room and even in the 'Smoke Hole', the whitewashed crowded room which had served as the Students Common Room since 1854 - the Athenaeum and the present library being major features of the new building. The Bedell was caught in the act of persuading the architect to increase the size of his own quarters.

The new College and the Home were opened on 23rd May 1887 by the Prince and Princess of Wales. They had first come to the London 23 years earlier to lay the foundation stone of the West Wing -the Alexandra Wing, and the Princess had since shown the close personal interest in the hospital that she was to maintain even after becoming Queen. In his speech in the new College Library the Prince referred to the school as being the first in which a complete curriculum had been established, to its now being a hundred years

The Library described by the Prince of Wales, later King Edward VII, as worthy of England's first medical school at the end of its first century.

old, and belonging to the largest hospital in the country. He was not to know that one of the surgeons in the audience, Frederick Treves, would 14 years later be operating on him for an appendix abscess on the day on which he should have been crowned . Nor could he know that the library he was opening, to replace one built a mere 33 years before - and now too small - would still be serving an even larger College in another hundred years time.

The splendid Victorian Hall provided as a Library in 1887 is now a handicap but then it, and all the other new and larger facilities, were of immense value. New teaching facilities were provided in the hospital also. The gabled clock-front which is so distinctive a feature of the hospital today was added in 1891, providing among other things a students room on the ground floor, a clinical demonstration theatre and an operating theatre with standing room for 250 students. It would

The clock-front added in 1891.

of course have been better to have built several theatres, each with room for a smaller number of

Sydney Holland, Second Viscount Knutsford: the portrait by Oswald Birley recently stolen from the London Hospital.

students but that was not appreciated at the time. In 1891 the London, with all its advantages, still lacked the man whose vision, fund-raising ability, administrative skill and devotion to it were to be its greatest asset from 1895 to 1931. Sydney Holland, later to become second Viscount Knutsford, joined the Governors of the London in 1895 and became Chairman the following year.

A 48 year old barrister with numerous interests, he had already had experience of hospital management at Poplar. He saw that hospitals were rapidly becoming complex organisations in need of clearly defined policies and of strong skilful administration to implement them. In his own words "a great forward movement in hospital administration was hurrying to its birth". He led the movement, providing both policy and administration at the London, devoting his enormous energies whole-time to the task, combining the enthusiasm of the dedicated amateur with the approach of the highly skilled professional. He prepared a plan for converting the existing hospital buildings to serve the changing needs of medical practice, virtually rebuilt it on site and then extended it. The rebuilding included of course much that was needed for medical education, not merely new clinical theatres (culminating in the Bearsted in 1923) but a floor of operating theatres, an Institute of Pathology, clinical laboratories, Xray facilities, an extended Receiving Room and a new Out Patient Department. In addition the College itself was extended three times between the rebuilding of 1887 and the first World War - and just to show that not everything at the London was utilitarian (and to commemorate her great interest in it) the statue of Queen Alexandra was erected by public subscription. Obtaining the vast amount of money needed year by year earned Lord Knutsford the title of Prince of Beggars but his dynamic leadership and total committment were even more important to both Hospital and College.

Sir Frederick Treves, surgeon and master mariner, friend of the Elephant Man and instrumental in founding the Club's Union.

iii

In view of the remarkable advantages of the London it is not surprising that it continued to attract staff of the same outstanding quality as the 26 teachers who signed the union of College and Hospital in 1879. While Andrew Clark, Stephen Mackenzie and Hughlings Jackson were still at the height of their powers, Frederick Treves took up the post of demonstrator in Anatomy and soon afterwards was appointed Surgeon. Others worthy of special mention who joined the staff before the turn of the century were Gustav Schorstein, Henry Head, Bertrand Dawson and Henry Percy Dean. Schorstein is remembered by the Lecture endowed in his name on his early death from diabetes. Henry Head's great contributions to neurology spanned the years from 1896 to 1919. Bertrand Dawson was also appointed in 1896, was the King's Physician and the country's most respected physician when he outlined his proposals for a National Health Service in 1918, and was still leading the profession at the time of his death in 1945. Dean was surgeon to the London only from 1892 to 1913 but his impact was long-lasting, being successful in his determination that 'the scientific subjects in the curriculum should be taught by whole-time professional scientists.'

William Bulloch was appointed as head of the department of Bacteriology in the College in 1897. Arthur Keith and Leonard Hill were appointed to whole-time college posts in Anatomy and Physiology respectively. R N Salaman was appointed Director of the Pathological Institute but on becoming ill was replaced by Hubert Turnbull. All five of these first holders of full-time posts at the London were to become Fellows of the Royal Society, though only two spent the whole of their working lives at the London. Bulloch, Hill, and later Turnbull all became professors after the University of London had been reconstituted in 1900 as a federal university no longer restricted to examining, and the College incorporated in it along with the other medical schools. Incorporation, however, made otherwise little difference to the College, which continued a Hospital medical school, run by the College Board, and self-financing.

William Bulloch, FRS,
first holder of the Goldsmiths' Chair of Bacteriology.

Between 1900 and the start of the first World War in 1914 there were many notable appointments. Among the surgeons were Hurry Fenwick, pioneer urologist; Harold Barnard who developed the sphygmomanometer with Hill, and whose contributions to abdominal surgery, including the classical description of subphrenic abscess, were cut short by his death at 40; James Sherren, the Master Mariner who became a student and then surgeon at the London, collaborated with Head in experiments on the afferent nervous system, and at the height of his fame as an abdominal surgeon, went back to sea; Hugh Rigby, surgeon to the King, and finally Serjeant-Surgeon; Hugh Lett, President of the Royal College of Surgeons; James Walton, surgeon to the Royal Household.

Among the physicians who were appointed between 1900 and 1914 were James Sequira, the dermatologist and Robert Hutchison who came as lecturer in Physiology, was appointed physician in 1900 and died in 1960 'a national figure, a great scholar and writer, a beloved and inspiring teacher and a distinguished President of the College of Physicians'. James Mackenzie worked on cardiac arrhythmia with Arthur Keith while still in general practice; he was then made lecturer in Cardiac Physiology and in 1911 was made physician in charge of a new Cardiac Department in the Hospital. In 1911 too a department of Physical Medicine, the first of its kind, was opened under Stanton Woods.

Sir James Mackenzie, FRS.

In the same period came four notable dental surgeons: Francis Farmer, Harold Chapman, George Northcroft and Evelyn Sprawson. Farmer developed the plastic repair of facial injuries in the first world war. Northcroft and Chapman fathered Orthodontics and Northcroft (aided by William Wright, the Professor of Anatomy who followed Keith and became Dean of the College on the retirement of the Warden, Munro Scott) successfully pressed the case for a Dental School. Evelyn Sprawson, as Director of Dental Studies, became responsible for its development.

Sir Francis Farmer.

During and immediately after the 1914-18 war came Henry Souttar, the most innovative of surgeons, Eardley Holland the obstetrician and John Parkinson the cardiologist. Then came the decision to start Medical and Surgical Units under whole-time directors. Henry Souttar became director of the Surgical Unit in 1920 continuing his activities in most fields of surgery including neurosurgery. He was not too happy to continue as director however, and in 1923 the unit was allowed to lapse and he returned to the honorary staff. Two years later he was the first to open the left auricle and stretch a mitral valve.

The Medical Unit was also started in 1920 with Charles Miller, physician to the London, as director with funds provided by the Government in implementation of the Haldane Report. When the University Grants Committee was founded it took over the allocation of the funds and decreed that units should be headed by professors. The London thereupon appointed Dr Miller a professor without appreciating that, since the College was now incorporated in the University of London, it was for the latter to choose the professoriate. The University declined to recognise Dr Miller who thereupon resigned and the Assistant Director, Arthur Ellis, was appointed to the Chair. He remained in charge of the Unit until 1943 when he went to Oxford as Regius Professor of Physic. Under him the Unit flourished, making not only important contributions to Nephrology but attracting, over the next twenty years, a stream of distinguished physicians which included Robert Aitken, Russell Brain, Ronald Christie, Archie Clark-Kennedy, Horace Evans, William Evans, Clifford Wilson, Leslie Witts and George Riddoch. Aitken, Christie and Witts moved to chairs of medicine elsewhere. Clifford Wilson succeeded Arthur Ellis and the remainder joined the part-time staff of the London.

Thus between the wars the London was well equipped to continue that advance in medicine which had been accelerated by the first world war. The huge size of the Hospital, the strong departments of pathology and medical sciences, the range and quality of the medical staff with its long-standing involvement in research and development were combined with the administration's determination and ability to find money for whatever was needed. More special departments

Viscount Dawson of Penn.

followed. Some like Urology under George Neligan, developed a well established tradition, others were in new subjects such as Neurosurgery under Hugh Cairns and Thoracic Surgery under Tudor Edwards. Donald Hunter was appointed physician in 1927 and began the research into industrial disease which was to bring Occupational Medicine and the Medical Research Council's Research Unit into being. Psychiatry was developed by Henry Wilson, assistant to Riddoch and Brain, leading to a joint department of Neurology and Psychiatry in 1942. Frank Valentine was appointed Reader in Chemotherapy. The Whitechapel Clinic, situated in the hospital but financed by the LCC continued to provide an exceptional department of Venereology under Ambrose King.

Thus, by the late 1930s there was already a wide range of new specialist departments mostly started by pioneers specialising from a strong basis of general medicine or surgery which some continued to practice and teach. The size of the hospital, with some 900 beds on one site, allowed the maintenance of large busy general medical and surgical firms. Pathological services were provided by central clinical laboratories in the Hospital under Philip Panton, and by the College departments of Morbid Anatomy under Turnbull and W W Woods, Bacteriology under Samuel Bedson who followed Bulloch, and Chemical Pathology under John Marrack. In addition, from the 1920s onwards, research funds provided full-time research fellowships which attracted men of the quality of Bedson, Howard Florey and Paul Fildes. Later, during the second world war, a separate department of Orthopaedics was started under Reginald Watson-Jones and Henry Osmond-Clarke, and one of Radiotherapy under Frank Ellis.

Such a resumé of the staffing of the London over the years between 1879 when the Hospital and College amalgamated and 1948 when they separated again, does little more than mention some of those whose contribution to the advancement of medicine keeps their names alive today. They are but a few of those who at any one time made up the staff - stars which for one reason or another shone a little brighter than others in the same galaxy. Thirty of those who held senior appointments as doctors or dentists over this period of less than 70 years received knighthoods or baronetcies, two became peers and one a viscount.

Such criteria of success, however, were not those used by students. They would have included many of those named above as great teachers who devoted themselves to the school and the students in it, but would have added numerous others like F J Smith, Thomas Openshaw, Theodore Thompson, Russell Howard, Robert Milne, Charles Donald, Victor Lack, Alan Brews, and still more. Nor were these great only in the eyes of students. They too were physicians and surgeons of distinction. Those of the London's staff in this period whose names are part of the history of medicine differed from their colleagues only in that they were, as the Lancet said of Dawson, 'in many ways a shade better than the average first class man.'

Sir Leonard Hill

Sir Arthur Keith

Chapter 5.

The Student Workers

Life in the London Hospital Medical College at any time between 1879 and 1948 was very different from that today, though students were being taught and patients cared for on the same site and - for the most part - in the same buildings that are still in use. Despite all the many advantages enjoyed by the London, the very fact that it was so extraordinarily busy, striving always, sometimes desperately, to keep up with the enormous demands of its exceptional community, meant that life was in many ways distinctly rugged.

The Whitechapel of the 1880s was that in which Treves found Joseph Merrick, the Elephant Man, on exhibition in a booth opposite the Hospital - in which he was later to be given sanctuary in Bedstead Square. Treves himself described the Receiving Room of those days: the place of 'strange scenes, some pathetic, some merely sordid, together with fragments of tragedy in which the most elemental passions and emotions of humanity are displayed...The most repellent thing in the Receiving Room is a low sofa. It is wide and covered with very thick leather which is suspiciously shiny and black. Its associations are unpleasant. It has been covered with blood and with every kind of imaginable filth and has been cleaned up so often that it is no wonder that the deeply stained leather is shiny' (19).

The post of Receiving Room Officer was created by the College Board in 1885. Until then it was manned by the duty house surgeon and house physician, fetched by the nursing staff.

This was the Whitechapel to which came Wilfred Grenfell - (later Sir Wilfred Grenfell of Labrador) as a student from Oxford in 1883 to find that the College, under the Warden Munro Scott, left students pretty much to their own devices so far as their theoretical studies were concerned. That must have suited him well, for he had other interests besides his growing missionary zeal (he started a boys' club and a branch of the Boys' Brigade) and the opportunity to participate in the work of a vast hospital.

'I was secretary in succession of the cricket, football and rowing clubs. I helped to move the latter from the Lea to the Thames and to start the United Hospitals Rowing Club. I rowed in the inter-hospital race two years and played in the rugger team the two years we won the Cup. I played a few times with the United Hospitals but my ways were not their ways, as I had been taught to despise alcohol and respect women. For three years however I played regularly for Richmond. I also threw the hammer in the United Hospitals Sports, winning second place in two successive years ' (7).

Grenfell's outline of the high points of his student life is so similar, give or take a few wins in the Interhospitals Rugby Cup, to those of other students in more recent times that it is difficult to realise he was at the London before the present College building was opened in 1887, before Jack the Ripper got to work in 1888, before the Clubs Union was founded in 1893, and the Gazette was started in 1894 (when Tower Bridge was built).

The Clubs Union resulted from the efforts of the staff, led by Treves who became the first President.

'At the unanimous desire of the Students', he wrote to Sir Andrew Clark, who had just retired, 'a "Clubs Union" has recently been formed, embracing all the Athletic and other Clubs formed by the Students of the Hospital and College. The Staff being anxious to encourage Athletics and add to the comfort and enjoyment of the Students have agreed to subscribe a large sum annually towards the expenses of supporting the Union.

'Owing to the action of the Staff a Field for Cricket, Football etc has been leased at Lower Edmonton, which was formally opened by Lady Clark in the presence of a large company of members and visitors on June 21st and for the first time the Students of 'The London' have their own Ground which it is trusted will prove a great boon to them.

'When discussing the arrangements for the Clubs Union, it was felt that you, who have always shown so kindly an interest in the College, would like to be associated with us in our endeavours to keep the Clubs Union and Ground in the highest possible state of efficiency and would be willing to help us financially, either with a small annual subscription, or a donation.'

Provision for recreation was certainly needed. Though not carrying as great a burden as house officers, most students worked hard in grim conditions, surrounded by infection in the Hospital, and living as near to it as they could find lodgings.

Sir Hugh Lett, PRCS.

In his history of the London, Clark Kennedy quotes Hugh Lett's memories of the 1890s: 'Lister's spray had been given up, but some surgeons still dabbed wounds with sponges soaked in carbolic ... rubber gloves were still unknown.'

He was disturbed by one of the surgeons with whom he worked who 'constantly forgot that he had to wear spectacles and so, after washing up and putting on a sterile gown, would walk over to the door, where his frock coat was hanging, and take them out of his pocket. He then returned, picked up a scalpel and made his incision'.

'There was only one registrar who was non-resident and not allowed to operate, his principal duty being to check and supplement the notes made by the house-surgeon and dresser. He was also required to approve the final diagnosis and treatment for entry in the register, attend the theatre, see outpatients in the absence of his chief, and report on microscopical specimens.'

The responsibilities of the house surgeon and dressers were correspondingly great. At night the House Surgeon had to decide for himself whether or not to call his chief down to the Hospital to see a patient. 'The telephone was relatively new and my senior chief refused to have one... a porter had to be sent to the West End in a cab with a note requesting him to come.'

Even then things were changing. Lett's junior chief was H P Dean, the man responsible for the appointment of whole-time scientists as pre-clinical teachers in the College. 'H P Dean was a tall, fine upstanding man with a large moustache of which he took great care, and a brilliant and progressive surgeon. He was also a pioneer of spinal anaesthesia. In his private practice his Spencer-Wells forceps were gold-plated. I remember, too, that in those very early days of motor cars he had two and always took both when going to an operation. He drove one and, in case it broke down, his chauffeur followed behind in the other.'

Minor operations were carried out in the wards - all of course large Florence Nightingale type wards - lit by gas brackets with two burners, placed at intervals down the middle. Screens were drawn round the bed and 'the necessary illumination was only gained by a nurse holding a paraffin lamp. Ether was thought the safest anaesthetic - induction was far from peaceful and dressers would be called in to help restrain a muscular patient.'

'Delirium tremens was common. Osteomyelitis and deep infected wounds required repeated painful dressings. Multiple incisions were performed for acute cellulitis and repeated fomentations and hot saline baths the order of the day.

'House surgeons, students and nurses suffered frequently from whitlows and infected fingers. Diphtheria was common too, and tracheotomy often urgently necessary - cries of "trachey" rang down the corridor, and the first resident to reach the trachey ward (in the small house near the gate) would perform the operation.'

Nathan Salaman* came to the London as a student soon afterwards in 1896, the year Knutsford became Chairman. Salaman, like Knutsford 20 years earlier, had been at Trinity Hall, Cambridge. Both were attracted to the London, like others before and since, because of its involvement in social problems. Knutsford because it was trying to meet the medical needs of the East End, Salaman because Stepney and Whitechapel were 'solid Jewish Ghettos, whilst dominating them and yet serving them stood the great London Hospital' (20). He decided his choice was a fortunate one.

'The London was a first class school of practical medicine; if it was weak on pathology I doubt whether any of the other great hospitals were at that time any better. Directly we reached the wards we became imbued with a sense of responsibility which increased as we advanced. Although as students we never originated treatment, we assumed automatically a sense of personal service and obligation to our patients. It was a great school in every sense, and not least in those lessons of human nature which can only be learnt through suffering and sympathy. I never was happier than during my "London" days. I had many close friends and a spirit of good fellowship permeated the whole of our set.'(20)

He found 'the atmosphere sincere, refreshing and intelligent; if we were favoured by the authorities - and I think we were - we certainly responded by our devotion to the work.'

In Salaman's case 'being favoured by the authorities' no doubt referred to having been 'swept off' about a year before his finals, by Henry Head to work with him in Sir Frederick Mott's laboratory at Claybury. Mott was a physician to Charing Cross who was also pathologist to the LCC Asylums. At Claybury he finally established that general paralysis of the insane

The Rowing Club's Annual Outing, much enjoyed by Treves.

*N.S. Salaman is best known outside the London as Redcliffe Salaman.

was due to syphilis and associated with the presence of the specific spirochaete. Salaman studied the histological changes of the nervous system in Tabes and 'drank in the inspiring atmosphere which permeated that remote and isolated focus of scientific research. The results of that intoxicating six months, my first scientific paper, were duly written up and published.'

He then returned to finish his studies. There being no grants, and schools being free to take as many students as they wished, students exceeded the minimum duration of the required course (shorter for conjoint than for a degree) by as long as they wished, or needed to pass finals, and could afford.

The spirit of good fellowship to which Salaman referred included, and was encouraged by, staff-student relationships. Besides the interest teachers took in individual students, close bonds developed between the two physicians or surgeons, the single house officer and the clerks or dressers of firms who worked together for three months at a time. Chiefs were held in great respect but were never distant, staff and students both being working members of the same team. Firm parties, organised by staff and not by students, were common, though not all in the same class as those provided by Tommy Openshaw, the surgeon who would take housemen and students on bicycles to Ascot for a day at the races. Clubs Union activities were equally well attended by Staff, including the annual picnic up river, reached after a long row, organised by Treves. The rule of the Medical Council requiring attendance at the Annual Reunion Dinner was strictly adhered to.

Such activities must have done something, as no doubt was intended, to offset the demands made on students, which reached a peak with midwifery at the end of the course. Students manned the 'White Charity' and Nurses the 'Green Charity'.

'We were privileged and protected' (recorded Salaman in his memoirs) 'by no more powerful weapon than our maternity bags. We could penetrate with impunity streets and alleyways which the police after dark visited only in pairs. Often as one passed by the entrance of some dark passage one would hear "Its all right, it's only the doctor". Usually we were welcomed warmly as we entered the home of the expectant mother and treated with respect and kindness. Rarely did we find ourselves regarded with hostility or suspicion.'

Many of the homes however were the poorest imaginable and often totally unprepared for the event. 'Once I attended a woman in a naked garrett, reached by a ladder. There was a broken bed with a single blanket, a chair without a back, a tin basin without a towel, and the poor mother herself practically naked. Of food and drink there was none...In the Jewish homes the conditions were immeasurably better for however poor the home there would be clean linen, hot water and several neighbours to comfort the mother and assist the doctor. The older Gentile tradesmen's

The District midwifery service. Nurses, in green walking-out uniform, ran the Green Charity — Students ran the White.

homes were generally clean - the main difficulty was to avoid their hospitality. Many a time I have been met with the invitation "Will you have a cup of tea, doctor, or a drop of methylated?"'

Lighting must have been a problem too. The Hospital was just beginning to install electricity at this time and the X-ray department was able to give up the use of batteries.

If in difficulty the student could send husband, child or neighbour to the Hospital for the Junior Resident Accoucheur. The patient might on occasion have to be removed to hospital in whatever transport could be found. George Neligan used to recount how as a student he took one of his patients with a post-partum haemorrhage to the London in a hansom cab at the gallop, peering as they passed the occasional street lamp to see the extent of the bleeding. There were stresses of other kinds too: Salaman discovered children being deliberately neglected with a view to collecting the life insurances taken out on them by their parents.

Students worked the district in pairs for a month at a time, alternating a week of deliveries with a week of follow-up visits. 'In the two weeks on duty' said Salaman 'we would each of us deliver not less than 54 mothers. I lost all sense of time, I did not know whether it was yesterday, today or tomorrow. It sounds absurd but it is true. The month we spent on maternity was in itself enough to undermine the stoutest constitution - but when that was finished we had our final examinations to complete and then without a pause took over a house appointment.'

Not all of course wanted or were lucky enough to get a house appointment, at the London or anywhere else. The majority went straight into practice, perhaps first as a locum. Some held non-resident out-patient appointments for a while. These were paid, enabling the holder to wait around until he could get a post on the House itself, with free board and lodging but no pay. Once on the House it was usual to stay for around two years, doing perhaps four different jobs of six months each.

At this period each firm had on average 70 beds and every 12 days went on full duty for four days, prior to which as many as possible of its 70 patients would be discharged. Throughout full duty the house physician gave anaesthetics for his surgical opposite number in the evenings and shared responsibility for all casualties coming in before midnight. During a six month appointment there was no official time off. The risks, of a pricked finger or infected throat combined with lowered resistance, were of course great but, Salaman wrote afterwards 'so keen was our interest, so happy our mood, that we were blind to the dangers which threatened us and, what was worse, the governing body and the staff were not less so.'

Some of the staff in fact, Treves and Openshaw and twenty-six nurses among them, had gone to the South African War and the governors were pre-occupied with that virtual rebuilding of the hospital on site which, over some five years without closing a bed, was to enlarge it and adapt it to the changes taking place in medicine. They were less conscious that 'the technical and clinical machinery of treatment had made corresponding demands on the time and attention of the trained personnel - in other words, the senior students'(20). The need to adapt their terms and conditions of service was not perceived. In their first year on the house one of Salaman's set developed a sore throat, collapsed, was put to bed, and in about a week, was dead. 'Before two years had passed, apart from those who fell sick and recovered to a greater or less degree, four more died in exactly the same way' (20).

In 1905 Nathan Salaman himself, recently appointed Director of the Pathological Institute, developed Tuberculosis and was forced to give up medicine.

Extra assistants were appointed as 'Emergency Officers' to allow each houseman a day off per week and before long the junior staff had been nearly doubled. Even so the work demanded of housemen and senior students remained heavy. Yet to judge by the many who left accounts of the years leading up to the first world war, the demands continued to be responded to with remarkable enthusiasm and cheerfulness, marked by outbursts of great exuberance on the rare occasions when 'the London' relaxed, the most notable being Christmas - which began on Christmas Eve when nurses and students decorated the wards; continued through Christmas day as troupes of residents and students moved in succession from ward to ward entertaining patients, nurses, students, the staff and their families; and was over but not forgotten by Boxing day morning.

From 1879 almost to the first world war the work of students and house officers included the extraction of teeth. The Dentists Register had been established in 1878 but the practice of dentistry was not restricted to

The Residents of Christmas 1913, 'The Inevitables':
George Neligan in the centre.

E J Burdon, College Secretary.

those with dental qualifications until the Second Dentists Act of 1922. So although the Hospital had a Dental Department the practice of dental surgery in the Receiving Room at any rate was pretty much a free for all. A poem published in the Gazette in 1910 entitled "The Long Pull" graphically describes the efforts of a dresser to help a dental patient:

'He sweated hard, this ardent youth,
To shake the owner off the tooth'.

In the same year Munro Scott, the College Warden, retired, the illuminated address with which he was presented stating that his 'firm yet tactful discipline had resulted in welding together the teachers and taught in one united effort to raise and maintain the prestige of our institution.' Professor William Wright was appointed Dean and E J Burdon Secretary. Wright, 'a man of formidable appearance and personality, although fundamentally kindly' (21) was known in the College as a great teacher of anatomy and outside for his studies of the bones of the little Princes in the Tower. Almost his first action as Dean, however, was to propose a School of Dentistry.

Two Dental Schools had been established in London back in 1859: the Dental Hospital and School which was later to become the Royal Dental, and the Metropolitan School of Dental Sciences, eventually incorporated into University College. Guy's later established a Dental School, but can hardly have done so at the speed with which the London proceeded. The proposal was first put to the College Board in January 1911, in February it was referred to a committee of physicians and surgeons which was requested to confer with the Medical Council, their report was received in March when a committee of three was deputed to go into ways and means, further advice was sought from Francis Farmer in May, and on Monday 19th June it was resolved 'that arrangements be made for the opening of the Dental School on 1st October 1911'. The arrangements included the appointment of six additional part-time lecturers - one of whom was Evelyn Sprawson.

The School was accommodated in the Out-patient building and four students were admitted in the first year. The College of Surgeons confirmed provisional recognition of the School in 1912 but the University of London was unable to do so at once. It had been at great pains, because so few students in London took its degrees, to get a Royal Commission established to look into education in London and it could not recognise any new dental schools until the Commission had reported.

Sir Evelyn Sprawson.

London Hospital crew 1912.

So 'dentals' began to augment the workforce of tudents and house officers on which so much of the burden of patient care depended. Considering the size of the London it is perhaps surprising that more was not provided for them. The College facilities were good, including the Athenaeum and the dining room which was shared by the resident house officers. The Clubs Union, founded to add to the comfort and enjoyment of students was extremely well supported, especially by staff. Residential accommodation, however, was not up to the same standard. Knutsford had at one time tried to improve that for house officers by seconding his own butler to care for them, but there was none for students despite the special difficulties they faced in finding somewhere to live in or near the East End. Then, in 1911, Numbers 52-60 Philpot Street were converted into a Students' Hostel.

In the same year the College received its first grant from the Board of Education, precursor of the University Grants Committee - small but welcome, though not in the same class as the endowment of £20,000 that Sir Alfred Yarrow gave to start the LHMC Research Fund.

In the years leading to the Great War, Christmas at the London was enlivened by this Dragon. It was designed by Arthur Rackham and built by Henry Souttar

The Rugby Cup 1913/14.

Chapter 6.

The Great War and After 1914-1939

The London received its first wounded from the Great War at the end of August 1914, a total of 300 on the first day, brought from Waterloo Station in horse-drawn vans unloaded in the hospital garden. The vans were supplied (no ambulances being available) by Messrs Lyons, whose Chairman was a member of the House Committee. The next to arrive were 200 wounded Belgians and thereafter a never ending stream of casualties to be cared for along with the civilian sick. In 1915 eighteen thousand patients were admitted and extra beds stood in every ward. Yet Sir John Lavery's painting of 'The First Wounded in the London Hospital' (now in Dundee Art Gallery, with two preliminary sketches safely hidden somewhere in the London) shows a world as calm, cheerful and orderly as any which gladdened the eyes of London students up to the second world war. Above each bed a rail standing out some two feet from the wall, blue and white chequered curtains either side, the blue treatment board and the white temperature chart hanging in between: at the foot of every bed a red blanket.

Hospital staff of all kinds were reduced to a minimum. Most students, with the exception of those about to qualify, joined the forces either as combatants in the Army or, like Donald Hunter and Monty Jupe (later to be Radiologist to the London) as Naval probationers serving as doctors in small ships. Retired Old Londoners were recruited onto the house, then American volunteers, and finally women students were admitted to the College, including Dorothy Russell - who one day was to succeed Turnbull as Professor of Morbid Anatomy.

In 1916 medical students who had joined the forces and still survived were sent home to complete their

'The first wounded'. Sketch by Sir John Lavery for his painting of the London in 1914.

studies. Archie Clark-Kennedy, who instead of coming from Cambridge to the London in 1914 had joined the East Surrey Regiment and gone first to India and then Mesopotamia, came back to the London in late 1916.

The College in 1917 by Hanslip Fletcher.

'The Medical College was a dim shadow of its former self. There cannot have been eighty students in it altogether... William Wright was still Dean... our lives were guided by the Secretary, E J Burdon, a frail, hard-working, helpful little man (who always wore a high, stiff white collar and had a nervous habit of gulping in his throat), assisted by Osman, the registration clerk, a little dark square man of Turkish extraction, and a friend at court of countless generations of Old Londoners... Martin Flack was about, engaged in research work for the Royal Flying Corps, Edward Mellanby taught us Pharmacology and William Bulloch bacteriology. But it was Turnbull's lectures that I remember best' (6).

Sir Robert Hutchison, PRCP.

Sir Henry Head, FRS.

'In the Hospital the teachers were Robert Milne Theodore Thompson, Percy Kidd, Cecil Wall, F Smith, Otto Leyton, 'Young John' (Jonathan Hutchinson Jr), Richard Warren and Russell Howard 'but the two most outstanding men were Hutchison and Head. The former, the dry Scot, said little. But every word he did say was worth hearing... a brilliant diagnostician who continued to ignore X-rays: in the summer he lectured in therapeutics. Not that there was much therapeutics in those days, but his lectures were worth listening to for the sheer elegance of his diction which matched his own tall, erect figure in that long, grey frock-coat. Henry Head, on the other hand, was talkative and histrionic, his public demonstration the high spot of the students' working week. I cannot actually recollect any of the many neurological cases I must have heard him demonstrate but it is a tribute to him as a clinical teacher that I can still see two others that he demonstrated as clearly as I can see the garden out of the window as I write. One was a case of chronic rheumatoid arthritis and the other a case of, as we called it then, chronic parenchymatous nephritis.' (7)

Thus the College continued through the first world war. In June 1917 German Zeppelins bombed Whitechapel, 207 casualties arrived in the hospital in less than an hour, 75 were admitted, 44 died and another 30 were brought in dead. Thereafter the local inhabitants sought shelter in the basement of the Hospital whenever there was warning of a raid: 5,000 on the first occasion but after that admission was limited to women and children and the gates closed after 2,000 had come in. In January 1918 four tons of TNT blew up at the munition works in Silvertown, two miles east of the Hospital, which catered for those who survived in a square mile of devastation.

In January 1918 too Archie Clark-Kennedy qualified after some 15 months as a clinical student - a rather short course for one destined to be Dean of the London for 17 years and one of its most distinguished clinical teachers. But characteristically while soldiering in India he had visited every hospital he could reach and obtained a certificate of attendance from each. He spent a few months on the house:

'I remember doing "tracheys" in the block which was still full of osteomelitis, erysipelas and cellulitis. Lobar pneumonia was very common, carcinoma of the lung was still rare and the differential diagnosis between it and aortic aneurysm (still common) considered difficult. Cardiac infarction had not yet been recognised. Blood transfusion was occasionally performed in the theatres, but never in the wards. There was no insulin yet for diabetes or liver extract for pernicious anaemia, or any form of treatment for sepsis (other than drainage and fomentations), or for any of the lung infections" (6).

In the Spring of 1918 the German offensive preceded the arrival of the Americans in France. 'I had still another month on the House but with all my contemporaries I was called up for service in the RAMC immediately.'

Londoners and "Old Londoners" served of course on all the different fronts in the Great War. Many lost their lives, many were injured, many were decorated but Neville Howes, awarded the Victoria Cross in the South African War remained, and still remains, the only Londoner to have achieved that distinction.

The women students admitted between 1918 and 1922 were few but they made their mark.

ii

The Great War, which changed so much and left so little as it had been before, brought no immediate revolution in medicine. It increased the tempo of change without altering its direction. The care of all forms of trauma was much improved. Surgery, especially abdominal surgery, aided by advances in anaesthesia, became much more effective. But throughout the period between the wars infection remained the main cause of morbidity and mortality and until sulphonamides were introduced in the late 1930s, good nursing remained the most important treatment for it, though often insufficient when resistance was lowered by the malnutrition and poverty which characterised the depression of the thirties.

Medicine continued to be predominantly concerned with organic disease: acute, florid and for the most part in young people. The average life expectancy of a man in the East End was in the forties. All who could manage to do so stayed out of hospital when ill, cared for at home or in a nursing home by the family doctor and visiting specialists; often nursed by members of the 'Private Staff' of a hospital like the London who when the illness was over would return there to augment the nursing complement until the next call came. Even so the need for admissions continued to exceed the ever-growing number of hospital beds but the presence of Municipal Hospitals allowed Voluntary Hospitals to be more selective in their admissions, choosing patients whose problems seemed more challenging or more 'suitable for teaching'.

So the London remained constantly full and despite specialisation the clinical problems seen by a student in the general wards and clinics as the Second World War approached were not fundamentally different from those of 1914, though treatment was often more effective. Students in the 1930s saw little of the kinds of conditions which were to fill the wards of the London in the 1970s. They gained their experience from the sort of problems which students in the 1970s would be likely to see only on an elective in the 'third world'.

Sir Arthur Ellis, first Professor of Medicine.

Sir Henry Souttar, first Director of the Surgical Unit.

Voluntary Hospitals found it increasingly difficult to make both ends meet but the London, thanks to the earlier efforts of Knutsford, remained better off than most. The College continued to pay rent to the Hospital for its buildings. Its income came from students' fees and from money paid by the Hospital in return for the services rendered by students. Funds from the University Grants Committee, via the University of London, met the salaries of the few whole-time academic pre-clinical and clinical staff. Most teachers received only a small token honorarium, medical education continuing to be a relatively inexpensive by-product of hospital care, the cost of which was itself greatly reduced by the fact that neither consultant staff nor house-officers were paid at all.

Medical education itself remained much the same between the wars as it had been before the first war. Matriculation was needed for entry to a degree course and all students were required to pass examinations in biology, chemistry and physics (1st MB) before proceeding to study the basic medical sciences examined in 2nd MB. The pre-medical 1st MB subjects were taught in many medical schools though not at the London whose students, if they had not taken the relevant examinations at secondary school, spent a first year at Queen Mary College.

Selection did not really exist between the wars. Virtually all eligible applicants gained admission provided they were male. Ambrose King, writing of 1918, described acceptance of a prospective student as 'little more than a formality; a brief interview with the Dean and evidence of educational achievement' (21). Harry May, when he joined as a clinical student in 1931 thought that the absence of interviews for the clinical course meant 'the College was far from flourishing' (22), but the situation was the same everywhere. Orford Dick and I applying in 1937 for admission to the clinical course were interviewed by Archie Clark-Kennedy, newly appointed Dean, in his rooms in Corpus Christi College, Cambridge. He asked a number of questions, all relating to the problem then exercising him, how to get the boat he had just built out of the room in which he had built it.

In 1938 the London had an entry of some 70 medical students, about one third of whom came from Oxford or Cambridge for the clinical course. The total number of medical students in the school including those taking 1st MB at Queen Mary College, was 469. UCH and St Thomas's had rather more, Guy's 593 and Barts 828. The remaining London Schools were smaller. St George's, Charing Cross, Westminster, and the West London had no preclinical teaching and took

Sir John Parkinson.

Sir Eardley Holland.

students from University College, King's College, Oxford or Cambridge. Charing Cross and St George's each had a total of students in all years of little more than 100. The West London had 38 women. In the Provinces the largest schools were Leeds and Liverpool with around 500 - and the smallest Cardiff with a total of 140. Neither Oxford nor Cambridge had clinical schools. Edinburgh and Glasgow were huge, both having over 1000 students, and there were three non-University Scottish Schools which now no longer exist - two in Glasgow and one in Edinburgh. There were over 1000 beds available for teaching in the main hospital used by the University of Edinburgh for a student entry of 200. The London had 840 beds available for teaching for an entry of 75 - Barts 650 for an entry of 120 - Charing Cross 300 beds for an entry of 30 (23).

About 95% of the students at the London in the late 1930s qualified by the Conjoint Diploma, which could be taken one part at a time a little earlier than any MB. Some 40% of those registering with a diploma later took an MB degree (23). The situation was the same in most other London schools. Nowhere was there any pressure, apart from personal considerations, on students to try to qualify at the first opportunity. In all schools some students seemed reluctant to change their student status. Ambrose King describes one with whom he went to Queen Mary College for 1st MB.

'Whether he ever went there to study I doubt. He spent most of his days at the hospital and played forward for the 1st XV. As far as I know he never passed an examination but continued as he was for some years until his poor father lost patience. Father was a successful GP in Wales and was heard to describe his son as the wickedest man who ever came from that country except Lloyd George.'(21)

At the outbreak of war in 1939 the London had one student, cultured, charming and elegant, who had been there so long, he seemed a kind of uncle to the rest. He did his best to adapt to the change in tempo brought about by war, but the effort was too much and he died before he could qualify. Very few, however, had the means to get into such difficulties. Many were, at best, impecunious. Most lived in lodgings. The present Hostel was opened by Queen Mary in Philpot Street in 1934. Old Londoners raised £8,000 towards it. £100 came from the trustees of the Knutsford Memorial Fund and £100 from Sir Gerald Spicer, father of two Old Londoners one of whom, like a number of Londoners, was killed in a climbing accident. £20,000 was borrowed on the security of the building - which was awarded the prize for the best architecture of the year. Though more expensive to live in than most 'digs', students could save on travelling. There was little other accommodation close to the hospital, compared with today. When Gwynne House was

The Hospital arms on the Hostel, opened in 1934.

ɔpened in 1938 its first occupants included students who found it as cheap to live in one of its flats as in the Hostel.

iii

'n the nineteen thirties the five year medical course :onsisted of five terms of basic medical sciences eading to 2nd MB and a clinical course of approximately three years, beginning four times a year with a 'our week clinical introductory course. Required ıppointments included a Junior Medical and Surgical 'irm each of three months, a Pathology course which ncluded Lunacy and Fevers, three months of 'Specials' ınd dressing in Surgical Outpatients, Obstetrics and Gynaecology which with Anaesthetics totalled 6 nonths, 3 months of Therapeutics and Medical Outpatients, and a Senior Medical and Surgical firm :ach of three months. At the end of the required course here were some six months free for 'Hospital Practice,' virtually a period of electives, in which the student :ould attend Out-patients, 'open rounds' on various 'irms, or arrange to be attached to a department.

A E Clark-Kennedy, Physician and Dean.

There were lectures too of course, most members of staff giving some. Despite an excellent Pathology course, the lectures given several days a week at midday by Hubert Turnbull were well attended and as much appreciated as they had been in 1916 when Clark-Kennedy had found 'the least intelligent of us perceived the truth which pervaded his lectures and the wealth of personal knowledge this contained.' Post-mortem demonstrations by Billy Woods drew a crowd of students every day. Clinical Lectures were divided into Elementary and Senior. The former provided a basic introduction to medicine and surgery, lucidly given by teachers such as Clark-Kennedy, who facilitated understanding, or Russell Howard who drove information into memory, with derisive comments on individual students. To a student arriving late in the Bearsted on a Saturday morning: 'Mr —, you wemind me of the undescended testicle., You cweep in late, you wiggle into position and when you get there you're no bloody good.'

Senior clinical lectures covered a wide range of subjects. Most reflected the personal experience of the lecturer. The least good suffered greatly by contrast with the majority. Public health lectures for example seemed to consist primarily of instruction in how to dig latrines by people who had never actually done so. Forensic medicine's popularity hinged largely on the more pornographic aspects of the content. The museum, constantly benefitting from the imaginative and energetic care of Donald Hunter (and the technical skill of John Edwards), augmented all teaching.

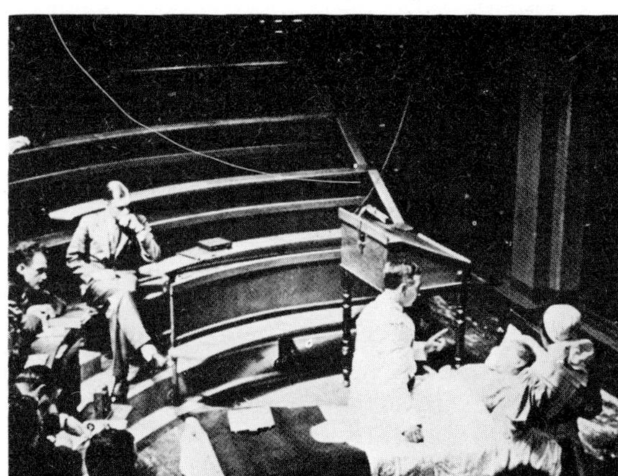

A demonstration by George Riddoch in the Bearsted.

Clinical demonstrations ranged from the sublime to the ridiculous. Neurological demonstrations by Riddoch or Brain were in the first category. The patients demonstrated may not have remained in the memory like those shown to Clark-Kennedy by Henry Head, but the student presenting a small ten year old to the Aberdonian Georgie Riddoch has never forgotten him slipping the boy sixpence to ensure an up-going toe, so that the students should not be 'confused'. At the other extreme were the sad and uninformative demonstrations of mentally ill patients which students travelled by tram to attend in Camberwell House Mental Hospital. The young man who answered a series of questions such as,'what day is it today, what year is it, who is the King?' all with the same 'I don't know, its been so hot and clammy lately' and then knocked the demonstrator unconscious, lives in the memory. Why either behaved as they did was never revealed.

In the wards and in out-patients, or when practising midwifery, students still had a useful role to play. The majority of their tasks required no great knowledge and the skills involved were quickly acquired with the help of a First Assistant, houseman, sister or senior student. They did lumbar punctures, drained ascites and pleural effusions, passed catheters, washed out stomachs, performed a range of minor surgery, and innumerable dressings. They prepared patients for operation, accompanied them to the theatre, placed them on the table, assisted or at least counted the swabs, and took the patient back to the ward. First Assistants watched over these procedures closely - often standing in the theatre, watch in hand, timing the process of placing the patient on the table, comparing it with the time taken by the previous firm.

The knowledge and skill acquired through such activities related more perhaps to learning about people and how to react to them, than to the rest of medicine. The experience was not directly helpful to passing examinations, but students were left in no doubt they they had a part to play in the medical care given by the hospital. They belonged, not attached to a firm but members of it, recognised as such by all and most importantly by ward sisters who, with the authority of many years service, would inspect hands for cleanliness and clothes for tidiness, and roundly condemn unpunctuality. Almost the lowest form of animal life in hospital (though in a different category from 'lay visitors' who passed from bed to bed leaving each patient with a smile, a flower and a small text such as 'Prepare to meet thy doom') students had responsibilities and were valuable. Because their duties mattered, however menial they might be, failure to perform them was noted.

First Assistants, successors of the Registrars of the past and predecessors of the Senior Registrars of the future spent much of their time in the wards, one for each firm, resplendent in long well-cut double-breasted white coats with four buttons on the back, checking on the activities of the students as much as on the care of the patients. Failure to fulfill responsibilities on time led to a 'flag' attached to the treatment board, its colour indicating the degree of urgency and importance - failure to comply leading to reports to the Dean's Office. During each spell of full duty, lasting three days, students remained under the First Assistant's eye, often rewarded by being allowed to perform at least one carefully supervised appendicectomy.

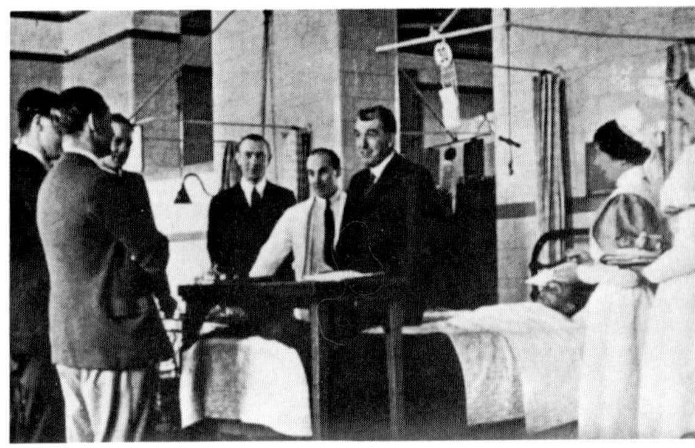

A ward round by Russell Howard in the 1930's.

Ward rounds were 'business' rounds and students part of the business, though never wearing white coats. (House officers wore short white coats). The patient's condition was discussed in front of him and the ward. Diagnosis was stated categorically, in terms of named diseases - 'he has an empyema' or, if it were thought necessary in the patient's interest terms would be used which he was not expected to understand, such as 'specific disease' in lieu of Syphilis. Advice or instructions to patients were similarly concise - impending operation might be announced, kindly and firmly, by 'I'll do you tomorrow'. Students received equally crisp advice, criticism and admonition, much enjoyed by patients. Robert Hutchison describing his paediatric clerks as a 'curious collection of crapulous cretins creeping from crib to crib' was enjoyed as much as Donald Hunter twisting his stethoscope tightly round a student's neck saying 'You stand on hallowed ground where Hughlings Jackson stood and you dare to tell me you don't know what this man's occupation is.' At the end of my first medical firm Donald Hunter exhorted us in ringing tones: 'Go forth and carry the bright torch of medicine into the abysmal darkness of the surgical wards.'

In Surgical Out-patients students helped with minor surgery and applied treatments as ordered, including the frequent application of Scott's dressings to limbs and other parts, heating the dressing over copper drums which would now be worth a fortune but which have long since disappeared. Medical Out-patients were different. The chief sat at his desk in the centre, the first patient seated at his side. The remaining patients, (each holding his or her notes fastened by a rubber band to a 6 inch long rectangle of metal) sat facing him on rows of benches. Behind him sat two or three rows of students, some of whom had earlier been deputed to examine selected patients. The problem of each successive patient was then considered in the midst of this interested congregation and discussed with students before a diagnosis was pronounced and recorded in the notes, along with the action considered appropriate - a prescription of medicine (never tablets) to be dispensed in the hospital out-patient dispensary, possibly a request for an Xray or some simple haematological measurement, or a letter to the referring practitioner.

The rows of patients emptied surprisingly quickly, despite teaching and despite, or perhaps because of, the inability of many (Jewish refugees, or lascars and seamen of other nationalities) to speak or understand English. Hospital notices (Do not undress until told) were helpfully written in both English and Yiddish. Those in whom evidence of organic disease was not apparent were diagnosed as 'Functional' and given to understand that, while their problem was not necessarily of their own making, it was from now on their responsibility. If referred by a general practitioner, often with a visiting card on which was written 'please see and treat', he would be informed of the diagnosis. But many patients would have been first to the Receiving Room and referred by the RRO with a small blue card on which he had written a few words outlining the problem and his diagnosis. This card would be returned to him the same day with on the back the out-patient doctor's, usually the chief's, opinion - both of the patient's condition and of the RROs competence, both expressed with equal sharp clarity.

Some patients were requested to attend again and on their next visit, while waiting to be seen, had the opportunity to read (if they were able to do so) whatever thoughts and findings had been recorded last time. A similar procedure was followed in special clinics - always well attended by students. An afternoon in the Cardiac Clinic offered the opportunity for students to listen, one after the other, to one murmur after another: and respond to William Evans' call to 'Take out your notebooks and write, "I vow that whenever I hear a third heart sound I will..."'

In the Skin department a stream of patients, for the most part scantily clad, would pass before W J O'Donovan who would point out the offending area, describe it in Latin and almost invariably intone (in the same Irish accent and ringing tones which inspired the people of Stepney and Poplar to return him to Parliament, where he seldom spoke) 'We will give him the Waters of Jordan.'

W J O'Donovan.

O'Donovan at times recruited students to accompany him on his electioneering tours of the East End, where his Conservative views not unnaturally led to heckling. 'Don't listen to him, he's only the pox doctor from the London' - to which O'D is reputed to have replied 'Ladies and Gentlemen, allow me to introduce one of my favourite patients.' The accompanying students had the task of ensuring, in the event of a rowdy reception at the street corner, that O'D, his hat and the Union Jack, all reached the taxi kept standing nearby with its engine running.

In all their various appointments students in the thirties worked closely with nurses, who also of course witnessed much of their clinical teaching and the discomfiture it frequently created. Social contact between students and nurses, however, was firmly condemned and if observed in hospital could lead to punishment of the nurse ranging from reprimand to dismissal. This naturally added an extra dimension to the attraction of nurses and stimulated great ingenuity in the arranging of meetings.

The simplest mechanism for making contact with nurses on day duty was provided by the lunch hour. As nurses walked across the garden to their lunch, passing the end of the tennis courts now replaced by the 'Garden Restaurant', students strolled around the courts in the opposite direction. Invitations thus delivered could be answered at the end of lunch as nurses returned and students reversed their perambulations. Nurses on duty at night could be reached by the back staircase at the garden end of each ward block; care being taken to avoid night sisters who, so that they might be reached easily in an emergency, hung their appropriate red or blue bow to the door handle of whichever ward they were visiting. Without doubt the vigilance with which nurses were protected from students added enormously to the enjoyment of life for young people in hospital and resulted in students spending more time in the wards than might otherwise have been the case. In 1936, however, another category of student entered the scene with the opening of the School of Physiotherapy, at the instigation of King George V, who had survived a severe illness (empyema) with care from London Hospital doctors and nurses, and had been impressed by the rehabilitation he was given by them while convalescing at Bognor. The first staff and students were transferred from the Westminster, then in the process of rebuilding.

iv

Between the wars the College itself remained essentially a male reserve apart from the relatively few women on its staff. What is now the general office was the shop; the office (where Mr Osman and Mr Webb perched on high stools) occupying the rooms and corridor leading to the Dean's room. The Athenaeum and the Dining Room were where the Blizard Club now stands, the Dining Room being large, L-shaped, and accommodating at lunch time the students, the house officers and first assistants, College Staff and usually a scattering of physicians and surgeons. The remainder of the senior hospital staff lunched in the Residents Room on the ground floor of the Alexandra wing opposite the Residents' Common Room known to all as the Billiard Room with its windows looking down on the Residents Tennis Court. The hospital 'administration', the Board Room and the House Governor's office were adjoining. Thus meal-times served to bring all kinds of staff and students into contact with each other.

The tennis courts.

Similar close contact characterised the activities of the Clubs Union, both in the College and outside. A majority of the thirty or so senior staff had special allegiance to, or held office in, one or other of the Sports Clubs. Societies were fewer but included the oldest, the Medical Society, always active under the aegis of each year's President, in arranging a series of talks from well-known people of his acquaintance on medical or non-medical topics. Of all clubs and societies the Rugby Club attracted most interest with a fixture list drawn from clubs such as the London Welsh, Scottish, and Irish, Rosslyn Park, Blackheath, Wasps, Northampton, Bedford, Leicester, Coventry, Rugby, Bath, Bristol, Cheltenham, Torquay, Portsmouth, Devonport and Aldershot Services, Neath, Pontypool, Aberavon, Llanelli, Swansea and the better Old Boy sides of London (24).

Christmas was the event which more than any other brought the entire community of the London together. Not even Sports Day attended by all at Hale End, nor Prize Giving held in the library with staff in academic dress assembled on the platform and guests, students, and parents seated below them, followed by tea with strawberries and cream in the garden to the accompaniment of a military band, could compete with Christmas - almost all of which was spent by almost everybody in the London. Christmas Eve was spent by students and nurses putting up the decorations which came down on Boxing Day. In the evening the Troupes gave a performance in the Library to a capacity audience in evening dress.

Carols.

'Very early on Christmas morning' wrote Dick Bomford, 'a long snake of sisters and nurses wound its way round the wards carrying candles and singing carols. Attendance by students was, of course, purely voluntary, but many came at least once.' The Residents (Father Christmas and the Fairies) took presents to patients and violets to nurses. 'Many members of the honorary staff paid a courtesy visit to their wards on Christmas morning and at lunch time the turkey was carved, if not by the chief in person, at least by the houseman. I have a clear picture of Charles Hill (now Lord Hill of Luton) tearing a turkey to bits with a determination which showed promise of his triumph to come. Students carried the lunch around to the patients and the more privileged of them were themselves given lunch in Sister's room' (25). Then came the Troupes, performing in sequence in each ward, returning finally to the Receiving Room for celebrations.

The Troupes consisted of the Residents, some four or five Troupes of Medical Students and the Dentals. With the exception of the Residents the cast of each troupe was seldom more than six; each of the Medicals having its own name, such as the Mercurians, the Pneumonics, the Flebites, the Cirrhotics and the Clerics. Traditionally the Residents produced a band. Each had around fifteen minutes performance time and included as much music as possible. Rehearsals took place in unlikely situations, often the crypt of St Phillip's Church. A dress rehearsal in the Library the night before Christmas Eve would receive blessing and censorship, usually from George Neligan, and directions from the Senior Resident Accoucheur who, as President of the Residents' Mess, was in charge of all proceedings.

A Christmas Troupe of 1938, showing the library's stained-glass window later destroyed in the Blitz.

A small theatre was erected by the Works Department in the proximal part of one section of each pair of wards, into the remainder of which could be crammed all patients considered well enough and everyone else connected with both wards including senior staff and their families. More seriously ill patients spent the day in the remaining sections of the wards. Scenery and props were of the simplest, each troupe having two theatre trolleys to move them and its own liquid refreshment around the hospital. The result was very much a family kind of entertainment, liberally fragmented by intervals, greatly enjoyed by everyone and most of all by most of the patients. Those who doubted its value to the sick, comforted themselves with the thought that at least it kept the young occupied and helped to avoid more of those outbursts of seasonal high spirits which were the subject of somewhat acrimonious correspondence between the House Governor and the Residents every January. The Residents, being unpaid and having very little time off, not unnaturally tended to view Christmas in much the same light as the ship's company of a tea clipper viewed their first night in harbour.

V

Such was life in the London as the Hospital neared its Bicentenary and the danger of a Second World War grew greater. So far as students were concerned it was in most ways similar to that in other teaching hospitals and caricatured by Richard Gordon in 'Doctor in the House': much service to patients, much memorisation for examination, not intellectually very demanding and a great deal of fun. What students saw, and did, is well documented in the hospital notes: the men dying of lobar pneumonia; the young women whose early death from rheumatic carditis was slowed a little by diuretics; the fearful speed of lethal erysipelas and the slow tragedy of tuberculosis; the rare attempts at suicide - all by violent means; the stream of children with osteomyelitis, acute rheumatism and acute nephritis - and the deformities of rickets; the boon of insulin, the remarkable results of partial thyroidectomy, partial gastrectomy and abdominal operations of every kind - with intravenous saline but very seldom blood; laudable pus, from every part of the body, and the interminable dressings. 'The London Hospital uses a mile (or was it two) of bandages every day' read the legend along the front of the Alexandra Wing, round which Out-patients poured into the Whitechapel Road carrying their great bottles of brown, green or red medicine, some stopping surreptitiously to sell it to a barrow-boy.

What else students saw, and what they felt, is less well documented. The memory of student days is always shrouded in a warm nostalgic haze. When enormous changes in medicine and everything else have occurred in the interim, the past seems a little unreal. It is easy to look back, only hard to believe what appears through the mist of time and harder still to remember how it felt. Archie Clark-Kennedy, in his eighties, was asked if he remembered the Blizard Club when it was the Athenaeum. 'I can still see exactly what the room was like when I first walked into it in 1916 - its remembering the me of 64 years ago that is difficult.'

The Pavilion at Hale End.

To students of the 1930s there comes back from the past the sense of wonder they felt at the amount of pain patients suffered, at the fortitude with which it was borne and at their gratitude for whatever was done for them which, no matter how little it was, seemed so often to exceed their expectations. There lingers in the memory too an acute awareness of medicine's inability to affect the poverty and ignorance which brought so many to hospital, and a feeling of nihilism at seeing them return to the same conditions from which they had just been rescued. Much stronger is the recollection of an all-pervading conviction that medicine's primary purpose was neither prevention nor cure but the relief of suffering. To that end the entire hospital community - doctors, nurses, students, porters and every kind of lay staff - seemed consciously dedicated; creating an accepted but seldom mentioned unity of purpose bringing its own rewards and making it seem quite natural that most were paid very little and many nothing at all. Nor did it seem the least surprising at the time that the whole hospital was clean and shining as a new pin and fequently quiet enough to hear one drop. Even in Philpot Street and Stepney Way (then called Oxford Street, hence the 'Oxford Arms') the notice read 'Hospital, Quiet please'. The thought, had it ever occurred to anyone, that it could one day be dirty and noisy would have been even more bizarre than the idea that sometime there might be married nurses or house-officers.

Hospital policy was clear to all, unchanged from that laid down in 1740 and reaffirmed by successive generations of lay governors therafter - to offer the highest standard of care to as many as possible of the local poor. The London Hospital, like Viscount Knutsford, was 'a friend to all manner of men', but it did not set out to be all things to all men, or in today's terminology to offer comprehensive medical care to a defined population. If, as was necessary from time to time, quantity had to be cut to conserve quality, it not only kept the hospital solvent but enabled it to maintain the standard of hospital care and set the pace of progress - functions vital to medical education and through it to the quality of health care in the future.

In the 1930s the London had reached the culminating peak of two hundred years of increasing development but there comes back no memory of a community resting on its laurels, satisfied with its facilities and results. Pride in an institution which had struggled always against the odds and yet achieved so much was accompanied by awareness of both the need to continue and the impossibility of doing so by the same means. Even students could see that the cost of increasingly sophisticated medicine was placing Voluntary Hospitals in an untenable situation - and what the teaching hospitals had to offer was now needed not only by the poor but by the middle class and the wealthy. Home was no longer the best place in which to overcome illness.

The idea of a National Health Service, put forward by Lord Dawson in his Cavendish lectures of 1918 had been taken up by the Ministry of Health (itself a recent innovation) resulting in the Dawson Committee Report of 1920; recommending a comprehensive health service which would provide for all aspects of medicine through a national network of primary (GP) and secondary (specialist) health centres which were to be mutually dependent. Further Committees had reported in 1921 on administrative machinery and in 1937 on the regionalisation of Voluntary Hospitals. The NHS was on its way, with the medical profession widely agreed that 'something must be done', even if divided as to exactly what.

Meanwhile parts of the profession, and some students, were equally convinced that radical changes were needed in medical education. There was no doubt that students were being well programmed to recognise most common conditions and respond to them in a given way, but the feeling was growing fast that more than that would soon be required. The expansion of medicine alone made it unlikely that students could become competent in medicine, surgery and obstetrics for very much longer. The rapidly advancing application of science to diagnosis and treatment meant that unless doctors acquired a greater command of the scientific method as students, they would soon be reduced to technicians applying the tools of science with little understanding of its limitations and dangers. It was clear too that before long students would not be able to acquire sufficient experience under supervision before qualification to fit them for independent practice immediately afterwards. The College of Physicians of London in particular was busy compiling evidence for the next review of the GMCs Recommendations.

In medical education as in medical care the end of an era was approaching. Archie Clark-Kennedy in a prize-giving address as Dean voiced a widely felt view: 'One day some scheme will be evolved which will provide a hospital service for all sorts and conditions of men, and at the same time afford wider scope for medical education and an extended field for medical research.' (26)

But as the Bicentenary of the London Hospital drew nearer attention was directed to Nazi Germany. Each act of aggression resulting only in appeasement leading to further aggression, the crisis of September 1938 found hospitals totally unprepared for the hostilities which suddenly it was clear might start within weeks or days. Hospital and College turned abruptly aside from the activities which had kept both so fully occupied for two centuries and made desperate efforts to prepare the buildings for the receipt of both casualties and enemy action from the air. Patients were still being evacuated and sandbags filled when Chamberlain's final appeasement at Munich bought respite by sacrificing the Czechs.

The wards filled again, students returned to their studies and the task began of making more adequate arrangements to meet the war which was now certain to come. The Emergency Medical Service was planned. London and the Home Counties were divided into Sectors each related to a Teaching Hospital - the London being allocated all the hospitals in east and north east London, Essex and parts of Hertfordshire and Middlesex. George Neligan and Archie Clark-Kennedy were given charge. The London itself was to be reduced to less than 200 beds with 300 in reserve for casualties. Patients were to be discharged or evacuated to the periphery. Doctors, nurses and students were to be disseminated over 46 hospitals. The dockland hospitals, other than the London were to be emptied and manned only by doctors and students as casualty clearing stations. The pre-clinical school would be reestablished in Cambridge and the Dental School in Claybury.

The task of how to dismantle the College and reassemble it again in working order in bits and pieces scattered over London and four counties devolved upon the Dean and his secretary Miss Koop, Mr Burdon the College Secretary and Messrs Osman and Webb. It was completed, down to the details of who was to go where and on which family each would be billeted, while the school continued its normal routine and the next year's new entry was arranged. Only in August 1939, as the last days of peace ran out in the summer sunshine, did the College come to a halt. Wards emptied and teaching ran down as students turned to piling sandbags against ground-floor windows of the Hospital, red crosses were painted on the roof, bunks erected in the basements and metal props placed between floor and ceilings down the centre of each ward. Surgical first assistants gave instruction to students on first aid and stretcher bearing in the garden and their medical counterparts took blood from students in the Medical Unit laboratories. Donald Bateman and seven other students were despatched to Acton to bring back eight icecream vans which would provide a mobile Blood Transfusion Service for the Sector.

Then activity gave way to waiting - students sitting in groups in the garden or strolling round the tennis courts in the sun. To Archie Clark-Kennedy emerging from the Dean's office the scene must have brought back memories of men waiting to go over the top in 1918. Confronting the nearest two students with the words 'We must find something for people to do' he marched us to Stepney Town Hall, demanded to see the man in charge and announced 'I am the Dean of the London Hospital Medical College. I have three hundred able-bodied men like these. What do you need doing?' Sadly, it appeared that the local authority, though ready and willing to face the worst that Hitler might send, shrank from even the thought of setting three hundred medical students loose upon the borough. We walked back slowly to the London.

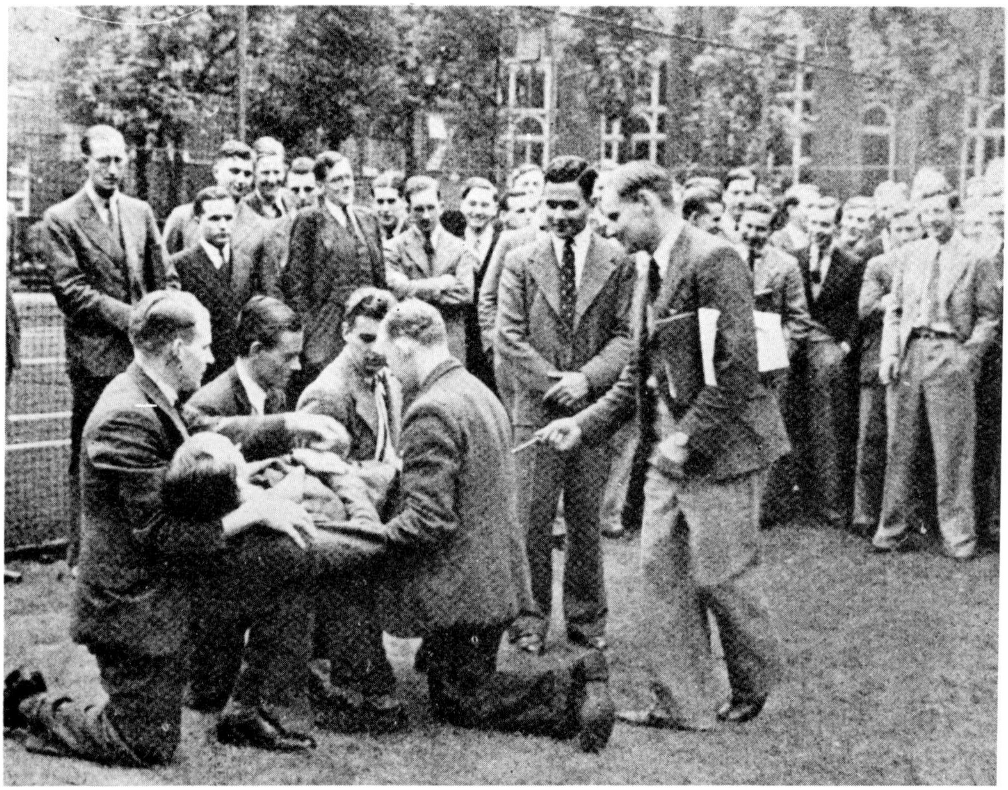

Instruction in stretcher-bearing 1938.

Next day, September 2nd, the time to move had come. The nurses left from Stepney Way in a long line of buses, the sunlight dazzling on their white aprons and caps as they waited to board. 'As we rumbled down the street' wrote Margaret Broadley, 'the excited chatter died away, as if the solemnity of the occasion had suddenly dawned on us all. We did not know whether we should ever see the familiar surroundings again and had only the haziest idea as to where we were going and none as to what lay before us' (27).

The nurses left from Stepney Way in a long line of buses.

Archie Clark-Kennedy assembled the senior medical students in the Anatomy Theatre and gave them 'their marching orders... promising that I would move them round from time to time and endeavour to keep the school alive and maintain their education as far as the forseeable future would permit. Then, as they gathered up their things and went their ways, I could not help wondering when or if I would see them all again '(7).

Those of us allocated to the Albert Dock Hospital forgathered in the Good Samaritan. The last to arrive was Ebbie Hoff, one of two brothers from the American Mid-West. Short and stocky, wearing his best suit of a peculiarly striking check, his tin hat on his head and the cardboard box containing his gasmask slung over his shoulder, he carried his suitcase in one hand and a basket containing cold chicken and salad in the other. 'Never go to war on an empty stomach' he said and so, fully prepared, we walked to Commercial Road and took the tram.

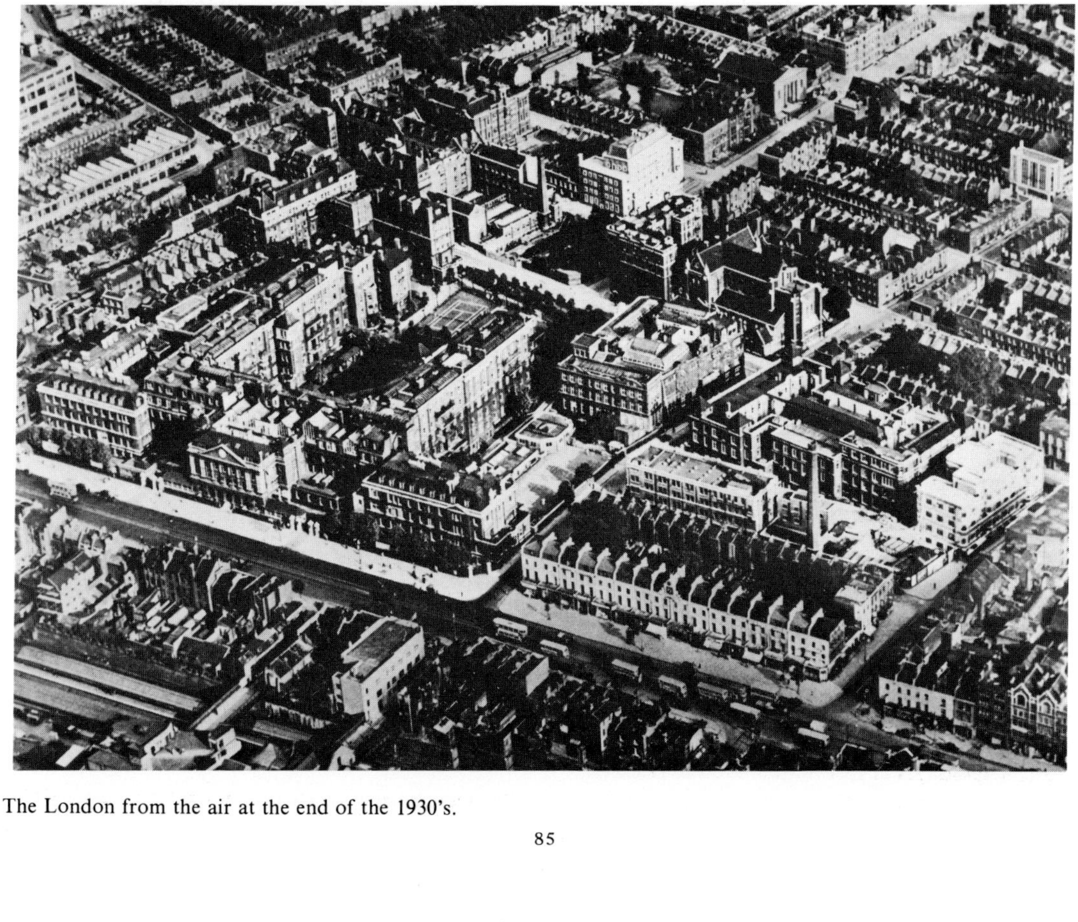
The London from the air at the end of the 1930's.

Chapter 7.

The Second World War 1939-1945

During September 1939 casualties at the Albert Dock were few and occasioned solely by the black-out. Wearing something white at night, achieved by old ladies who left the pub at closing time by tucking their skirts into huge white bloomers, was good protection from being knocked down in darkened streets, but none at all against falling into the docks. Students, accommodated in the nurses home where each bedroom door carried the name of a well known ship, had little to do except to see whether their ship had been torpedoed in the night and attend talks on surgery by Pete Reidy, (the surgical first assistant in charge) and one on the 'First World War at Sea', formally delivered to all twelve of us by the elderly Earl of Cork and Orrery in his admiral's uniform. In October, being of little use to anyone, we were moved to join students in various other hospitals.

The General Hospital, Southend-on-Sea provided a different experience. The town had been evacuated and declared a restricted area, but a residual population augmented by the Services maintained a steady flow of patients. A reduced hospital staff and some twenty students from the London formed a close-knit community, on good terms with the fighter squadron across the fields at Rochford. The Hospital community was knit still closer by three quarters of it spending much of every day digging trenches, until the flat ground round the airfield was deemed unusable by enemy aircraft. That completed, something approaching a miniature medical school was established with clinical teaching in the wards, outpatients, and theatres from enthusiastic Southend Staff of the quality of Rodney Maingot and Rowland Hill, and an equally enthusiastic junior staff comprised of Andrew Monro from the London and a number of the excellent postgraduates from New Zealand and Australia to whom the hospital had long been an attraction.

Before Christmas a reasonable rugby side was in action and at Christmas a review entitled 'The First Born' was produced by Charles Keogh (the London's staff representative) and his wife Barbara, in one of the local schools. Its small chorus line included Albert Kagua from Uganda, A H E Marshall later to become Reader in Histology at the London and J M Ledingham destined to be Professor of Medicine. Either because nothing quite like their dancing had ever been seen before, or because no other form of live entertainment was available, the show met with such a warm reception that under Charles Keogh's management it went on tour - first to the London where it was produced in the library and then to Portsmouth where it entertained the troops.

Such was life in one of the fragments into which the College had been scattered. Not all were as good but each had a character of its own and in each London and local staff combined to provide all they could for students. Early in 1940 the College itself came to life again and students were withdrawn from most of the smaller hospitals. More were concentrated on the London (to which the Dental School returned) but sizeable groups remained in each of the larger hospitals in the sector, moving every few months from one to another or back to the London. Many Londoners of the early '40s were to remember with gratitude for the rest of their lives the teaching and experience they gained at places like Billericay, Goodmayes, Chase Farm and Southend.

The Dean portrayed in the Gazette as 'Our Liaison Officer'.

As the war advanced the nature of the experience gained changed with it. In the summer of 1940 the students at Southend not only had Billy Woods teaching them Pathology but saw their first battle casualties - German airmen with shattered bodies and to us, shattering confidence in the certainty of their early victory. Through them we learned much about the treatment of casualties and were encouraged to make the hospital section of the Local Defence Volunteers as efficient as possible. A week's small arms course with the Highland Light Infantry did nothing to forward this aim, owing to an impassable language barrier, but the section turned out smartly enough to provide a guard of honour for the Dean on his monthly visit. It turned out too when invasion was thought imminent and spent the night guarding the approach to the airfield, fortunately troubled only by the fact that noone could find the key to the ammunition locker.

Similar incidents and excitements enlivened life in other groups - at Cambridge where the pre-clinical students joined a mobile cyclist batallion of the Home Guard, at Chase Farm where more pathology teaching was centred, at Billericay where Clifford Wilson and Hermon Taylor were developing an exceptional teaching programme, and at Goodmayes where Donald Hunter was insisting that the London nurses were properly fed and where later he was responsible for organising a remarkable Christmas show aided by Vera Lowe. Back at the London life approximated more to the pre-war norm, students no longer divided into day and night dressers as in September 1939 but attending wards, out-patients and lectures. Then came the Battle of Britain and then the Blitz brought experience of a different kind.

7th September 1940.

ii

From the first daylight raid on the docks on September 6th (when from the balconies of Gwynne House it seemed as though the whole East End was rising up in smoke almost to reach the wave after wave of bombers passing in close formation slowly overhead in the sunshine) to the last great night raid in May 1941, bombing continued almost every night with only a short break in 1940 and longer ones in 1941. The London was hit first on September 8th and altogether was hit eight times by high explosive and innumerable times by incendiary bombs. There were two serious fires and countless small ones. But in the whole nine months it was never once put out of action. On its two hundredth anniversary a large bomb struck right at its heart, in the garden between the main ward blocks close to Queen Alexandra, and failed to explode. A week later it was exposed, twenty feet down. Proving impossible to defuse it was detonated underground with minimal damage.

Every evening the familiar front of the Hospital was the last sight above ground for the long line of East Enders passing into Whitechapel Station, loaded down with their blankets on their way to spend the night in the tube stations up West. Every morning as they emerged again into the Whitechapel Road the Hospital was still there standing out from the ever increasing devastation around it. Those of us who had joked in 1939 about the old place being sure to collapse like a pack of cards if a bomb fell anywhere near it, began instead to believe in some special providence; a belief which turned to conviction one morning in March when daylight revealed large sections of the railway line from Whitechapel station lying on the Residents Tennis Court. Over the whole period of the Blitz the London took in 1,330 casualties and not a single member of its staff was seriously injured.

Hospital and College were fused into one relatively small community with a corporate spirit unlike any before or since, and an upside down element to existence; night seeming to predominate over day, bunks in basements replacing going up to bed. Without question the whole institution was extremely well run, untroubled by contentious issues of future policy, concentrating solely on the cares of the immediate. The leadership of George Neligan, Medical Superintendent, Henry Brierley, House Governor, the acting Matron Miss Burgess, and the Hospital Surveyor Norman Oatley, brought a total response from every kind of staff and student. Not one of the descriptions of this time left by anyone, fails to mention the impression made on the rest of the team by the women of Whitechapel who every night got down on their hands and knees and scrubbed the hospital clean, unaware that their example of business as usual shone more brightly than their polished floors.

George Neligan, MC, FRCS.

Luckes and Alexandra Homes.

The King and Queen visit the London on the Hospital's Bicentenary 1940.

Everyone looking back on the London in the Blitz sees the same long dark background but for each it is lit by a different series of flashes in which particular incidents are seen again in startling clarity, complete with sound and smells. The receiving room with the imperturbable George Neligan sorting casualties: a young and very pretty girl climbing back into her frail emergency ambulance at the front door and driving off again into lurid red smoke billowing from burning buildings: the operating theatre in Matron's office (the post-war RR), bright lights shining on its twin tables, the gowned surgical teams bent over them and the familiar faces of Victor Dix, or Basil Page or Robert Percival: the ground floor wards full of sick patients, quiet enough to hear the drone of planes preceding the noise of guns and bombs: first floor wards receiving casualties with nurses working by torch light, soft faces contrasting with their hard tin hats: dark stairways up which porters and students stumbled with casualties on stretchers: a deputation of students in the House Governor's Office suggesting that movement exacerbated shock: the resulting extra resuscitation area on the ground floor in Crossman, the smile of a twelve year old saying thank you for morphine, and the never to be forgotten smell of blood on blankets.

Inevitably those who knew the London at that time developed a very close personal attachment to it, as sailors come to feel for their ship which assumes an identity of its own. Students helping to put out fires started by incendiaries acquired a special affection for those parts of the buildings involved - and a proprietorial attitude towards the local houses which, standing empty at night, provided unusual opportunities for breaking and entering in the public interest. An incendiary which fell at the foot of the plane tree next to the library exploded as two students were putting it out. One of them still feels the pain, not of the explosion, but of the tree being felled more than thirty years later, to make way for the Radioisotope Department.

The Blitz made perhaps a longer lasting impression on students than on anyone. The 25 or so at the London carried no final responsibility for anything - but they were useful in many different ways. Living in the Hospital (the Hostel was occupied by the Friends' Ambulance Unit) they were in close contact with every kind of Hospital personnel - including the senior staff with whom they shared the evening meal in the basement of the Alexandra Wing. That alone, with people such as Neligan, Clark-Kennedy, Arthur Ellis, Turnbull and Henry Wilson was a learning experience as rich as it was enjoyable. It was not an easy context in which to prepare for finals, but students learned much about the care of casualties which was to stand them in good stead later in the war, and what they learned about people (including themselves) was of incalculable value. People so seldom turned out to be exactly what they seemed from the outside. When morale sank a little in the mess it was Professor Turnbull of the interminable lectures who spotted the reason, went up off West, and came back proudly clutching a new piece of billiard chalk.

iii

The Blitz was also, though noone knew it then, the last time the Hospital was to function on a single site. In 1941 the London Hospital Annexe opened in a hutted hospital at Brentwood. By 1942 it had over 300 beds and by 1943, 350. 100 more beds were reopened too in the London itself early in 1942, putting its complement up from 350 to 400.In 1941 it admitted 6,000 patients and in 1942, 8,000. Outpatient attendances rose from 42,000 in 1941 to over 56,000 in 1942. It was easier, however, to reopen beds than to man them, particularly with medical staff depleted by the many who had joined the forces and still strained by duties in sector hospitals. Students grew accustomed to finding the same two medical registrars, Michael Vaizey and Alastair Hunter, at work in all the different specialty clinics and Joe Fathi whenever surgery was needed. House officers combined the care of inpatients with attendance in OPs. As each of the two medical and two surgical firms had some fifty beds, and was on full duty alternate days, there was ample opportunity to acquire clinical experience. There was also the closest collaboration between the clinical units and departments of radiology and pathology. Housemen gained enormously from being able to drop in at any time on the laboratories where John Penfold would advise and the everlasting 'Butch' and 'Dickie' unveiled the mysteries of haematology and clinical chemistry. There was contact too with exceptional people who had volunteered to help maintain the hospital service, notably Norman Shumway, an American physician who gave invaluable service and endeared himself to everyone.

The policy adopted in the second world war, unlike the first, of keeping the medical schools in action and maintaining the training of doctors, included requiring new graduates to serve upwards of one year as house officers before joining the services. In those months those who qualified in the early 1940s were more than able to make up, especially at the London itself, for the disruption of their course at the start of the war. Except that they were paid £18 per month by the Emergency Medical Service their situation closely resembled that of the senior students of fifty years earlier - caring for an endless stream of acutely ill patients in close contact with those to whom they were responsible. The house-surgeon who asked in 1941 for a weekend off during his six month appointment was given it but led to understand that he should reconsider his suitability for clinical medicine. He did in fact later become a pathologist.

Life in the early war years was not, however, without its highlights and the London's traditional celebration of Christmas was maintained in all the hospitals where London staff and students were stationed. In Whitechapel the Christmas Show of 1941 took place in Rachel Ward which being on an upper floor was not in regular use, with one performance also in the library. A short and very successful revue was put on by nurses while the nine residents and slightly larger number of resident students performed a musical entitled 'Pstink-on-Don' inspired by the invasion of Russia, reminding the audience of Napoleon's unsuccessful Russian venture and of the fact that

'Now again in forty-one
Comes another smaller one
With intent to wash his face in
The snowy waters of the basin
Of the Don.'

The wedding scene in which Natasha ('who of this woman is the giver, are you sure you've finished with her ?') married the hero Boris Turnov and became Natasha Turnova, was as colourful as many peace-time productions even though the costumes came almost entirely from the operating theatres.

Wartime housemen also had the inestimable advantage of working with the older and therefore more experienced people in almost every category of hospital staff - the younger members having 'gone to the war'. They were guided in the wards by sisters of immense experience, in the Receiving Room they benefitted from what the male orderlies, Pascall and Ransome, had acquired over years of service, and in the theatres it was Ovary, the most senior of the renowned pre-war theatre men of the London, who brought them up. The most fortunate had additional advantages. Not long after I had been appointed an RRO I was sent for by the Dean whose house physician I had been for six months. He told me an emergency situation had arisen at the Annexe in Brentwood and I was to report there next day as house surgeon. On arrival I found that the chiefs whose beds I was to look after included Messrs Moore, Butler, Hermon Taylor, Goulden the Ophthalmologist and Mollison the retired aural surgeon from Guy's who was helping the London. There was no surgical registrar or first assistant. Each surgeon operated at least once a week and at first 'finishing off the end of the list' was something of a nightmare but there were two tables in the theatre and Clive Butler would let me work at one while he hummed encouragingly as he 'chipped away' at the other. I learned more ophthalmology from Charles

The Christmas Show 1941: seated left to right —
Noble, Ross, Ellis, Warren, Dick, Golden, Rogers.

Goulden in the 'Robin Hood' the nights before he operated than in three months as a student. When emergency admissions were clearly beyond me Allan Brews came from his home in Brentwood. It was impressive and encouraging to see a gynaecologist dealing so deftly with a mangled leg, setting the compound fracture of the femur and washing out the open knee joint with Dettol. The result was equally impressive.

Nor was research left out of life at the London in the early war years. Squadron Leader E A Pask (later Professor of Anaesthetics at Newcastle) found that some aircrew who ditched into the sea were held face down in the water by their life jackets while unconscious. Remembering the nurses swimming pool from his student days at the London he brought a team of physiologists from RAF Farnborough and conducted experiments in the pool, at great risk to himself, which eventually resulted in a life jacket that could be worn in the confined space of aircraft and yet keep unconscious aircrew with their heads above water.

iv

By the end of 1942 the London had 770 beds in Whitechapel and Brentwood. By the end of 1943 it had a total of 870 and when another 100 were reopened in Whitechapel it had more in action than it had had before the war began. So the dual task of caring for patients and training doctors, dentists and nurses, continued in the second half of the war with less difficulty than in the first. The pre-clinical school returned from Cambridge in 1943. In June 1944, however, the flying bombs began just after the landing in Normandy, the first dropping in Bethnal Green. From then on the London turned again to the care of casualties. On August 3rd it suffered worse damage than any inflicted in the Blitz when, in the early hours, a flying bomb demolished half the East Wing, killing two patients, seriously injuring two nurses and blowing in most of the windows in the Hospital. Despite all this and the consequent evacuation the hospital did not close to admissions and by evening 263 beds were ready for use.

Postmortem: Profession Turnbull and W W Woods inspect the Bernhard Baron Institute.

The East Wing after a direct hit from a flying bomb.

The London suffered no further serious damage from flying bombs and survived the rockets which followed and the rain of long-range rockets which fell from November 1944 to March 1945 - but throughout that period received waves of casualties from less fortunate areas all around. Its last special war-time effort was to send 12 students to help with the appalling horror of Belsen - one of them, John Hancock, contracted typhus.

For the London as for so many hospitals the Second World War was a chapter in its history of which it can be justly proud. It is fully described in Archie Clark-Kennedy's account of 'The London' except in regard to the part he himself played, not merely as a physician in Whitechapel throughout the War, but in planning the integrated hospital service of the whole sector (the London's sector included 32,000 hospital beds, 500 doctors, 6,000 nurses and served 4 million people), in planning how to keep, as on September 2nd 1939 he promised the students he would, 'the College alive', and above all in keeping his promise. His was a magnificent achievement. What it cost him not one of the countless people who benefited from it can begin to assess, not least because to every individual with whom he came into contact (his patients, his house staff, his students scattered round London and East Anglia, all the medical nursing and other authorities with whom he dealt) he gave the impression that everything was well in hand and that he was more often than not enjoying himself. Very probably he was - for without doubt he was the man of the hour, possessing all the qualities needed to rise to the occasion and win.

The Receiving Room, drawn by Hanslip Fletcher in the first world war, proved an effective casualty clearing station in the second.

s his house physician in 1941 one would never have uessed that he had any other care to contend with but hat of his patients, and the well-being and upbringing f his students. Only occasionally did he show signs of nxiety that a student might be likely to miss some nportant experience. One evening he announced: There's a young chap at Trinity Hall who might be uite good. He's been offered a scholarship to do his linical in America but that would be an awful waste. I've told him to come and see you next Wednesday. Just take him round the wards, show him the patients and make him realise he'ld much rather come to the London than go to Harvard or some such place'.

So a rather weary HP called Ellis took a rather gangly fairhaired youth called Floyer round the wards, neither remotely aware that both would one day succeed Archie as Dean of the London.

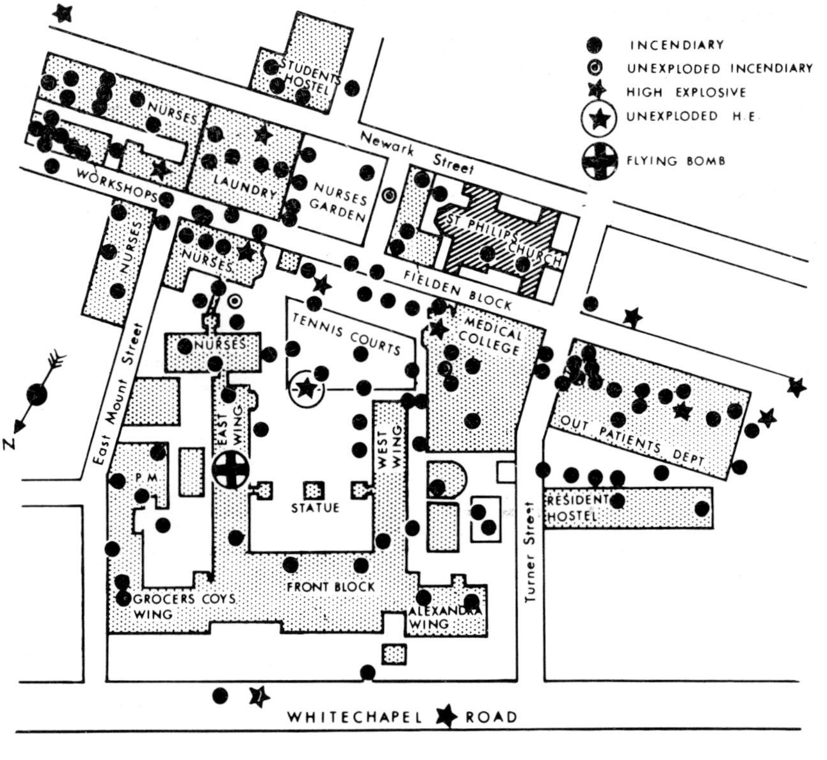

It could have been worse.

Chapter 8.

The Turmoil of Peace 1945-1948

The kind of training pioneered by the College in its first half-century and consolidated in the next, was brought to a peak in the 69 years between 1879 and 1948 during which College and Hospital were united and run virtually as one. Hospital medical schools were at their most successful between the wars, as were the voluntary hospitals which ran them, but although this golden age was ended abruptly by war, the very success of the system was sowing the seeds of its own destruction before ever the war began. The advance of medicine, to which hospitals and schools both contributed so much, was ensuring that hospitals could not be run much longer on voluntary subscriptions alone, and that students could no longer acquire in a medical school course all the knowledge and skill needed by a safe and efficient general practitioner.

Even in the midst of war, work continued on planning the changes in medical care and medical education which had become essential. In the darkest period of the war, in October 1941, the Government announced plans for a post-war State Hospital Service, and in March 1942 set up an interdepartmental Committee under Sir William Goodenough to enquire into the organisation of medical schools and their facilities for clinical teaching and research, and to recommend how they should relate to the future hospital service. So, soon after the fall of Singapore and months before Alamein, urgent consideration began to be given to the future of medical education and continued through the two years between the end of the Blitz and the start of the doodle-bugs. During that period the Beveridge Report was published in December 1942.

The Committee had to consider not only the effects a national hospital service might have on the training of doctors, but also what kind of medical education would be required to prepare doctors for what was clearly going to be a rapidly advancing kind of medicine different in many ways from that taught before the war. Major changes had already occurred and the effect that antibiotics like penicillin might have could begin to be glimpsed.

Obviously much practical training would have to take place after qualification. The process which had been going on before the war of handing over to qualifie house officers much that had previously been done b students would be accelerated by the continuin advance of medicine. It would be expedited still furthe by a National Health Service because patients i teaching hospitals would cease to be objects of charit and become people with a right to more highl qualified medical care - it would become increasingl difficult for students to take responsibility for the care and in the process learn by doing.

Sir Henry Bedson, FRS.

At the same time if medicine were to continue t advance as it was doing, or at even greater speed, the (even if the pattern of disease did not change, as it we might) doctors would have to be able to deal wit situations about which they had never been taugh They would need to be equipped to face the unfamilia to think and reason things out for themselves. The would need education as much as training. In medical school they would have to have both, with all the technical difficulties the mixing of education and training brings, because the one encourages the student to question all he is told and the success of the other depends upon him doing what he has been told without question. So the medical school course would inevitably become a very complex area of higher education and would differ from others in being dependent not only on a university but also on a hospital (designed, staffed and equipped to care for patients) where the necessary training could be provided on an economical basis. The medical school would be the meeting place of university and hospital and its success would depend on its ability to alternate education and training and on its capacity to relate its students to courses and teachers so as best to meet their varying needs.

The Goodenough Committee reported in 1944 and came out clearly and categorically with the recommendation that the medical school course should 'provide the student with a university education on broad and liberal lines' and that it should be followed by a compulsory 'pre-registration' year of internship for all, and postgraduate training for those entering the specialities. During the internship year students would be qualified and given provisional registration enabling them to practice as house officers under supervision in posts approved by the GMC on the recommendation of a university.

The Goodenough Report recognised that medical schools would have to be provided with the same educational facilities as universities and with a great increase in the number of university-appointed whole-time teachers. The schools would in effect have to be rebuilt and re-staffed and the Goodenough Committee recommended that the enormous cost should be met by government as a necessary investment for the nation's future. It considered whether it would be better (i) for teaching hospitals to continue to run medical schools, (ii) for teaching hospitals to be run by a university or (iii) for equally independent schools and hospitals to work together.

It opted for the last and recommended that each of 12 London schools (it recommended closure of the West London) should become an independent corporate body, with strong University representation on its Council of Governors, able to deal on equal terms with the teaching hospital; and thus marry the needs of care with those of education. The Committee also recommended that some of the London teaching hospitals be resited and that all medical schools should be able to relate to, and make use of, not just one hospital but a group of hospitals which, with the medical school, would together comprise a university medical centre.

The Goodenough Committee Report was published when all attention was focussed on the Allied invasion of Normandy. Its remarkable recommendations for adapting British medical education to the rapidly changing nature of medicine and the forthcoming National Health Service went unnoticed by the public, the medical profession and the medical schools while the war went on, victory in Europe came and Japan finally surrendered. With the end of the war came a widespread longing to see as soon as possible that bright new world which, as the war progressed, had come to symbolise that for which it was being fought. The new world would respect the rights of man and foremost among them the right to health care. A National Health Service being an integral part of that eagerly awaited social revolution its long gestation period had to be brought quickly to a close and delivery expedited.

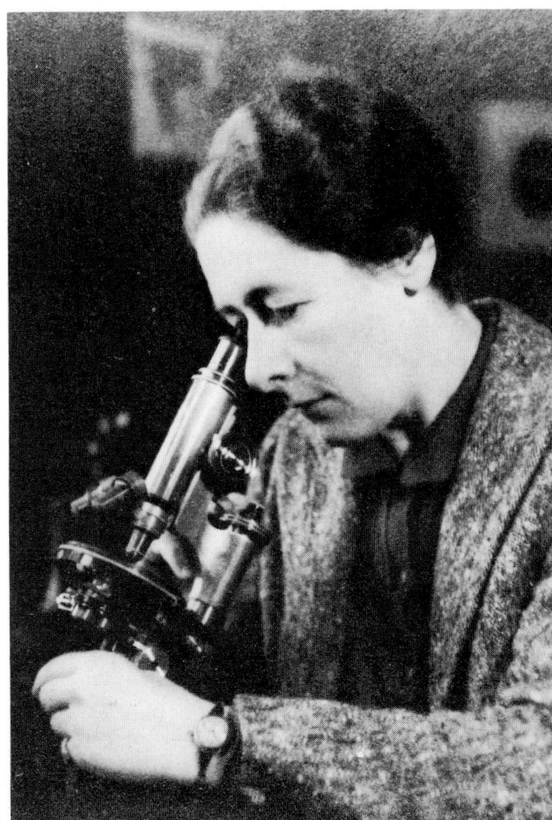

Professor Dorothy Russel.

The original plans were reshaped, not to take account of the fundamental changes in medicine during the six years of war, but so as to gain the agreement of the various interests involved. The plans for the hospital part of the service were of course far advanced and hospital doctors accepted the principles of salaried appointments (part time for those who wished to continue private practice) subject to the teaching hospitals in England having Boards of Governors responsible direct to the Minister of Health. General practitioners on the other hand were not prepared to become salaried members of a National Health Service and so it was agreed that they would remain outside it. They could undertake to provide certain services as independent contractors.

So a National Health Service originally intended to rest on the cornerstone of general practice operating from primary care health centres, was quickly altered to one without health centres and with general practitioners as independent contractors outside it. The Medical Act bringing it into being was passed in 1946, leaving many with the impression that the NHS had, by some kind of political wizardry, been conceived, planned and delivered in little more than a year. Not much public attention was paid to the future of medical education in the debates which preceded the Act but the government accepted the Goodenough Report, and those of its recommendations which required parliamentary legislation were implemented in the Act. So Parliament decreed that on the appointed day (5th July 1948) the London Medical Schools would become independent corporate bodies each with its own Council of Governors empowered to run its finances and own its premises, and each incorporated as a Medical College of the University of London, financed by the University Grants Committee.

While these momentous changes were being debated and decided the College itself faced problems requiring immediate answers. No sooner were VE Day and the Victory Dance in the College Library over and demobilisation begun than the numbers seeking to take up medicine swelled enormously. Men and women returning from the forces, including many who had intended to take up medicine or had actually begun but who had joined the services instead, sought admission along with the school leavers of the year. Left to itself the College might perhaps have continued to take only men. The admission of women which had begun in 1918 had ceased in 1922 and there seems to have been no great local pressure for it to be reintroduced. But the University Grants Committee, its policies based on the Goodenough Report, indicated that the funding of Medical Schools would be linked to their acceptance of women. State funding was still only part of the income of hospital medical schools but the London, which had been granted £15,000 in 1939 received £50,000 out of a total income of £67,000 in 1946. It was decided to admit women and like all schools to admit as many new students as it was thought possible to provide with a good course.

The staff in 1946 consisted of 30 academics and 2[illegible] technical staff. There were six professors - one of whom, Evelyn Sprawson, Professor of Dentistry, was part-time. Clifford Wilson was appointed to the vacant chair of medicine, Arthur Ellis having gone to Oxford in 1942 as Regius Professor. Dorothy Russell replaced Turnbull in Morbid Anatomy and at the instigation of the University Grants Committee a Surgical Unit was established in 1947 and Victor Dix appointed professor. Other replacements and additions followed - J d'Silva in the chair of Physiology and Miles Weatherall replacing W A M Smart in Pharmacology. Readerships were filled in Bacteriology, Chemotherapy, Histology, Dental Surgery, Morbid Anatomy and Chemical Pathology, and William Warren appointed to the chair of Biochemistry.

Regrouping of the administration was needed also. The Dean, Archie Clark-Kennedy, remained as indomitable as ever despite losing the sight of one eye from a detached retina and with a cataract impairing vision in the other. Harold Osman and Fred Webb continued to manage the functions of the Registrar's Office giving every indication that the turmoil of peace would no more disrupt the performance of their duties than six years of war had done. But the Dean's Secretary, Miss Nesta Koop, who had survived being alone in the College when it had received a direct hit in the Blitz, now retired and was replaced by Miss Kay Reynolds. In 1946 too Mr Burdon, the College Secretary retired after 43 years of service to the College. He had been Secretary for 36 years. In 1916 when he had been in that post for only six, Clark-Kennedy had described him as a 'frail, hardworking, helpful little man', but frail or not he had carried on his hard work and helpfulness for another thirty, and no record remains of anyone ever saying a word against him.

Burdon was replaced by Hugh Laird, a graduate of Corpus Christi College Cambridge who had left the coal industry to join the army at the start of the war. He was captured by the Japanese on the fall of

Singapore, but despite his experience as a Prisoner of War in the Far East noone could ever have described Hugh as either frail or little. Like his predecessor, however, he was hardworking and helpful - and very, very much more besides. Devoted to the College, he rose always to the occasion and there were always occasions to rise to in his 32 years as College Secretary, especially at the start and at the finish, and if they did not occur spontaneously he was not averse to creating them.

College policy continued of course to be decided by the College Board whose chairman, Colonel Marlborough Pryor, had been chairman since 1921. The six hospital governors and six representatives of the Medical Council were augmented by the professors in post and advised on dental matters by the Dental Education Committee. Their greatest problem arose from the state to which the hospital had been reduced by the war. The Whitechapel buildings were badly damaged. The most sensible policy was clearly to rebuild the hospital not where it stood, but on the land which it owned to the south of the existing buildings. Meanwhile however the beds in the Annexe at Brentwood were of little use for teaching and those in Whitechapel were insufficient for the necessarily increased number of students. In addition facilities had to be provided for young doctors needing a period of time back in hospital as supernumerary registrars on demobilisation from the Services.

Attention turned therefore, in 1947, to taking over Mile End Hospital with its 400 beds, as recommended in the Goodenough Report. Opinion oscillated. At one point a Joint Planning Committee of Hospital and College came down firmly in favour, subject to the eventual rebuilding of the London not being prejudiced. Then the idea of taking over a hospital which already had its own medical and nursing staff met with opposition. The possibility of merely using the beds for teaching purposes was entertained but no firm coherent policy was forthcoming and the opportunity was lost. Had it been realised that the London Hospital would remain for the next 20 years with some 600 beds only in Whitechapel and 350 in Brentwood, the decision might have been different. At the time the evil consequences of such a division had still to become fully apparent and in any case there were many who, despite the vast number of damaged and dilapidated hospitals across the country, found it difficult to imagine that the London, the country's largest voluntary hospital for about 100 years, would not be quickly rebuilt.

So, when the Act of 1946 was passed and the College Board began to plan the kind of Council of Governors and Academic Board by which it would be replaced the College prepared to enter the third phase of its existence not as it had entered the second in 1879, in conjunction with a hospital which had all the advantages a school could want, but linked with one which had already lost many of those advantages and was itself about to move into an unknown future in which many grave difficulties could already be seen.

Clifford Wilson, Professor of Medicine.

Victor Dix, first Professor of Surgery.

PART III

THE UNIVERSITY MEDICAL COLLEGE

Chapter 9.

The Nineteen Fifties

Looked at in 1985 the Goodenough Report of 40 years ago reads like a statement of the obvious. Medicine now, (as much concerned with disorders of function, of mind and body, as with disorders of structure) is clearly as different from that of the 1930s as that was from the medicine of Blizard's time. The hospital beds which once were filled with acutely ill children and young adults now contain those with more chronic disorders, and elderly people suffering from the complex interaction of physical, chemical, psychological and social problems. Injuries and acute disease which threaten life require intensive care from specially trained teams in specially equipped premises.

It is obvious now that students cannot share in the care of patients in the same way and to the same extent their predecessors did and that the knowledge and skills of current practice are mainly acquired during post-graduate training. It is equally obvious that medical students need to acquire not only basic knowledge but the ability to solve complex problems, think and learn for themselves, and that they need those learning situations and teaching methods which develop such intellectual capacities. No one now seriously questions the need to adapt the old training that was so superbly given in the Hospital Medical Schools, so as to include new aims and methods without losing its insistence on clinical method, patient care and service.

But such things were not at all so clear in 1948 when a National Health Service designed to provide the entire population with the medicine of the 1930s went into action with a war-weary disorganised profession and a collection of out-of-date war-damaged hospitals none of which had had any regular maintenance for six years. The public had high hopes that the NHS would do what was expected of it and provide everyone with that medical care which in the 1930s was available to the rich in their homes and the very poor in hospital, but only with difficulty obtained by the many in between. It seemed likely that antibiotics would make a considerable difference to treatment and that a whole host of advances made during the war would increase the power of both diagnosis and treatment, and maybe enable some diseases to be cured and others prevented. It was assumed that the wider availability and fairer distribution of medical care would, with its increased effectiveness and combined with a rising standard of living, reduce the need for help.

The East Wing stood wrecked and empty for 12 years.

The fact that people would soon want and need medicine of a very different and far more expensive kind, for many different types of illness, was not apparent in 1948. No one could have believed how quickly change in social, cultural, economic and every other aspect of life would combine with the new medicine to alter the whole pattern of disease, reducing acute illness in the young, allowing people to live long enough to suffer cancer and the disabilities of old age. It was not anticipated that the demand for medical care would escalate, along with an inflated concept of its capacity to right all ills; or that diagnosis would

Staff and students add to the parking problem.

frequently come to depend on the most careful, time consuming and costly assessment of the interaction of physical, chemical, psychological and social variables; or treatment range from that safely given by rule of thumb in ancient hospitals, lock-up surgeries or front-bedrooms, to that requiring a team of many kinds of professionals, with complex equipment and purpose built premises. It was thought that people might seek medical care who had never done so before, but not that many would come to interpret the right to health care as a right to health, with little or no personal responsibility for maintaining it. Above all it was not foreseen that the growing ability of the medical and allied professions to give help would be accompanied by a considerable risk of doing harm.

The centuries old tradition of British medicine still held - that the care of the individual patient was the yardstick by which everything to do with medical care should be measured. The doctor's duty was seen by him and the public, as it had been seen for so long, to do his utmost for Mrs Brown. There was no reason in 1948 to suppose that good personalised care would be so time-consuming and costly in the late twentieth century as to cause conflict between the care of the individual and that of the community. Community Medicine still had only a nice warm 'homes and gardens' connotation - nothing to do with the cold estimation of the community's needs and the dispassionate setting of priorities.

Had it been possible in 1948 more accurately to forecast how greatly medicine would change, it would not have lessened the public desire for a National Health Service and maybe its initial structure would still have been that which was then agreed. Those arrangements might however, have been seen as the best that could be made at the moment and inevitably requiring much change and adaptation as time went on. Instead the Act of 1946 and the arrangements embodied in it came to be identified in the public mind as the Service itself - an NHS to which much should be added but from which nothing, no structure or function, should be taken away. New hospitals, better diagnosis, new therapy and more powerful drugs were expected but even if neither the butcher nor the baker could deliver to the door, the doctor would still bring comfort into the bedroom. The closure of an antiquated hospital or the imposing of a personal contribution to the cost of ever increasingly numerous and expensive prescriptions would inevitably appear as a breach of faith.

On July 6th 1948, it is true, the medical profession was less convinced than the public that the millenium had come. General practitioners were inclined to feel that general practice in the 1930s had been good and to hope that as independent contractors they could continue to maintain it as it was. Hospital doctors had been aware in the thirties that hospitals were in trouble but during six long years of war, dispersed around the globe, pre-war hospital medicine had acquired a rosier glow reflecting the happier days of peace. Having spent the 'forties' either in the Emergency Medical Service or one of the Forces, hospital doctors in 1948 were not quite ready to be conscripted into a new and untried NHS. With no experience of management in medicine beyond that of the individual patient, a hospital firm, a general practice, or in rare cases a department, most had been brought up to regard management as 'admin' or 'politics', and not a proper pursuit for a clinician. Hospital administrators were needed to facilitate the doctor's work but not to decide what that work should be, or where and when it should be done.

It was obvious enough that existing knowledge, much of it based only on empirical evidence, had already grown beyond the capacity of a single mind to apply effectively, necessitating the specialisation which would hasten its further increase. The educational implications of this phenomenon however occasioned little anxiety in the profession as a whole. After all, few felt that they themselves had learned all there was to know at the time of passing finals or that they had been greatly inconvenienced by having since forgotten much of what they had once known. It was, as it always is, difficult for doctors to believe that medical students should be armed with intellectual capacities the doctors themselves do not possess, or that students could become so endowed by means of educational methods that doctors themselves have never experienced. Most doctors, and many medical teachers saw no need in 1948 to change a training which had been so good for so long.

ii

As had been foreseen by Goodenough the National Health Service affected medical education in many ways - not immediately but gradually, almost insidiously - and its effects were of course soon magnified by the changes in both medicine and society.

Teaching hospitals which for so long had provided almost exclusively for the poor were now open to all who might benefit. They contained most of the specialist units in each region and until new ones could be established elsewhere the Health Service enabled those who needed specialist care to be transported to the teaching hospitals, which quickly filled with patients from far afield, limiting their capacity to serve their local populations (even where much reduced in size as a result of war) and altering the kind of clinical experience available to students. Well within the first few years of the Health Service the pre-war picture of doctors travelling to care for patients in their homes began to change to one of patients travelling to hospital. Attitudes to admission changed too, from fear of entering a place in which in the past so many had died to the fear of being denied the care and safety which hospitals seemed to offer and which all had a right to expect.

Attitudes changed within hospitals also: patients no longer being in receipt of charity, grateful for whatever could be done even if only by students, but having now a right to expect the best of modern medical care from trained staff. Few declined to contribute to teaching but many did not expect, or relish, the combination of care and teaching which had been the basis of the rounds by physicians and surgeons in the past. The outpatient consultation of the past, conducted in full view of assembled patients and students, no longer seemed acceptable to anyone.

Teachers who had previously been rewarded for their work in teaching hospitals by past students referring patients to them, were no longer dependent on private practice but received a salary from the hospital and a token of acknowledgement from the school for teaching. The Goodenough Committee's recommendation that part-time teachers should receive a salary for teaching was seldom taken seriously. Only a very few teaching hospitals ensured that part-time consultants had a session free from clinical responsibility in which to fulfill their educational functions.

Research was also affected. While increasingly important if a medical school were to give the kind of education which would ensure the intellectual development of students, research became increasingly difficult to engage in (even if the many necessary facilities were available) when employed in a National Health Service

The changing face of medicine — the student waits his turn.
(JPB).

to provide patient care for most of every week. As the part-time clinical staff of a medical school became more wholly committed to patient care their way of life and attitudes began gradually to differ from those of pre-clinical teachers and the few whole-time academic staff in medicine, surgery and pathology. Whole time research workers, so invaluable to the climate of a medical school, also became few and far between, not least because of the difficulty in providing accommodation for them. At the London, for example, where before the war research fellows like Bedson, Florey and Fildes had been numerous, facilities could be found only with difficulty for the occasional one or two like Denys Jennings, the radiologist who inspired the post-war generation of physicians and surgeons.

All such developments had secondary effects on the medical school course, altering its structure as new specialised subjects were added to the curriculum, changing the content of the clinical years, widening the gap between them and the pre-clinical, altering the relationships of students to both staff and patients - and with the advance of medicine many of the duties previously performed by students, such as dressings, became either no longer necessary or so sophisticated as to necessitate qualified care.

The number of qualified junior staff increased rapidly. In 1953 the pre-registration year became compulsory, requiring every newly qualified student to complete two house appointments. Most then spent two years in National Service and on return many sought further posts at the Senior House Officer or Registrar level. The NHS provided large numbers of paid posts in hospitals throughout the country in which young doctors could acquire practical experience under supervision. Training programmes were of course totally lacking but the other requirement of postgraduate training - a method of paying the trainee - was solved. Almost without anyone realising, the preparation for medicine changed from a medical school course to a three-stage process of undergraduate studies, a pre-registration year and a postgraduate training for a specific branch.

Meanwhile the inevitably slow process of adapting the medical schools to new circumstances had also begun. The Government's acceptance of the Goodenough Report had not only resulted in legislation establishing the London medical schools as independent corporate institutions but had also provided funds with which to begin the rebuilding and reequipping necessary to provide the country with the kind of university medical schools recommended.

The University Grants Committee, faced with the unusual problem of where to spend money, found the schools outside London more easily able to change than those in it. Each provincial school being an integral part of its University and working closely with its Hospital Board of Governors and its Regional Hospital Board was well positioned to proceed. London, with twelve schools and a new Postgraduate Federation was in a more difficult situation. There were over thirty medical University institutions, relating to over thirty boards of Governors and liasing with four Regional Boards. University governance allowed little opportunity for participation by medical schools as such and the Medical Faculty was subdivided into a series of Boards of Studies, each naturally primarily concerned with its own subject. London failed to attract the same degree of financial support for development as the medical schools elsewhere.

Although the recommendations of Goodenough had been accepted by Government and provided guidelines for the UGC, they had not necessarily been accepted by individual schools or universities, or even studied closely by all the many teachers involved - nor had the General Medical Council pronounced on them. As it got ready to do so it sought opinion and one of the organisations ready to give a carefully considered opinion was the Royal College of Physicians of London. Its President, Russell Brain, had reestablished its Teaching Committee early in the fifties and set it to work. Its members included four Londoners beside himself - Clifford Wilson, T F Fox - Editor of the Lancet, Alastair Hunter (a Londoner by virtue of serving it throughout the War) and John Ellis. The last was sent to North America, Scandinavia and round all the British schools, to study present practice and future aims in each place and report back. The College's eventual evidence firmly supported the Goodenough Report and advocated that the GMC should revise its Recommendations so as to facilitate its adoption by the schools.

Lord Brain, PRCP.

In 1957 the GMC abandoned its system of controlling standards by prescribing a minimum time-tabled curriculum and issued new Recommendations urging the schools to instruct less and educate more, and giving them freedom (which it said should equally be regarded as a duty) to experiment with the course. The College of Physicians then invited all the bodies concerned with medical education to join with it in setting up an association which would provide them with a forum for discussion and a means of studying the subject. The result was the Association for the Study of Medical Education which started in 1957 with Russell Brain as Chairman and John Ellis as Secretary. It was first accommodated in the basement of the College of Physicians in Trafalgar Square and then moved to premises of its own in No 53 Philpot Street at the back of the London Hospital.

Whilst all these developments were taking place however the schools themselves were confronted with a further problem -student numbers. To those leaving the Forces after upwards of six years service were added all those leaving school who wanted to complete their medical studies before doing National Service. At the same time the provision of annual grants to eligible students by Local Authorities removed any financial barrier to taking up medicine. No ceiling was put by any authority on the number of students a school might admit and all took as many as they thought they could provide with a reasonable course. All became crowded and had at the same time to help hospitals to give young doctors returning to civilian life some kind of rehabilitation. The selection of medical students began but schools were soon to find difficulty in providing the teaching and clinical experience necessary for the large number of students they were taking, and in the mid-fifties, many, including the London, began to reduce their intake. Under pressure from the British Medical Association the Government set up a Committee to enquire into how many medical students were really needed. At that time the schools were between them producing about 1,500 qualified doctors per annum, of whom over 200 came from countries such as South Africa or Norway, to which the great majority returned. In 1957 the Willink Committee decided that, unlike most other countries where a great expansion of medical education was thought to be urgently necessary, Britain was producing too many doctors and recommended a reduction in the total number of student places.

Intakes were reduced but almost at once doubts arose as to the wisdom of this astonishing policy which was totally at variance with the experience of the rest of the world. By the end of the 1950s the problem of how to expand medical education as quickly as possible without lowering its standards, had been added to that of adapting it to a new kind of medicine in the context of a National Health Service.

iii

The new activity of selecting medical students began at the London with the establishment of 'An Advisory Committee on the Selection of Candidates for Admission'. The Chairman was Mr Roy Hobson, one of the lay governors, and the members Professors Bedson, Boyd, Wilson and Dix with George Neligan and the Dean. With the College Secretary and the Assistant of the Dean in attendance and a representative from Queen Mary College, the group seated around the College Board Room table must have seemed impressive to the young candidate seated alone at its foot - especially as not infrequently the older members of the committee at the far end of the table were still arguing over the last candidate while the interrogation of the next began. To a small girl of fifteen, peering out from under a huge school hat, the echoes reverberating from the other end of the room must have been off-putting - 'Well at least he'd driven a tank, damn sight better than being a stretcher bearer like the chap you want'.

Academic requirements for entry remained for some years related to school certificate and matriculation and posed few problems. The choice between ex-service candidates and schoolboys was more difficult, and the required consideration of female applicants was considerably complicated by the fact that none of the selectors had had much recent experience of little girls or seen the inside of a girls' school. Gradually, however, a different, more effective and certainly kinder system of interviewing evolved, with the candidate meeting two or three members of a selection panel in a more informal setting.

At no time, of course, have the decisions taken met with the approval of all candidates or of those connected with them. Always there are some who feel that attributes they see as essential to good doctoring have been under-assessed. The attributes widely considered essential have however altered somewhat over the years. Intellectual ability was not generally seen as important in the early fifties (and there was even less confidence then than now in the accuracy with which it can be measured by examinations) and other qualities were thought by many to be more essential. Hence the letter from the distressed mother of an unsuccessful applicant 'so that you can see what you are missing we are sending, under separate cover, an example of his woodwork.'

A questionnaire enquiry of headmasters and headmistresses conducted by the BMA in this period showed wide support for the view expressed by one: 'Medicine has always attracted the weaker brethren, and in recent years the brethren have got perceptibly weaker.'

Whilst the College struggled on with the task of selecting its students, it wrestled too with the problem of caring for them and providing them with the best possible curriculum. Clark-Kennedy had found when he became Dean in 1937 that the responsibilities of preparing the College for war had prevented him from paying the attention he wished to individual students and the course. He realised that dealing with the problems of post-war re-orientation would do the same and saw the need to involve others in the work of Deaning just as Jonathan Hutchinson and Walter Rivington had done in the late nineteenth century. So in 1947 A G Allen was appointed Dental Sub-Dean and soon afterwards, no doubt because as senior lecturer on the medical unit I had been much involved in designing a new clinical introductory course, I was invited to Cambridge for the week-end.

A G Allen, Dental Sub-Dean.

Walking round Grantchester, trying desperately to keep up with Archie, I listened to his views on medical education in general and on the London in particular. He outlined the problems of the College and the needs of the students as individuals. As we reentered Cambridge he asked if I would like to help and I had just enough breath left to say yes. Soon after, I was appointed Assistant to the Dean, a title later changed to Sub-Dean. After appointment I received a written list of the first things Archie wanted me to do. Much of it related to the care of students and how we should work on this together, but other tasks followed one on another covering most aspects of College life, making me wonder how many were compatible with a full-time job on the unit. They included straightforward tasks expressed in classical Clark-Kennedy style: 'Reorganise the Clinical Lectures...Find out what the hell is going on in the... department...Start work on a new curriculum'. There was interesting advice also: 'Beware of professors - they get carried away by their subjects...Remember that popular teachers are those who do the students' thinking for them'. The envelope was marked 'Strictly Confidential' - the paper itself was headed 'KEEP THIS - TO YOURSELF'.

No one could have had a more stimulating, outspoken but delightful person with whom to work and from whom to learn. We shared the Dean's Office until I was given a desk in the six foot passage between the general office and the shop. When Miss Reynolds announced the approach of anyone whom Archie was disinclined to see he would invariably say 'Show him in' and adding (in what to him was a whisper but which echoed from the ceiling) 'All your's,' he would slip quietly out through the back door. He furthered my education also by sending me to the 'Conference of Metropolitan Deans and their Representatives' which met every month at the Middlesex Hospital to consider all matters affecting the medical schools - an extra-university committee in which (in those days) what should be done in the faculty of medicine was previously decided by a group of remarkable men most of whom had been Dean of their respective schools for many years. As formidable as they were powerful, and almost all part-time physicians or surgeons, they were nonetheless punctiliously courteous to a young beginner and took pains to introduce him to their strange world. My naive suggestion that Deans should themselves oversee the approval of posts for pre-registration house-officers was effectively dealt with by the decision that Regional Post-graduate Deans must be appointed and that at the next three meetings Dr Ellis will not be served with tea.

One of the main recommendations of the Goodenough Committee was that at the start of the clinical course 'the work of students must be facilitated by a methodical organisation, so that at the beginning of their clinical studies they may see diseased conditions in an orderly development of experience and not in the random ways of routine hospital duties.' This orderly development was to be achieved by a four-month introductory clinical course, under the direction of the Professors of Medicine, Surgery and Pathology with integrated teaching from their assistants, using carefully selected patients drawn from the whole hospital. Its aims were to be, to help students adjust to new conditions of work and study, to show them the relation to clinical studies of their previous study of the structure and function of the body, to encourage them to acquire methods of scientific thought and criticism, and to assist them to acquire, without loss of time, the ability to observe and interpret the physical signs of disease.

At the London Clifford Wilson and Clark-Kennedy were determined to provide a better Introductory Course than any other school, using its Medical and Surgical Units in collaboration with the Pathologists, and mobilising its vast range of patients both in the wards, in out-patient clinics, and in the patients' own homes. It began with four weeks introduction to clinical method and continued over eight further weeks to give a bird's eye view of medicine arranged system by system through selected patients (examined and presented by students). The organisation involved was daunting and the course was given twice a year. Irrespective of how well it achieved its objectives it welded the incoming students into a cohesive group and brought a wide range of patients and of specialists to them. It also did much to offset the disadvantages students would otherwise have suffered from the hospital being scattered over several sites.

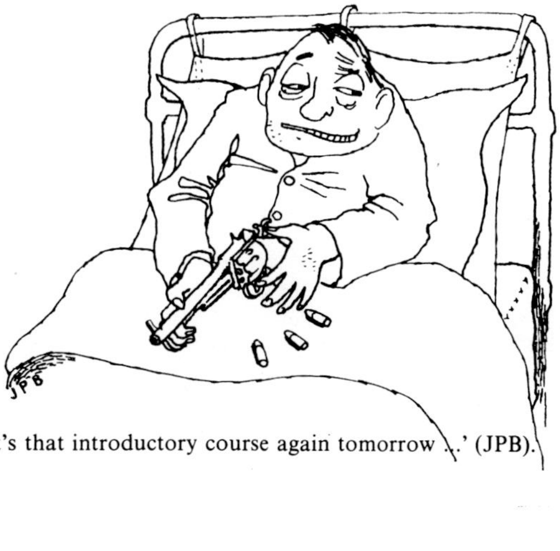

'It's that introductory course again tomorrow ...' (JPB).

Another effect of the course, however, was to extend the required elements of the clinical curriculum, which, with the addition of time for new specialties, quickly exceeded the total duration of clinical studies demanded for some degrees. Thus students took finals at Oxford or Cambridge and qualified before completing the curriculum, their main holidays having been taken at the expense of some part of the course. So in the early fifties the curriculum had to be reorganised, reducing its length and restoring a free period at the end for integration by the student and revision. At the same time the main clinical lectures were arranged on a systematic and integrated basis, physicians, surgeons and others all contributing to each system - and the museum arranging an exhibition appropriate to it. This was a far cry from the old system of every member of staff giving some lectures to senior students at whatever times he found most convenient - but it was a more difficult system to maintain and easily eroded as time went on. Clinical teachers, however willing to give priority to students' needs when arranging their own time-table, cannot easily alter health service commitments.

Donald Hunter.

For a period, however, the arrangement met with some success. The Sub-Dean, whose task it was to arrange the lectures, found Donald Hunter, the Curator of the Museum, an enthusiastic collaborator in mounting the exhibition which accompanied the lectures on each system. Care was taken to include anything which students, now excluded from the wards at certain times of the day, might not see - such as the drugs patients were given or the diets they ate. A technical hitch occurred when hungry students ate all the demonstration diets as soon as they were displayed. They proved less interested in the lecture in each system billed as the history of that particular part of medicine. Donald Hunter correctly assumed that this was due to mentioning the word history, substituted titles such as 'Big fleas have little fleas' and there was standing room only in the lecture theatre.

The whole atmosphere of medical and dental education was also affected very soon after the war by the availability of grants to students. Whereas in the past each could proceed very much at his own speed and certainly take finals at whatever time suited him best, now all who entered on the same day (almost all of them were entered for an MB degree) were expected to pass each successive landmark at the same time and qualify together. Grant-giving authorities had difficulty in differentiating between university courses lasting three years, at the end of which everyone passed with a degree of one class or another, and medicine with its pass or fail examinations which some failed at the end of five years. Education Committees of town and county councils found it hard to believe that those who failed were good students who would make good doctors and should be financially supported for a further six months - and in the early fifties the failure rate for first time takers in the London MB was 61%. The passing of examinations 'on time' became more important, and the taking of them more frightening than ever before.

With these new complexities in mind Clifford Wilson proposed a tutorial system to help students during the clinical course. Initially based on first assistants, or registrars as they were beginning to be called, it was agreed to raise the number on each medical firm from one to two, the College continuing to pay the Hospital a contribution towards the cost. It had done so for many years in acknowledgement of the first assistants checking the work of students - just as the Hospital had paid the College for the services rendered by students to patients.

At the start each tutor was appointed individually and formally by the Academic Board, considerable apprehension being voiced, when first the name of a female first assistant was put forward, as to whether medical students could be helpfully tutored by a woman. This innovation in medical education, followed slowly by other medical schools in Britain, has remained a special feature of the London. Its intention was to provide each student with a guide to the clinical course who could also help him to overcome any learning difficulties and develop regular profitable study habits. Such high academic aims are not easily achieved particularly by those who are in the process of postgraduate training and have not themselves experienced the benefits of academic tutoring or been introduced to the techniques involved. Yet for some students at the London over the past thirty years, the clinical tutorial system has provided perhaps their most formative educational experience - and in time more than half the tutors were senior members of staff. Some students have gained little or nothing, some have received more teaching than education but many have formed lasting friendships, and the great majority have enjoyed valuable personal help in pulling together the diverse strands of the course in preparation for finals.

A less successful innovation in the fifties was a three week course in Nursing in which students were attached to a ward as auxiliary nurses. The most enthusiastic students were from the start those who least needed the experience. The reluctance of the remainder quickly diminished what little enthusiasm ward sisters had for the scheme at the start and it was soon abandoned. On the other hand the photographing of each student at the start of the clinical course and the distribution of his portrait ahead of his attachment to a firm or department, came to be accepted, like the wearing of white coats and name badges, despite much initial opposition and cries of 'Gestapo'.

A still more important innovation dating from the same period was the introduction of the intercalated BSc course, allowing selected medical and dental students to spend an extra year after 2nd MB studying Anatomy or Physiology (and later Biochemistry) in depth, and take an Honours BSc degree. This was perhaps the greatest single advance made in British medical schools in the immediate post-war period, its only weakness being that it was applicable to so few.

One other familiar feature of the medical education of today began in the London in the middle fifties. Groups of students were brought from carefully chosen schools, first in the United States and then

The museum.

elsewhere as well, to spend an 'elective' at the London. They were as delighted as they were amazed with a kind of clinical teaching to which they were totally unaccustomed. Equally they amazed many of the London's teachers and most of its students by asking distinguished chiefs such questions as 'what's your evidence for saying that ?' - at a time when a much respected teacher would complain to the Sub-Dean 'Two of the boys on my round today confessed to having been reading the Lancet: this kind of thing has got to stop', and another proposed to the Academic Board that the library should be shut in the daytime because students had been seen reading in it.

The receipt of students from elsewhere encouraged the despatch of our own. The first three were sent to carefully arranged programmes in Western Reserve and the University of Virginia. As they appeared to be none the worse for the experience (all three are now consultant physicians, two of them at the London where one is professor of medicine), the experiment continued, financed for a period by Singer's Sewing Machines.

Meanwhile the Dental School continued a curriculum similar to that of before the war and less affected by changes in hospital practice. The four year course began with one year of pre-clinical studies, proceeded with a year devoted mainly to prosthetics and dental mechanics (part of the second floor of the College being used for demonstrations on the Phantom Head) and followed again by two years of carefully controlled clinical practice during which students treated large numbers of patients under personal supervision, while also attending courses in General Medicine, Surgery and Pathology. The number of students was small, a total of 40 in 1946, but the system of training necessitated a high ratio of staff to students, especially as most teachers were part-time. The system depended also on good organisation - much of it devolving on the Dental Sub-Dean, the post occupied first by A G Allen and then by A M Horsnell.

One other activity in the fifties which brought the London wide-spread recognition was the mounting of post-graduate courses -the Fellowship Course and the Course in Advanced Medicine which were justly renowned and brought postgraduates to the London from all over the world.

iv

The students who came to the London in the nineteen fifties were not too concerned as to whether the course was old or new so long as it enabled them to learn. John Blandy, now Professor of Urology, began Medicine at Oxford in 1946. He spent the Long Vacation of that year in the Anatomy Department at the London.

'My first impressions are still vivid: the uncleared rubble in the bombed East Wing: the garden still a garden, with tennis courts and a cricket net: and most of the covered way between the wards and the nurses' home remaining despite the blitz. Then as now, the trees in the garden were heavy with their evening crop of starlings: everywhere there were strikingly beautiful nurses. At the front door, smart ex-service porters firmly directed me round the corner to the Turner Street door of the medical college - students were not supposed to use the front entrance to the hospital - but I wanted from the first day at the London to feel part, not just of the college, but of the hospital.

'The dissecting room was run by Drs Harper and Peacock: Harper polite, pawky and infinitely patient: Peacock quick and cockney, with a bright eye and particularly long forceps. Gerald Tresidder was then demonstrating anatomy - his first love then, and for another forty years, especially popular because he made the dry bones live and each muscle tell a story illuminated by his surgical experiences in India. For the first time I understood why those meaningless descriptions of fascial planes occupied so much space in anatomical texts - they really existed in the living body to confine pus, or facilitate surgical exposure: nobody had ever explained this at Oxford.

'There were moments to be treasured: Harper (to a student starting his first part:) "Are you Conjoint ?" "No sir: I'm Fistein".

'Nor can one forget the smell of the formalin-fixed cadavers in that sun-baked room: no matter how we tried to wash it off in lifebuoy soap and cold water it clung to the greasy copies of Cunningham's dissecting manuals and followed us to the Atheneum where students and staff shared a cafeteria so crowded that many of us crossed over to the Black Bull or the Good Samaritan.

We were always aware of the Hospital, reminding us that what we were learning in the dissecting room and the laboratory, however meaningless it might seem, would one day be useful in the wards - which was where we really wanted to be. My cousin, Sister Rachel, invited me to her ward where a seemingly immeasurably Senior doctor, Chris Bartley, took time to explain physical signs to a very ignorant preclinical student. It was not to be the last example of the special quality of the London - its friendliness - and the active association between clinical and preclinical schools. From that moment on there was no other choice for my clinical training, but in fact, the London was recommended to me by my tutor at Balliol, Sandy Ogston, who had done some secret work on British Anti-Lewisite at the London with Clifford Wilson. They were listening to the Boat Race: the batteries of the wireless had run down. Applying his stethoscope, Wilson offered one earpiece to Ogston so that each could hear the commentary, from which Ogston drew the conclusion that the London must be a good clinical school.

I was interviewed by Professor Boyd, the anatomist, who smiled continually (though not from mirth) and by dear old W A M Smart. They accepted me.

In the introductory course of 1948 there were nine ex-servicemen for every ex-schoolboy. It was a wonderful mix. The ex-servicemen were heroes to us - whether their decorations were for parachuting into Yugoslavia or Germany (like John Ross and Derek Richardson) for action at Anzio (like David Brown), for flying resistance agents in and out of occupied Poland (like Jack Strain), for service in the Atlantic (where Eddy Keel had lost a leg), or for working with the Friends' Ambulance unit in the Far East, like Ernie Mold. The war was too recent for memories to fade, but the ex-servicemen wanted to make up for lost time, to get on with the job of becoming doctors as soon as possible.

'They worked very hard, and both steadied and stimulated the younger of us, who could sometimes offer discrete help with studies. It was a happy relationship, not least because of the strange contrasts which would occur from time to time. One particularly bossy registrar with a reputation for being uncivil to students was put in his place when it turned out that one of our year had been his commanding officer a few years previously.

'Things were by no means all solemn and serious. On the contrary, there was a seething boisterousness in the fifties: almost anything was an excuse for a party: but it was still a time of rationing, of coupons and of austerity and we were all of us very hard up, so that none of our excesses were ever very excessive.

'The introductory course began with a lecture by the Dean -Archie Clark-Kennedy: "What is Man?" he began, and went on to discourse about free will and atoms. Visiting Bishops usually chose this text for sermons at school, and although C-K knew more about the subject than most Bishops - some of us were not ready for his wisdom.

The Introductory Course began with a lecture from the Dean. (JPB).

'The Introductory Course was administered by Clifford Wilson and run by his brilliant group of young teachers - John Ellis, John Bolton, John Dew, Jack Ledingham, Michael Floyer and Stuart Mason. They taught us how take a history: how it begins and ends with being polite: how if you listen carefully enough the patient will usually tell you the diagnosis. They taught us the rituals of eliciting physical signs, and we did our best to hear crackles, râles and heart sounds, and to feel the tip of the supposed spleen.

'Much of what we learned to do, has, because of modern technology, now to be supplemented and checked by more accurate means of measurement, but we learned how to make contact with patients, and when we came to our first firms at the London we enjoyed the luxury of being surrounded with a great many patients, most of whom were very ill indeed, and all of whom delighted to tell us their life histories. What we learned at their bedsides remained forever.

'The surgical firms at that time were Perry and Moore, Neligan and Taylor, Donald and Butler, and the Surgical Unit. On the firm of Donald and Butler the senior, Charles Donald, was a tall, saturnine figure of great charm and charisma, who resembled Charles II without the wig. He carried still the air of dash and derring-do from his days as a flying ace in the First War. He chaffed his students and we loved him: "Examine this testicle Mr X. What do you think?" "er, er, it seems a bit large, sir." "Jealous, Mr X?"

'Donald's junior was Clive Butler. He had been the first ship's surgeon on the Queen Mary in 1935 and before the War he had carried out pioneering work on the early antimicrobials - prontosil rubrum and sulphanilamide - in the septic block. In 1948 his operating was bold and innovative and his results for carcinoma of the colon and parotid far ahead of his contemporaries.

Charles Donald at the Hostel Christmas Dinner.

'A young Maltese boy had a tuberculous ankle joint for which the normal treatment then was amputation. Clive Butler irrigated the joint continuously for weeks with streptomycin: the boy kept his foot. Butler belittled his own achievements, and had absolutely no self-consciousness or side: one of his endearing habits was to hum as he worked. "Lead kindly light" was a favourite during sigmoidoscopy though the light was not always kindly: once as we watched him diathermising a rectal polypus the resulting explosion blew off his eyebrows. The firm applauded.

'Abdomino-perineal excision of rectal cancer had just been introduced: on Saturday mornings Hermon Taylor and Clive Butler would perform the procedure synchronously - a daring innovation. The results were excellent, and it was at the end of one of these that Butler suggested sewing the bowel directly to the skin, hitherto unheard of.

Robert Percival and Clive Butler.

'Hermon Taylor radiated charm and confidence: his technique was a joy to watch - the tissue planes opened up for him and nothing seemed to bleed. He was a pioneer in the use of the gastroscope - commonplace today - but then regarded with suspicion. It was not easy to introduce the enormous rigid brass tube past the incisor teeth under local anaesthesia. The dresser's task was to restrain the patient from moving her blindfolded head. "Keep still, Mrs Smith, this is not an operation. If you move you might damage my instrument".

'George Neligan - beloved of so many generations of students was always amiable and courteous. After the Second War he had become increasingly breathless, and we would watch with apprehension whenever Georgie enucleated a prostate, as, between coughs, he became increasingly cyanosed until the adenoma was retrieved and he took breath again. He continued the long London Hospital tradition of urology. I will never forget my first glimpse down a cystoscope held by George Neligan. In those days men and women were cystoscoped under local anaesthetic in "Hoppy's end" of surgical outpatients. Hoppy's end was "clean", as opposed to "Spital's end" which was "dirty". There was a kind of armed truce between Hopkins and Spital, both ex-RN sick-berth attendants, each with a wealth of experience. On Saturday mornings dressers were allowed to "help" Joe Fathi in Hoppy's end, in the stricture clinic. Joe Fathi was a large lazy-seeming but remarkably competent operator who had been a first assistant throughout most of the war. He was very experienced indeed and a great teacher: in the stricture clinic he took pains to show each generation of students how to pass a Clutton sound without anaesthesia or pain. In these manoeuvres he was helped by Hopkins who would model the stricture in lead wire so that the student had a three-dimensional concept of where to direct the instrument.

'When, in 1951, after George Neligan had retired, the new subterranean department of urology was opened little old men were heard to ask: "I see Mr Dix's name on the door, and I see that nice young Mr Tresidder's; but where's Dr 'Opkins's ? Dr 'Opkins done my stricture for twenty years and I'm not changing now. "

'Just after the Second World War the London was enriched by a plethora of "supernumeraries", men returning after 4 or 5 years of war to brush up their skills. They were to fill the large numbers of new specialist appointments that were required for the new National Health Service. They were always around the wards, and we soon learned to get them to sit down in spare moments and talk about Mrs Smith or Mr Jones. Personal tuition was available anywhere in the London at any time of day or night.

'This was especially valuable when a firm was on Full Duty. Students lived in the hostel, and whenever there was a slack moment, could hang around the Receiving

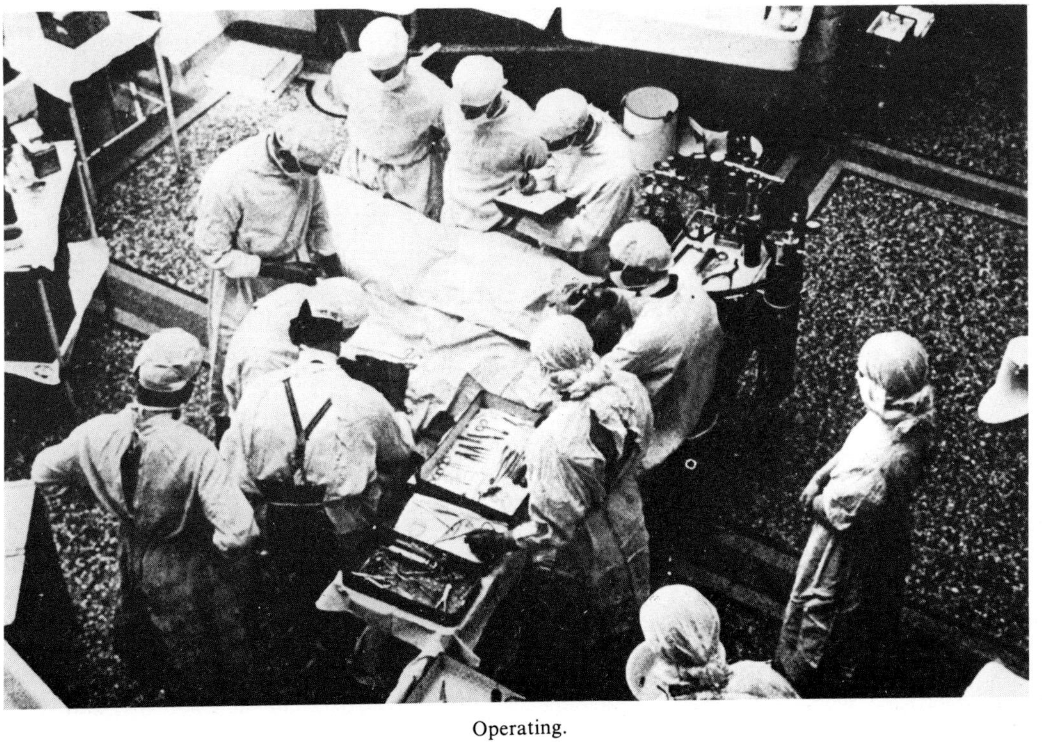

Operating.

Room. There Dai Pugh - another war-time hero - would teach us hour after hour - without ever seeming to. He also took care of students who were sick or injured - especially the crop of fractured ribs and collar bones returning from Hale End every Wednesday and Saturday.

'Medical and Surgical registrars would be called to the receiving room to see cases who needed to be admitted. Tony Walton, Terence Kennedy, "Percy" Warren , Michael Reilly, Dai Evans - no matter how busy or pressed they might be, always had time for an impromptu "tutorial", beside the bed, in the laboratory, or in the Grave Maurice. No money could purchase such teaching.

Dressers wore rubber gloves. (JPB).

'The job of being a surgical dresser had changed with the introduction of penicillin and the sulphonamides: pus was uncommon and dressings were changed as little as possible. Nevertheless it was still quite hard work, for it was still our duty to shave and prepare the patient for operation - and we had first to learn how to sharpen the open razor which was the only implement permitted. Dressers assisted at all operations on thei patients. This could be an ordeal. The chief and th first assistant changed into cool theatre clothes Dressers removed collar and tie, donned a rubbe apron which covered them from neck to toe, an Wellington boots. Rubber gloves for students, sterilize by boiling, were wet, wrinkled, put on with glycerin difficulty and discomfort. Assisting at a long operatio was a protracted and sweaty ordeal.

'Removing all this gear gave unbelievable relief. I those days we changed in a little room overlooking th consultants' car-park. One August evening Bori Fistein disrobed with vigorous relief: a blood-staine Wellington boot sailed out of the window to lan beside Arthur Lister in his open Lagonda. Dea Arthur Lister: he made no fuss.

'It was then the custom for chiefs to wander up an down the theatre corridor to look in on what was bein done in their colleagues' operating rooms. A P appeared in his dressing gown, without a mask, i Richardson's theatre. Two dressers, who did no recognise him, quickly moved to remove the intruder thinking that an insufficiently premedicated patien had escaped his escort: "But I'm the Senior Surgeon." "Yes, dad, and I'm the King of England."

'Expecting A P to be furious, the students hastene to report this unfortunate outcome of their goo intentions to the Sub-Dean to whom A P was wont t send notes "Mr X brushed by me in the front corrido today. Please see and deal with him." On this occasio A P made no complaint.

'Alan Perry conducted his outpatient clinic in the old style. He sat at a desk in the middle of what is now the waiting room. The interview was conducted fortissimo because A P was becoming a little hard of hearing. Patients, clutching their notes, sat all around the wall: "How are you, Smith ?" "Well, Sir, I've this awful feeling that comes on about twenty minutes after I have eaten and ..." "Splendid, splendid. Come and see me in six months' time." (Dumping was unknown after A P's gastrectomies.)

'Perry's junior was "Dinty" Moore, who was something of an enigma. A remarkable teacher, he operated less often than most surgeons.

'Heading the Surgical Unit in the fifties was Victor Dix, tall, fair and strikingly handsome, he had been a Flying Instructor in the First War and served in the

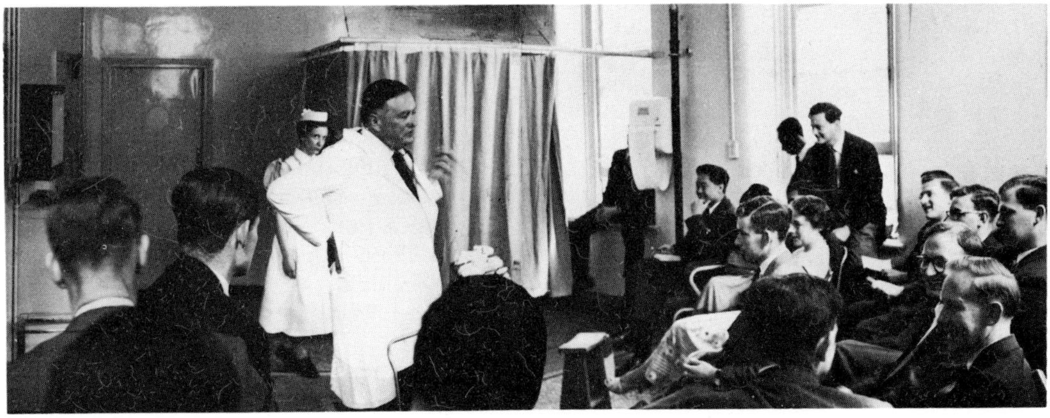

A M A Moore teaching in out-patients.

RAMC in the Second. He was notably skillful and delicate in any kind of urethral instrumentation, in the old London Hospital tradition of urological surgery. Some of the instruments he used had belonged to Frank Kidd, and others had been used by Fenwick. In those days even simple cystoscopy took considerable skill. The little mignon lamps would burn out just at the critical moment: the more powerful diathermy machines had all been withdrawn during the war to be used in the nose-cones of Blenheim bombers as radar detectors, and those in use were too weak to cut under water. There was no transurethral resection, so prostates and all but the smallest tumours were dealt with by open surgery.

'His junior was J E Richardson, always known as "Sam". After a brilliant career as a student, and having been torpedoed twice during the war, he had just returned from the Massachusetts General Hospital where he had honed his already formidable surgical skills, bringing back to the London a new style of operating, and a new interest in electrolytes and endocrinology. His operating theatre was the cynosure of a surgical generation. To watch him perform a gastrectomy or thyroidectomy was, to another surgeon, to watch Nureyev dancing. It may be too soon to evaluate his full contribution to British Surgery, but his teaching of its craft is commemorated every day in a hundred operating theatres all over the world.

'Most of the teaching on the firm was done by Tony Walton: whose operating was unusually gentle: the nurses knew, and his pupils soon learned that this meant that his patients did unusually well. Like so many of the first assistants of those days, he always seemed to have time to spare for those impromptu teaching sessions which made experience at the London so valuable.

'On medical firms the emphasis was on taking a history and making a physical examination, writing it all down, and having it corrected by the first assistant. The notes were written on harsh yellow paper, destined to be destroyed, which spoiled much of their significance. How Donald Hunter protested against this, ever pointing out that most of the really useful information was recorded in the students'notes. The first assistants took endless pains to correct our efforts. They used to teach us that if we took a proper London Hospital History, and made a proper London Hospital examination, the diagnosis would become obvious. To a large extent this was probably true.

'On the medical firm of Hunter and Perry the first assistants, Paddy Hamilton and Tony Tasker, spent hours screening patients with tuberculosis and refilling their artificial pneumothoraces. Students were allowed to put in the needles and play with the Maxwell box. We drew off ascites with silver trochars and cannulae. We aspirated empyemas. We set up transfusions using huge needles and tubing made of red rubber. The wards were still full of young men and women with tuberculosis, many of whom would die, and all who survived were condemned to a year or two in a sanatorium. Streptomycin had just come in, but not PAS or INAH. Students still caught tuberculosis fairly often. One of my year "Kite" (who wore a silver plate in his forehead from a wound received in his Spitfire) got tuberculous meningitis. Housemen took turns to do his daily lumbar puncture and inject his poor theca with streptomycin. He survived, but lost his sight and had to give up medicine.

'Donald Hunter's ward rounds were a high point. Arriving late, in a tearing hurry, he could then spend hours beside the bed of an interesting patient - emphasising points to students by "strangling" them with his stethoscope, or knocking their heads together. (Boris Fistein and I still carry scars, I suspect of the subdural haematomas we simultaneously sustained in this way though I have long forgotten what I was supposed never to forget). The ward round over, we swept off in a run across the garden, halting only to note the vestiges of W A M Smart's herb garden - foxglove persisting in the corner despite the bombs - to the museum, to look at bits of beryllium, asbestos, or some illustrative pot from his wonderful collection. Donald Hunter bubbled over with enthusiasm and fun. He set us all on fire.

Sir Alun Rowlands.

'Others were attached to other medical firms. "Daddy" Rowlands was famous for the slow progress that he made, and how he never forgot a face. As a consulting Rear Admiral in the Royal Navy during the war it was said that he had been smitten with an attack of vertigo from Menière's disease when entering the main gate at Portsmouth Dockyard, and gained the distinction of being the only Rear Admiral to be taken to the guard-room suspected of being drunk and disorderly. On another occasion when piped aboard a battleship he recognised the boatswain as a former patient, took off his hat, shook hands and asked after his abdominal pain and his sister in Llanelli. Sir Alun Rowlands was nothing if not methodical. Taking a history in the proper London Hospital style could easily occupy him the entire day, leaving little time in which to reach a diagnosis. Fortunately Mike Haggie was his first assistant, and made sure that patients got their necessary blood tests and Xrays.

'All those on Russell Brain's firm admired him greatly, but most students came to know him mainly through his neurological demonstrations in the Bearsted. He made major contributions to neurology, published a most readable textbook, and became in time FRS, a peer, and President of the Royal College of Physicians, while continuing to share in the running of a general medical firm all his time at the London and seldom if ever missing a ward round.

'Dick Bomford (the country's most successful Radio Doctor) was universally liked and one of those chiefs who gave much of his time and effort to running all kinds of activities: students' clubs and students' societies, secretary of the Medical Council, the Medical Club and the Old Londoners' Dinner. Horace Evans became perhaps the most distinguished physician of his day, with a private practice which included the Royal Family. Horace was the idol of his students and his housemen, for his never-failing courtesy and commonsense. The Dean, Archie Clark-Kennedy, known to all as C-K and very tall and thin, looked like a heron as he stood at the bedside requiring students to think for themselves about patients and bet on probabilities.

Lord Evans.

'To cope with the revolution in chest disease in the decade immediately after the Second World War two physicians had been appointed on the same day, Lloyd Rusby and Kenneth Perry. For a long time tuberculous patients were sent to the Brentwood Annexe, and generations of students were taken by bus to make rounds in breezy wards filled with young men and women with active tuberculosis. Before combination chemotherapy was available, the lungs had to be kept as still as possible by the mutilating operation of thoracoplasty, or by keeping the pleura filled with air, and under Vernon Thompson and Geoffrey Flavell an active thoracic surgical department developed.

'Flavell operated at amazing speed and with unsurpassed panache: "What's the time, sister ?" "Ten o'clock, sir." "How many thoracotomies have we done ?" "Four, sir." "Just as I thought: half the day gone and nothing done".

'In the cardiac department William Evans had been joined by Wallace Brigden. Willie continued to make his students "take vows" with him. Wallace taught in a different style. There would be a patient with a murmur. One by one each member of the firm had to listen and declare what he had heard. Only when each had committed himself irrevocably would Wallace reveal the truth: we learned by having to put down our stake money. It was a memorable way of making us listen and be honest. In those days electrocardiograms were commonplace but noone could explain what they meant in terms of electricity and physics. It was a curious gap. I tried to learn from Mr Dicks, the long suffering chief technician in the cardiac department: this was firmly put a stop to: the ECG was a mystery not to be understood: our duty was to get the rules by heart.

'There were curious anomalies too, in practice. Anticoagulants had just been introduced and their rôle in cardiac infarction was hotly disputed. Willy had no doubts: "I will not have you give my patients rat poison".

'The most exciting of all the medical firms was the Unit, where Clifford Wilson had collected a team of able young doctors who, with the supernumerary registrars, nearly outnumbered the patients. Students were treated to day after day of intense teaching in small groups, whether by the bedside or in the outpatient clinic.

'Later we were each assigned a personal tutor, under Wilson's new scheme, then unique to the London. John Vallance-Owen, and later Richard Balme, would meet two or three of us once a week and discuss our problems. Sometimes we would read an essay: sometimes present a patient. More often we talked about the prospects for the Rugby Cup. During the run-up to finals these already hard-worked first assistants gave us extra coaching. Perhaps more important, they became life long friends.

Enthusiastic teacher, Geoffrey Flavell; student Gordon Seward decides to take up oral surgery.

'There are always differing views about the value of the old-style didactic teaching by lectures. There were a good many on offer at the London but in general they were not compulsory. The worst were prolix and dull, providing through the ear what could be absorbed in half the time from a book. The best, like Donald Hunter, were inspired. Everyone went to Donald Hunter's lectures. They were better than a music hall. One of his best turns was a lecture on lead poisoning. D H would enter the old Bearsted Lecture Theatre in complete silence, tiptoe to the lectern, carrying an immense jar of white powder. In silence he would pour out a heaped handful of the powder and then suddenly clap his hands: instantly a choking white cloud would fill the Bearsted: "Stop Gentlemen ! Do not breathe: this is the most poisonous dust in industry !" And then followed an unforgettable and passionate lecture on the perils of lead oxides in batteries and paint.

'He was equally impressive on anaemia. At that time haematology was poised on the brink of discovering the secret of pernicious anaemia, and we were full of misinformation about folic acid and "sprue" and tended to forget about iron. D H would seize a gigantic waste-paper basket full to the brim with ferrous sulphate tablets, and in a mighty sweeping gesture scatter the entire contents throughout the Bearsted. Pills fell like rain. We were never to forget that iron deficiency is the most important cause of anaemia.

'To the fortunate students who had been taught by Howard Florey at Oxford or Harry Dean at Cambridge, the teaching of Morbid Anatomy at the London was no novelty, except in the Post-Mortem room where Dorothy Russell became enthusiastic: "What a beau-oo-tiful septic spleen." Her lectures were handwritten in chalk on the blackboard. If you copied them all down you ended up, after a complete cycle of several years, with a textbook. Some of us found it less trouble to get much the same information from a book. In the practicals Jerry Landells was stimulating, and one could always ask him or Billy Woods the " why" of things and not merely the "what".

'After "firms" came Specials. These were inevitably a mixed bag. O'Donovan was still teaching Skins. He may have known more about dermatology than he let on, but students got the impression that the whole performance was a sham, most of the patients neurotic, and the treatments of no value at all. He told us that Xrays worked just as well whether the current was turned on or off so long as the machine made a noise. Biopsies were unknown so there was no discussion about the pathology of what was going on in, or under the skin. These were the days before cortisone, so for any dermatological disorder there was, instead of one, a choice of two remedies: if the rash was dry, you made it moist with linimentum calaminae; if it was wet, you dried it with lotio calaminae. Neither did good nor harm. Dermatology must have been different in the days of Jonathan Hutchinson or James Sequira.

'Psychiatry was brilliantly taught by Henry Wilson. I shall never forget how he could interview a patient before a room full of students without occasioning any loss of dignity for the patient or embarassment to us. We learned a great deal from him, mostly about good manners and listening, but also in his spare time, much more about the technique of water-colour of which he was a master.

'Fevers, especially poliomyelitis, still killed many people in those days. They were taught at the Eastern Fever Hospital where of supreme importance were the mysterious Koplik's spots, which were said to have something to do with meazles. Koplik's spots were always there yesterday, or would appear tomorrow, but they were never actually there when our firm attended. Instead we were shown coloured pictures of what they would have looked like had we come

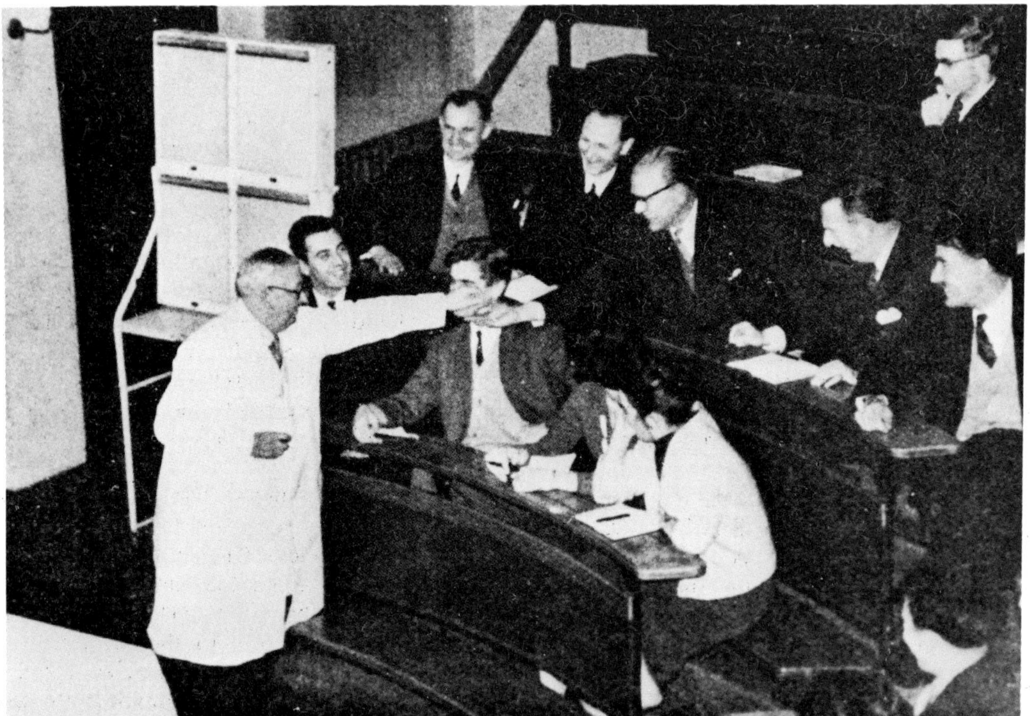

William Evans, in his last teaching session in the Bearsted, administers Trinitrin to Dick Bomford, watched by Arnold Woods, Byron Evans and Wallace Brigden.

'esterday or tomorrow. (Forty years later, I have still ıever seen a real live one). Second in importance to Coplik's spots were the table of incubation and ıuarantine times which were to be got by heart. Since hese went very easily on the back of an envelope, tudents could escape to take part in the more mportant matters of attending to the Christmas Show. The only difficulty was that because attendance ıt the course on Fevers was statutory: one had to be ıigned up. Fortunately one member of the firm could ısually be persuaded to sign for the rest and the equally bored instructor did not demur at lecturing to ɔnly one and receiving an attendance roll with fifty ıames on it.

In contrast Microbiology was wonderfully well taught ɔy Sam Bedson and his department. He had gone to he trouble of providing every student with a textbook nterleaved with blank paper. We could read up the subject the day before, and add our notes. As a result ıe did not have to waste time - his or ours - in going hrough routine information - it was all there in front ɔf us. He could spend time talking to us individually - and by the second laboratory session knew the entire class by name.

'One of our statutory duties was Vaccination: by the end of the course we had all vaccinated the Professor ɔr each other. What a tragedy that my classmate, Henry Bedson, Sam's son, should have been hounded to death by the media after the laboratory accident involving the very smallpox virus which he and his father had done so much to eliminate from the Earth. Bedson was one of the very great men of the London and yet he knew each one of us, talked to us as equals, listened to our questions with sympathy and answered them with erudition.

'Haematology was a matter of measuring haemoglobin and counting different sorts of cells. Even then it was obvious that for the most part it could be done by a fairly simple machine, and today it is. We were taught little about clotting factors, I suppose because little was known about them. The wonderful deeds of modern haematology were still in the future.

'Paediatrics was taught by Kenneth Tallerman, a beloved character, always on the point of rage. The most important thing in the world was to know by heart exactly how many scoop-fulls of National Dried Milk per pint of water would make up a feed for a baby. Tallerman had a curiously shaped head. Once a child burst into laughter as he came into the ward, shrieking : "Funny head, funny head, funny head" "Sister: that child is a lunatic. Have her sent to St Clements".

Kenneth Tallerman.

'The great London Hospital tradition of otorhinolaryngology was kept alive by Keogh, Bowen-Davis and Lindahl, the latter pioneering ultrasonic treatment of labyrinthine disease. Charles Keogh looked distinguished, was an excellent draughtsman and painter, a superb operator, and would spend hours teaching every student exactly how to use the auriscope. We came away from our brief sojourn in his clinic competent to deal with most of the straightforward emergencies and common conditions of the throat nose and ears. Charles Keogh was a leading light in the Clubs Union, urging us to arrange Art exhibitions, offering the prize, and bringing a supply of sherry to the hanging party. In the operating theatre there was always a skull on which he would explain exactly what he proposed to do so that we could follow every step of the procedure. He was a proponent of radical surgery for carcinoma of the antrum, a formidable operation which he did in conjunction with Arthur Lister - this was always worth watching. Arthur Lister as taciturn as Charles was demonstrative.

'John Ayoub and Arthur Lister taught us eyes in the outpatient clinic, and we spent happy hours playing with slit lamps and measuring visual fields but we were not encouraged to attend operating sessions or ward rounds. (I recall to this day the first operation I ever saw was John Ayoub repairing a lacerated cornea.) Arthur Lister was very eminent in his field, but had a noticeable tremor, which steadied only as his forceps approached the eye. One of his amiable house surgeons who had a pronounced stutter, ventured to comment one day "Mr L-Lister, s-s-sir: you have a b-bloody awful t-t-tremor today." "Not as bloody awful as your stutter."

'For most of us it was only when we started midwifery that we felt real doctors. There was an active "District" practice, whose boss was Miss Haines - "Aunty Glad" to generations of Londoners. Whitechapel was still a tough district, where policemen went in pairs after dark, but the midder boys on their cycles, with the big black box on the carrier, could safely go anywhere. We delivered children at the top of vast tenement buildings, where the only water might be one cold tap on the landing. There was a lot of waiting, and there were difficult moments when the midwife would be doing something important to the mother, and the midder-boy was invited to give his expert opinion to the assembled family, over endless cups of tea. "Will it be long now, Doctor ?" "Oh - er - not long at all". "So you'll be staying then." "Of course". Enter District Midwife: "We'll be off now. Nothing's going to happen until the morning".

'Deliveries were much as they had been in Grenfell's day: poor light and minimal asepsis. It was dear Miss Haines' practice to defer to the "doctor". "And now Doctor's going to examine you, Mrs Smith, when Doctor's washed his filthy hands": and "Doctor says its a girl, doesnt he Doctor?". We wore ourselves out: but it was tremendous fun. When it was not our turn to play doctor on the District, we hung around the labour wards hoping to be allowed to deliver another baby.

'After a month at the London we spent a second month in a peripheral hospital. At Oldchurch the midder boys were made welcome: the hard-pressed casualty officer let them stitch cuts and open abscesses: the surgical registrar was always glad of another assistant. At the end of midwifery most of us could count on having delivered more than 50 babies.

'In contrast, we learned little gynaecology. There was a litany of the classification of ovarian cysts which had no particular rationale and there seemed to be only one operation - hysterectomy, with variations on the theme. But we did get to know Victor Lack, "Bonzo" Brews and "Bush" Percival - who went out of their way to get to know the students. Bonzo was prodigiously slow in all his movements, writing or operating. (Russell Howard is said to have chided him - "Bwews, you know what'll happen to you, you'll be wun over by an 'earse"). In fact although Brews may have appeared to be slow when he was operating his cases took no longer than his colleagues: to the careful observer of his technique the secret was that he never wasted a movement.

'Venereology was compulsory. Names were ticked off. This was necessary, for the lectures were of unparalleled tedium. We snored through the 57 varieties of congenital and acquired syphilis and the 39 steps in diagnosis of a gumma, but never saw a new case of either. It was not our teachers' fault: at that time, and for a brief interval just after the War, gonorrhoea and syphilis had been extinguished by penicillin: a false dawn, as events were to prove, but we did not know it then. However tedious the lectures we all admired Ambrose King. He had a reputation for fearlessness. From time to time there would be a small disturbance in the waiting queues of patients outside and it only took a whisper from Ambrose to command instant and respectful silence.

'Neurology demonstrations were a popular event: Henson and Russell Brain would demonstrate physical signs upon a patient with an anatomical lesion, and give a masterly exposition of how to pinpoint the lesion by applying the details of intracranial anatomy. Having discovered the lesion however there seemed to be precious little one could do about it. I found it more exciting to follow Douglas Northfield on his neuro-surgical ward rounds. Alas, students were unwelcome in his operating theatre, where he insisted on complete silence, as he did in the wards. Douglas Northfield resembled the hospital barber: "'ere, Barber: come 'ere: I want a shave." "My friend, if ever I shave you I promise it will be the closest shave of your life. Now be quiet, or I may make a mistake." Angiography was then in its infancy, and very dangerous: without CT scanning, the diagnosis of an intracranial tumour required the utmost in clinical skill. Watching North-field elicit physical signs was to watch a master craftsman in action, not a showman.

Every student had to learn to give an anaesthetic. We were taught by John Challis: ex German Prisoner of War, crippled with breathlessness from emphysema, nevertheless he took endless trouble during the long gynaecology list to teach each one of us how to administer the sequence - Pentothal, gas, oxygen, trilene and ether. At the crucial stage in the procedure we were taught how to pass an endotracheal tube through the nose. Today this is regarded as "blind, septic and unnecessary" but it was essential in our first year on the house when any doctor at tea in the billiard-room might have to dash upstairs to the delivery room to give an anaesthetic for one of the registrars - Charles de Boer, Tony Pearson, or Tony Alment.

'Bonzo' Brews.

'The entire house changed over just before Christmas. I do not think I ever finished the curriculum. In December 1951 I was taking Finals at Oxford while rehearsing the star rôle of Front Legs of the Camel in the Christmas Show, and on New Year's day 1952 started on the House as the junior of two house physicians on the Medical Unit. The first three months of this house job were spent in the clinical laboratory. Tutored by "Butch" and "Dicky" in the day, the Medical Unit HP provided the entire laboratory service of the London Hospital from about 4.30 pm until 9.30 am and at week-ends. I measured blood urea and glucose by boiling little flasks which could explode without warning and give interesting but inaccurate results. The method for estimating cholesterol required me to match a shade of yellow with one of blue - it was wildly inaccurate but since there could never be any reason why this should have to be done in the middle of the night my results were never questioned. The emergency microbiology and haematology investigations were much more interesting since they could determine clinical treatment. It was a wonderful education, not least because it taught me the possibility of error in laboratory investigations and a considerable respect for the labour which seemingly simple tests might entail for laboratory staff.

'Especially dangerous was cross-matching blood for transfusion, for which our methods were very simple. The London, for some reason, supplied blood to the big liners which still came up to the Pool of London and suddenly required blood. We also crossed matched blood for some of the nearby hospitals - an arrangement which seemed then, and in retrospect still seems, as bizarre as it was dangerous. Cross matching blood for exchange transfusions for the "Rhesus babies" was a harrowing exercise, and it is wonderful to think that these tragedies are now prevented.

'Thirty-five years ago the range of laboratory tests which were in common use was very small, and they were all done by hand. There was a single flame photometer which could measure some of the plasma electrolytes, but only in the hours of daylight. It was locked up at night, when these estimations could not be done.

'At night, besides doing the laboratory work, the junior medical unit houseman was on call for the wards. It could be busy. One night Stuart Mason admitted a patient from a mental asylum where the astute psychiatrist had observed that this patient's recurring attacks of madness looked exactly like those experienced by patients undergoing insulin therapy - then in fashion for schizophrenia. Sam Richardson was warned, and throughout the night I ran up and down the three flights of stairs to Rothschild, arriving as the patient was lapsing into hypoglycaemic coma. I had just time to draw blood for a sample, inject glucose, and dash downstairs to repeat the boiling-up-explosion-method for measuring blood sugar. This took me so long that by the time I had finished the patient was in coma again. However, by the morning I could show Sam a dramatically jagged graph of the blood glucose. Unfortunately at laparotomy the islet cell tumour was found to have metastasised to the liver. To my joy, Sam used the graph for a paper in the Lancet.

'The discipline on the Medical Unit under Clifford Wilson was of the best kind: he simply expected everyone to do their best, and we all tried. Clifford took me on one side to tell me to be sure to telephone him, whatever the hour, if there was a real problem. "The firm really consists of us two, " he said "all the rest of these clever young chaps are just learning the job." (Most of the clever young chaps are now retired professors).

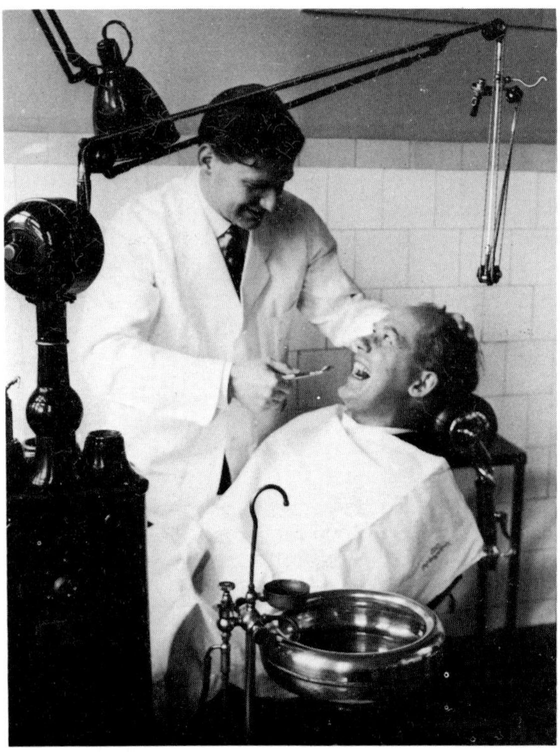

Patients sat up for dental care in the 'fifties'
(Ted Renton and Bill Russell).

'"What is this patient's history" (I gave it - it was very long and involved and interesting, but all weeks old). "Does he have any complaints now?" (There were, in fact none.) "What are the physical signs ?" (There had once been all manner of interesting things, but to tell the truth, there were none now). "Then why is he in hospital ?"

'It was distressing for a newly qualified doctor to be able to do so little for anyone who was really ill. We had sulphonamides, and penicillin: Tetracycline had just come in, and Streptomycin was available for tuberculosis. We had morphine, we had aminophylline and digitalis. Compound F had just been described, and in 1952 Will Tegner brought the first tiny supply of it back from America for a patient with rheumatoid for which it was to be the magic bullet.

'Ambrose King always had one or two men with Reiter's Syndrome. Treating them was exciting. They were placed in an insulated container and broiled by means of an artificial fever caused by more or less dead enterococci given intravenously. Denis Ford was aspirating fluid from their knee joints in the hope of identifying pleuropneumonia organisms. Coley's fluid was sometimes given for metastatic cancer, without benefit: it was my first brush with oncology. Of course the medical unit houseman, like any other, learned more from the ward sisters and his colleagues on the house than from anyone else.

'On the surgical unit things were, paradoxically, more quiet. The work was less intense and far more straightforward, partly because of the excellence of the staff. On the Surgical Unit Dix, Richardson and the First Assistant Tony Walton were all such good craftsmen that complications were seldom seen. Junior housemen would spend hours trying to tie knots and sew imaginary suture lines in their style - and to tell the truth - some of us still do.

'Treatment was very simple. There was remarkably little of it. We had blood, intravenous glucose and saline, but no other fluids. We could measure urine chlorides, but none of the blood electrolytes. Sam was continually frustrated by this, having learned in Massachusetts how to diagnose and remedy serious deficiencies of potassium: but there was no help for it: the flame photometer was locked up at night and even in the day time it was hard to get these measurements done. I remember J B, a young man with a partial gastrectomy, who developed a terrific diarrhoea - no doubt from superinfection with some intestinal organism. He poured his extracellular fluid out through his colon and looked as though he must die. Sam and I, with the help of Miss Reynolds (Sister Talbot) estimated his fluid losses as best we could by weighing his bed-linen, and spent an anxious hour calculating from Gamble's tables how much potassium he must have lost. Meanwhile J B had lost consciousness.

'To give potassium intravenously in those days was a heinous crime. (Everyone knew it would make the heart stop.) At dead of night I got the key to Mr Sykes' dispensary and found the shelf of potassium chloride tablets. We had calculated J B's deficit. There was no means of sterilising the tablets, but poor J B was certainly going to die. I flamed two tea-spoons, ground the tablets between them, and added the powder to litre-bottles of saline, praying that a few more germs would make no difference.

'There were no ECG monitors in those days, so I sat beside the bed, feeling his pulse, waiting for it to stop until eventually I dosed off. In the morning Miss Reynolds found me and packed me off to bed. J B was sitting up, grinning, and demanding something to drink.

'Surgical house jobs were far less demanding than medical ones in those days. The operations were on the whole relatively minor by today's standards. The biggest one on the unit was a partial gastrectomy. For a porto-caval anastomosis or an abdomino-perineal excision of the rectum a whole Saturday was set aside. Oesophagectomy then, as now, caused anxiety: the treacherous anastomosis broke down no less often then, and we had no parenteral nutrition. I remember being woken by a porter in the morning with a "slip" from night sister: " Mr Y in Talbot ward is doing very well. He has drunk two litres of milk through the night, but I think you should know that his chest tube has drained two litres of thin pus."

'Intestinal obstruction was still formidably dangerous, for without means of measuring electrolytes replacement was by guesswork. Septicaemic shock struck without warning especially on the urological side of the firm, and was invariably fatal, since nobody understood the pathological changes that were taking place: they bled to death into their own extracellular space. We were decades away from intensive care.

'Housemen in the fifties had no official time off, except on the medical and surgical units where one of the pair would cover for the other except on full duty, or if there was any "corruption" on their side of the firm. The Units were favoured, because one could expect two or three half-days during a six months' stint. Not so the other housemen, though a certain amount of latitude was permitted. When the firm was quiet, one houseman would cover for another - but the chief always had to be asked for his permission, and some never gave it.

'I stood in for a friend on another firm one weekend, when he went off to be best man at a wedding, having forgotten to obtain the chief's permission. On Sunday an assistant matron developed a carbuncle on her bottom: the registrar had to phone the chief. My friend was dismissed on Monday.

'One might think it was impossible to pursue any kind of normal life. In fact, it was tremendous fun. Good sportsmen could still turn out regularly for the XI or the XV, and we still managed to see our girl friends. If, for example, she happened to be a staff nurse, contact was strictly taboo, but love has ever laughed at locksmiths. On full duty one arranged to "lodge" emergencies in the ward of one's beloved. Elaborate relays of signals were passed from ward to ward, giving up-to-the-minute information on the situation of each of the two night sisters. If surprised in the ward one hid in "bluebeard" (the London Hospital name for the linen cupboard). One sporting night sister, seeking linen, found X cowering in Bluebeard, clutching the ritual "blockbuster" -(iced-Horlicks and cocoa) - ignored him, took the linen, helped the blushing nurse to finish changing the bed and vanished with the barest flicker of an eyelid. Nothing was said.

The Athenaeum.

'As the new intake made its way through the medical college, so the character of the House changed. By 1952 nine-tenths of the new house were ex-servicemen, mostly married, many of them to London Hospital nurses, but nurses were strictly forbidden to enter the Residents' Hostel. Matron unbent. She caused a notice to be put up: "Members of the nursing staff may visit their husbands in the Residents between the hours of 10 am and 4 pm." Marriage beneath the rank of Sister was however, out of the question. X proposed to Y, then just about to take her state examination: Y was dismissed: it did not stop X later becoming a professor in the medical college, but it did stop Y from becoming state registered.

'About 10 pm each evening on the House we would foregather in the old dining room for toad-in-the-hole, fried eggs and coffee. The full-duty surgical first assistants would be there, a mine of help and information. X was miserable. At paracentesis faeces came out of the cannula: what should she do? A council of war was held. After a good deal of discussion the consensus was to pull out the cannula. She did, and we all took turns to watch the patient through the night. No harm came of it at all. Y had the misfortune to pierce the rectum with a catheter intended for the bladder. The surgical registrar telephoned the chief who made understanding noises having done the same thing himself many years previously. A suprapubic tube was placed and all went well. Y later became a consultant to the London Hospital though in a field far removed from urology. '

Perhaps not all students saw things in quite the same way. Clifford Wilson's personal interview of every student at the end of the Introductory Course revealed a wide range of reactions - which may indicate that students do differ and react differently to the same course, or that consumer reaction is an uncertain method of evaluation.

Nor can any record of the period be complete without reference to the difficulties faced by ex-service students or tribute to the way they overcame them. Many were married, some had families, and few were well-off. Some, for one reason or another, depended on a gratuity received on demobilisation. One gratuity at least was lost in the necessary attempt to double it by investing in paper hats to be sold at the seaside on August Bank Holiday - someone else scooped the market the day before. Some found the transition from war to peace hard to make. Survival in a midget submarine having depended on the minutest attention to detail made it difficult not to try to memorise the whole of medicine. As examinations approached breakdown threatened in students desperately striving to memorise more than their tired minds could hold. One who decided he could do no more and must go home to shoot his wife and himself, went first to say goodbye to the Sub-Dean but accepted his offer to check that the gun was properly loaded and politely handed it over. He went on to a long and successful medical career.

It was not always easy for the ex-serviceman to ignore his past. One, busy on duty in the Receiving Room, on being told Captain Brierley (the House Governor) wished to see him in his office at once, not surprisingly replied 'Tell Captain Brierley, Colonel Dick will be glad to see him here at any time.'

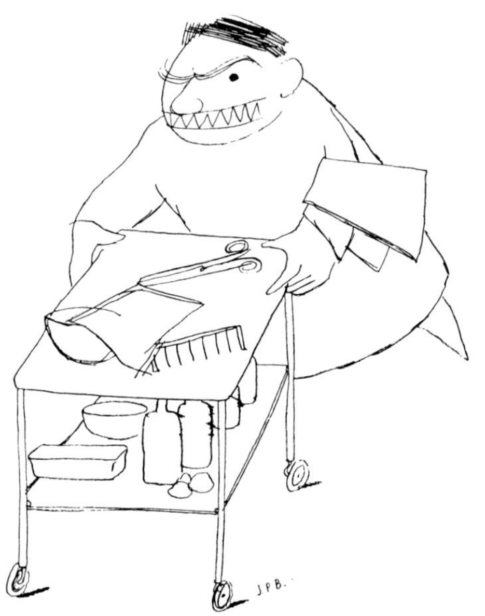

"I like doing my P.F.O.'s.
I like doing my P.F.O.'s.
I like doing . . . ."

Lacking the more interesting tasks, students began to resent the less interesting.

The unusually large number of students made competition for house jobs in the London exceptionally keen, and strained the time-honoured procedure for selection. By tradition all applicants presented themselves in the College Board Room standing around the table at which sat the Hospital staff watching as

Osman (and after his sudden death, Fred Webb) touched each candidate on the shoulder and pronounced his name. A full round, calling every name without hesitation or error, was expected, almost always achieved, and greeted with warm applause. The applicants left and business began. Those not offered jobs at the London were left to try elsewhere. Some ex-servicemen felt the need to go straight into practice - but after 1953 all had to find two jobs somewhere. A house appointment in 'one's own teaching hospital' was nonetheless still regarded as a pre-requisite to a successful career even though often offering less satisfactory accommodation (especially for the married) and more arduous work. The suggestion that the newly qualified should be consulted about their aims and circumstances, made at his first Medical Council meeting by the Sub-Dean (now a newly appointed physician) was regarded as very strange, but also, mercifully for him, almost hilariously amusing. Investigation of a series of breakdowns on the house, however, was traced to the strain of firms having beds in many different wards, and action was taken to concentrate them.

As the fifties wore on and medicine changed rapidly, the working life of both students and housemen changed too. Students particularly were less and less able to participate in the care of patients, partly because there was less that they could do and partly through fears of medico-legal problems arising from procedures conducted by them. Lacking the more interesting tasks students began to resent the less interesting, many of which (like preparing patients for operation) were taken over by others.

V

Throughout the fifties the student body remained 'boisterous' - its cheerfulness and vibrant activity contrasting with the austerity of life in general and the war-time scars still disfiguring the Hospital. The Clubs Union had little space. Every facility was crowded - the Athenaeum's single ancient desk unable to accommodate the records of clubs and societies, which is no doubt why so many have sadly disappeared. Clubs of all kinds flourished and met with great success including the inter-hospitals Rugby Cup in 1955 and 1957. The destruction of the pavilion at Hale End one night by fire was unconnected and successful activity continued whilst a new and better pavilion was built, and opened by C B Fry in 1956.

The new pavilion.

Tennis on the hard courts between the Library and the Old Home provided exercise for some and lunch-time entertainment for many, the style of R D Caterall long remaining in the memory.

Lunch-time tennis.

'Pinafore' in the Library.

Clubs Union Societies were equally active. The Music Society augmented its periodic concerts with a phase of Gilbert and Sullivan productions, beginning with 'Trial by Jury' and a masterly performance of 'HMS Pinafore'. Dramatic Society productions were interspersed with Play-reading meetings - usually in the homes of staff and enjoyably incorporating the visiting American students. The Art Society was formed in 1949. Its annual exhibition in the Athenaeum added extra interest to Prize Day and for some years the Society provided the main means of decorating the College for the newly instituted Autumn Ball. At the first, the entire wall of bookshelves in the library was covered by a reproduction of the Bayeux tapestry drawn out on the floor of Charles Keogh's flat and painted in the basement of the College, where the so-called 'Games Room' offered suitable space for activities of various kinds. Balls concluded of course with the traditional 'lilly white boys' performed not as in the past by the housemen alone, but by all who could still stand. Great efforts were made on these occasions to beautify the halls and staircase of the College - fountains in the well of the stairs calling for much ingenuity.

Most activities were well attended by senior staff, and each club or society well cared for by its President and Vice-Presidents. Even so, with the increase in staff, a smaller proportion was involved than in the past. From the end of the war too it became customary for end-of-firm parties to be given by students for staff, replacing the old system of staff entertaining students. It was clear that clinical teachers particularly would not be able to maintain the close interest in the Union taken by their predecessors at its start. So in the late fifties its constitution was overhauled and changed to include a Student-President who it was hoped would be free of the day to day union duties carried up till then by whichever student held the office of Secretary.

A much greater change in tradition had to be made in regard to that peak of the year at the London - Christmas. Entertaining by the Troupes in the wards had ended at the outbreak of war and the Hospital administration was adamant that the old custom of the Troupes touring the wards should not begin again. After the war a Christmas Eve entertainment was put on in the library - consisting of four seperate shows, by the Residents, the medical students, the dental students and the nurses. The audience was saved from death by exhaustion only by the unexpected delivery of an impromptu speech by Aneurin Bevan who happened to be visiting in his capacity as Minister of Health. After this experience College and Hospital administrations met formally in the College Board Room to consider the future.

The College argued that some kind of communal entertainment at Christmas was important, and a useful means of bringing together all the many different groups working on the campus. The Hospital was not wholly convinced but prepared to collaborate provided that no performance was given in the Hospital itself. Agreement was reached that the College should put on a Christmas Show in the Library, and that the Hospital would contribute to the cost and the Works Department help with the stage. As none of the nurses who had shared in the Music Society's production of 'Trial by Jury' had come to any lasting harm, it was agreed that Nurses and Physios could participate in the Show if casted.

The first of this new kind of Show was produced, according to the old tradition, by the President of the Residents' Mess, the SRA - Adam Turnbull. It included a number of nurses so the Hospital sent a Sister to rehearsals to chaperone them. The College responded by sending the Sub-Dean to chaperone the students and noone being available to protect either Sub-Dean or Sister, this practice was abandoned. Due largely to Adam Turnbull, the show was a great success. The only serious weakness at the Censors' preview was the final portion which had been reserved for the Residents, but which in the absence of the SRA was a somewhat scratch affair. The night before the first performance it was rewritten around a sketch from the Southend Show of 1939. Rehearsed the next day it was warmly received that evening. The Show ran for a week and included a matinee to which selected patients from all over the hospital were brought by teams of students.

New style Christmas Show (Blandy, Weeks, Betts).

By 1949 the new Christmas Show had become a well-organised event. A student of that time recalls: 'The first Show I took part in was directed by Frank Grave and I had a small part in some unmemorable sketch vaguely to do with Hippocrates. The following year we did a pantomime for which David Oppenheimer (B.Mus) wrote and orchestrated brilliant and original new music. The plot was simple: the hero - banished for the heinous crime of drinking theatre sister's tea, makes good and rescues the heroine from the wicked Griffin (Oppenheimer) who was changed in a flash of magnesium into Colonel Cahusac, the deputy House Governor. The music was memorable and catchy, and included a final chorus with the lines

'Early to bed, early to rise
Gives a man ulcers and rings round the eyes
Laughter is free, nylons are dear
Where are the Film Stars of yesteryear'

'In the following year the Griffin was reconstructed by John Samuel and Keith Giles and converted into a two-humped camel, capable of protruding its tongue, rolling its eyes, and passing its water. The part had to be learnt by the two humps while they were at Oxford doing their finals and on the first night the crib fell off the back of the front hump to which it was pinned and the back hump "dried" - but the other physiology of the camel did not and it made a watery exit.'

Thus the present type of show began, moving in turn to the nurses Swimming Pool and then to the College Hall - losing the ability to entertain patients in the process, and losing perhaps in atmosphere but gaining in facilities. For as long as possible it was kept close to Christmas, the final performance taking place on Christmas Eve, mainly reserved for Staff and followed by a party. It helped maintain the spirit of Christmas past even in the year when notices in the Hospital announced 'Christmas Day will be on December 26th'. After the first show it became clear that the task of producing it was incompatible with the responsibilities of the Senior Resident Accoucheur and the show became two: one produced by the Students after long weeks of rehearsals and a shorter more spontaneous contribution from the Residents.

Blandy's Griffin succeeds Souttar's Dragon.

In pre-war days a special issue of the Gazette recorded the script of each of the Troupes supplemented by many photographs. Gramophone records were made of many of the post-war shows but no complete collection has been kept. "Never-to-be-forgotten" lines remain in the memory of performers showing how themes persist while variations on them change. From time to time history repeats itself as another batch of students applies more modern technology to the production of monsters similar to those with which their predecessors entertained past audiences. Thus the Griffin referred to above bears a close resemblance to that designed by the artist Arthur Rackham in 1913. The framework was made by Henry Souttar, the canvas and painting by his fellow registrars. It took 3 weeks to make and cost 23s 9d. Motor power was supplied by clerks and dressers (28).

The Children's party.

The fact that the Christmas Show could not quite reproduce the family festival of pre-war days led to the idea of a College Childrens Party. The first of these brought together the 60 or more children of students, junior doctors and staff, their parents, a load of onlookers and the students who gave the party. On arrival children received from the Old Lady who Lived

From the Christmas Show of 1955 (Hass and Bass).

in a Shoe (an enormous boot erected in the College front Hall) a ticket entitling them to travel in a train of open carriages (decorated laundry trolleys) past the Board Room, through the Dean's Office to the Library steps where each was greeted by the Dean. Games in the Library and Athenaeum preceded tea in the Dining room prior to films and singing in the Bearsted. Then back to the darkened library to watch from the windows as Father Christmas (Charles Keogh) rounded the tennis courts in his sleigh (a horse-drawn United Dairies float) to emerge with his sacks of presents in the library as the lights went up. Most of the younger children distinctly saw the antlers on the reindeer.

As each successive year the Clubs Union Committee met to plan the next party, efforts were made to discover a more deserving group of children. Invitations were sent to Dr Barnardo's and declined because the children already had a surfeit of parties. Nowhere in the early fifties was it possible to find in the East End of London a less privileged group of children than those of the students and junior doctors of the London. Throughout the fifties junior doctors were in fact sadly exploited. Until the middle sixties they worked extremely hard for long hours in poor conditions for such low pay that most could make both ends meet only by taking on extra work, usually in general practice, at night, week-ends and in lieu of holidays. So the Childrens Party was maintained until there were few such children left - and then after a gap it was replaced by the Old People's Party.

One further event of importance to student life at the London which took place in the fifties was the extension of the Hostel which, with the College Hall, was opened by Queen Elizabeth the Queen Mother as Chancellor of the University in 1959. For the first time, officially, women took up residence in the Hostel, and the Hostel Club was reconstituted.

vi

Whilst the students of the nineteen fifties, despite their difficulties, enjoyed life at the London and remained a cheerful cohesive group, the same could not be said of the staff. The hospital began the post-war period both battered and bewildered. It had more beds than before the war but scattered between Whitechapel, Brentwood, a small Maternity Hospital in Hampstead and Convalescent Homes south of the river. Before long it was to take on the Hora Home in Woodford and a home for sick and elderly retired nurses in Kent. By the early 1950s a much larger clinical staff was building up - representing numerous different interests and no longer residing, as for the most part their predecessors had done for so long, in a single area of central London, but scattered around the metropolis. Many had as many sessions at other hospitals as they had at the London. By 1955 the senior staff had increased by 45% and the junior by very much more.

The new Board of Governors, which included representatives of the medical staff and the Dean with professional and lay representatives of the College, was appointed by the Minister of Health and was responsible directly to him; the Finance and General Purposes Committee replacing the old House Committee. But whereas in the past the Hospital governors had been free to decide their policy for themselves in relation to whatever funds they could collect, the new Board operated within a budget decided by the Minister. It was faced with meeting both the demands for care (including specialised services for much of the North East Metropolitan Region) over which it had little control, and the needs of the Medical College, the provision of which was the reason for its own existence independent of the Region. It had to meet these conflicting requirements in a scattered hospital, the main part of which was badly damaged.

It was not an easy time. With each year the need for an overall plan of phased rebuilding grew greater. Out of it emerged the concept of a new block linking the main East and West ward wings, which would allow modernisation of the old wards - and a many-storied tower block at the extreme North East corner of the site. Together these would provide the in-patient facilities of a rebuilt London Hospital of around 800 beds. Tower blocks were popular with many in the nineteen-fifties but the idea of accommodating the major part of a hospital in one on the corner of the site appeared to some more likely to cause problems than to make best use of the twenty three acres available. Detailed planning continued nonetheless.

In 1956 a Joint Sub-Committee of the Medical Council and Academic Board made a further attempt to get a London Hospital Group established, combining St Clement's and two other local hospitals with the London itself. The Regional Board's decision to close St George's-in-the-East provided an opportunity for this scheme, but nothing came of it.

The Medical Council, consisting of the medical staff holding consultant rank, continued to meet monthly in the Medical Society of London near Portland Place. It elected representatives to serve on the Board of Governors from which it otherwise remained somewhat distant. It also elected nine of its members, including the Chairman, to serve on the Academic Board of the College, and continued to discuss matters relating to the medical school as in the days when it had been the Medical Council of the London Hospital Medical College. But it no longer had any de jure place in the constitution of the College and did not include in its membership any academic staff other than professors and readers in medicine, surgery, morbid anatomy and bacteriology.

The College, under its new constitution approved by the Privy Council, now had a Council of Governors including representation of the Board of Governors of the Hospital and of the academic staff of the College, together with representation of the University and lay members elected by the Council itself. Colonel Marlborough Pryor, the previous chairman of the College Board, became the first chairman of the College Governors, and was succeeeded by his son, Mr Matthew Pryor, in 1956. The Academic Board, created to advise the Governors, took office in 1948. It had a membership of 22 - 10 part-time medical teachers (including its chairman, Russell Brain, also chairman of the Medical Council) one part-time dental surgeon (A G Allen, Dental Sub-Dean), 7 Professors (one of whom was a clinician), 3 Readers and the Dean, himself a part-time physician. Thus while cross

Decoration for the Autumn Ball 1955 drawn by Charles Keogh and painted by the Art Society. "London won the Cup".

representation of College and Hospital had been achieved in the management of both, the new independence of the College was more nominal than real. It was highly dependent on the Hospital for clinical resources, facilities and teachers - and ironically for management, as part-time consultants outnumbered clinical academic staff on the Academic Board. The Hospital on the other hand was no longer dependent on students and, faced with the immediate problems of providing specialist services for a vast catchment area, it was difficult for the Board of Governors to appreciate that it owed its relative independence in the Health Service to the College or that the Hospital's long-term future would depend upon it.

Conflict of interest between Hospital and College developed inevitably on two major issues - beds and space - and began to undermine the previous unity of purpose. The College needed beds for general medicine and surgery for the students, beds for clinical academic units, and space for research facilities for academic staff - and it needed them all in Whitechapel. The Hospital needed beds for specialised departments with their rapidly growing waiting lists, and facilities for the increasing number of specialists - and it needed them in Whitechapel. Brentwood was of relatively little use to either and created stress and a sense of isolation for those who had to work there.

The situation was of course made worse by the fact that so much accommodation in Whitechapel had been damaged or destroyed, like the Bernhard Baron Institute of Pathology. In 1948 the Bacteriological Laboratories of the College, engaged in research rather than service, were reconstructed in the Hospital main building but the starting point for the Medical and Surgical Units was two rooms each, one for each professor and one for each assistant director and any senior or junior lecturers. Inadequate though this was for whole-time academics it compared not unfavourably with the locker in the Staff Room which was all that could be provided at the time for most part-time physicians and surgeons.

The consequent struggle for space occasioned in this way inevitably began to focus attention on underlying differences of aim and attitude between Hospital and College: the one battling with the cares of the immediate, the other committed of necessity to developing the kind of university medical centre on which the future depended, but at a time when few at the London had, or wished to have, any active contact with a university. Nor was there anything the College itself could do to provide accommodation except to buy from the Hospital the strip of land between its northern border and the residents' tennis court and erect additional preclinical laboratories.

Five years after the end of the war, Clark-Kennedy, though not due to retire until 1958, announced his intention to resign as Dean in 1953, by which time he would have completed seventeen years in post. Dr H B May, the whole-time Director of the Clinical Laboratories who was appointed to replace him, later described this change in the administration of the

College as part of 'a steady evolution towards self-government from the Hospital, although this was by no means obvious at the time'. The election of Dean was conducted at a private meeting of the Consultants o the Hospital (the Medical Council) at Chandos St W1. There were three members of staff willing to accept the office. In order of seniority they were Dr Bomford, later to become Treasurer of the College of Physicians, myself, and Dr Ellis. The three of us sat by he fire in the hall while the consultants debated. The whole matter was decided in half an hour'(22).

Although that was undoubtedly just how the consultants saw the matter of the appointment of Dean it was nonetheless considered by the Academic Board which passed its views to the Council of Governors of he College who actually made the appointment. Dr May accepted an appointment for five years not to be renewed except in exceptional circumstances, the Sub-Dean accepted a further five years part-time in that position on the understanding that he was to be made Dean, and all returned to the formidable tasks of adapting College and Hospital to a new era.

Progress was made in numerous ways. Research aboratories for the Medical and Surgical Units were opened in the Hospital in 1954, many parts of the College were renovated and a new animal house built on the roof. In 1957 the Research Laboratories built by the Hospital were opened in Ashfield Street and much of the space made available to College staff. The College's annual income rose too, reaching the £300,000 level, but College and Hospital still had difficulty in finding a common policy by which both could go forward together. Ironically the more senior members of the medical staff of the hospital could more easily see the need for change, in both medical education and the organisation of medical care, than could many of the more recently appointed and more specialised consultants who, increasingly suspicious of university influence, were more inclined to hanker after a return to a kind of hospital medical school in which the curriculum and the students followed loyally and unquestioningly in the wake of hospital organisation.

Matters came rapidly to a head in 1957 when the time came to appoint a Dean once more. The Academic Board set up an advisory committee of College and Hospital members which recommended that the Sub-Dean be appointed Dean in accordance with the plans made in 1953. Some perceiving this to imply (as it did) a move towards the policies recommended by Goodenough more than a decade earlier (and now reaffirmed by the GMC) were strongly opposed. In the ensuing struggle the unfortunate Dean and Sub-Dean became pawns in a game in which, to a few, the end seemed to justify the use of any means, however threatening to the maintenance of trust and amity in a relatively small community. Dean-making in a medical school, if it once gets out of hand, can make the Wars of the Roses or junior house-matches, appear pale by comparison.

The Academic Board, on whom decision rested,

tensed itself and responding or not, as the case might be, to the strings attached to it from without, voted 50% in favour of the recommendation of its Sub-Committee, and 50% against. The Chairman wisely declined to give a casting vote. The Council of Governors thereupon decreed that exceptional circumstances existed and the following month the Academic Board approved a proposal recommending Dr May as Dean for the next five years and the creation of a post including the opportunity for research into medical education for the Sub-Dean. Agreement on the details of this post proved difficult to achieve and so as to counteract the proposal that proxy votes be used in the Academic Board and to prevent further unrest the Sub-Dean decided to resign and look for part-time employment elsewhere. Jack Crawford, second neurosurgeon to the Hospital, was appointed Medical Sub-Dean.

As is usual in such situations the decision as to which individual to appoint was of little importance compared with the manner in which the appointment was made. The latter resulted, on this occasion, in creating not so much two hostile groups as a state of shock which brought inertia rather than conflict in its train. The London entered the 1960s with the conflict between town and gown, which all London Schools were bound to go through, already over, but it was numbed by it and for the first time in its history had no clear and agreed goal. Perhaps it was too much to expect that the school which had pioneered the old form of training and brought it to a peak would also be equally successful in promptly pioneering its adaptation to changed circumstances. Nonetheless Clifford Wilson, Professor of Medicine, redoubled his efforts to steer the London (College and Hospital) in the way the future beckoned, the way it had to go, and the way in which eventually it went.

A quick thrust.

and a long haul.

Soccer Final.

Hockey Final.

Rugby Finals provide a variety of interest.

Prize Giving:
left to right —
Prof Dorothy Russell, Col Marlborough Pryor,
A E Clark-Kennedy, H P Laird, Lord Adrian,
H B May (Dean), Miss A Bloom.

Tea on the lawn — Charles Keogh, lower right.

Chapter 10.

The Nineteen Sixties

i

As the fifties ended so did Britain's peculiar refusal to see the need, recognised everywhere else in the world, for many more doctors. There was great pressure to start new medical schools, one government minister proclaiming that no less than twenty-four should be started at once. The University Grants Committee, however, was convinced that the need to maintain quality was as great as the need to increase quantity and that it depended upon modernising the existing schools to provide them with the facilities and range of staff recommended in the Goodenough Report. It decided therefore that, apart from one new school at Nottingham, expansion should be combined with modernisation, beginning with the schools outside London.

The first wave of expansion began in 1960 and describing it the University Grants Committee stated: 'as a result, most of the provincial schools will have major additions to their buildings and will each be able to take an entry of 120 to 160 students by 1970. This is about double the capacity of the typical school up to the early sixties. Quite apart from the pressure of student numbers, both academic and economic considerations point to a larger teaching unit, particularly in view of the large specialist staff needed to deal with an extended range of subjects with supporting technical staff and costly equipment' (29).

This bold and far-sighted decision was very different to that taken in most other countries, most of which concentrated on providing new schools. In the long term it saved money but at the outset it called for a vast national investment in medical education, necessitating not only the rebuilding of medical schools but also the provision of a second main teaching hospital for most of them, together with arrangements for teaching in associated hospitals.

In addition, from 1962 to 1967, as in the previous quinquennium, the Scottish and Provincial schools were provided with increased revenue to enable them to appoint the necessary academic staff and in consequence to make innovations in teaching methods and curricula. By contrast the London undergraduate schools received little more than in the fifties. In total, of course, the amount of money received by the University of London for medicine was very great but when divided some thirty times between 12 undergraduate schools and the many postgraduate institutes no single place could make much significant development and remained heavily dependent on part-time clinical teachers who, as employees of the National Health Service, had far more difficulty in finding time for teaching than their unpaid predecessors had done.

The situation was complicated by the development from 1948 onwards of the Postgraduate Medical Federation with a view to improving the provision in London of post-graduate training for visitors from overseas and to advancing each specialty by academic endeavour. At the time it seemed easier to base this development on the single-speciality hospitals which had grown up in London rather than in all, or some, of the general teaching hospitals. In the event the postgraduate hospitals often proved reluctant to establish academic units and the general hospitals were unable to do so even though carrying an increasing burden of specialised care.

So in the sixties the London medical schools had great difficulty in making new academic appointments even though some now wished to do so. In dentistry however the situation was different. Faced with a suddenly realised need to improve and expand dental education the University Grants Committee had decided in the late fifties that three metropolitan schools, including that of the London, should be rebuilt and had taken the unusual step of ear-marking additional revenue funds for dentistry.

Geoffrey Slack was appointed to the chair in Dental Surgery in 1959, Livingstone Ward having been made Dental Sub-Dean the year before, and the Dental School entered a period of exciting growth. Ronald Fearnhead was appointed reader in Dental Anatomy in 1961, Gordon Seward reader in Oral Surgery the following year, Francis Fish professor of Prosthetic Dentistry, Dennis Berman reader in Child Dental Health in 1965, Roy Duckworth reader in Oral Medicine, J P Waterhouse reader in Oral Pathology and Harry Allred reader in Conservative Dentistry in 1966. To conduct this galaxy of dental talent Slack became Dean of Dental Studies.

The medical school had little opportunity to establish new academic posts. In 1959 however the Medical Research Council decided to move its Social Medicine Research Unit to the London and its Director, J N Morris, was given a personal chair in Social Medicine. This was some compensation for the loss of the MRC unit for research in Industrial Medicine when Donald Hunter retired soon after, like many of his contemporaries who had joined the London's staff before the war. Donald continued to teach with all his old enthusiasm however, first at the Middlesex and then at Guy's. In 1970 he wrote to Dick Bomford in characteristic fashion: 'Hippocrates is dead, Osler too, and I don't always feel very well myself. Therefore I enclose material suitable for my obituary... and now to cheat all of you by living to 95.' Henry Wilson who had started the department of Psychiatry (the first of its kind in London) was another who retired in the sixties, but before the decade was out a chair of Pychiatry was established and Desmond Pond appointed to it. A few years earlier Francis Camps was given a personal chair in Forensic Medicine, Rea Johnson one in Histology and Jack Ledingham in Experimental Medicine. With help from the Hospital Roy Simpson was given a personal Chair in Anaesthesia, started an Academic Unit of Anaesthetics and developed an Intensive Therapy Unit.

Jack Crawford — Medical Sub-Dean.

Geoffrey Slack — Dean of Dental Studies.

The site selected for the new Dental Institute (its clinical facilities financed by the NHS and the school by the UGC) was in Stepney Way immediately south of the Out-patient Department. NHS and UGC combined also to rebuild the bombed Bernhard Baron Institute of Pathology immediately south of the main hospital on the site of the 'Garden of Eden' so long enjoyed by the nursing staff as a green oasis in the east. Neither the Ministry of Health nor the UGC however, had funds for rebuilding the hospital itself. Both found the tower block scheme unsatisfactory and when its proximity to the underground line to New Cross was realised it had to be abandoned. It seemed likely that the East Wing would remain for another decade as a memorial to the flying bomb which had destroyed it.

Then it was decided to use Endowment Funds to build the Link-Block, which would join the two main ward wings, enable those wards to be modernised, and the proximal half of each wing to be converted to provide much needed facilities such as treatment rooms, ward laboratories, teaching rooms, offices for ward sisters and rooms for relatives. A small clinical theatre could be provided on the ground floor on each side.

The restored and modernised East Wing and the Link Block itself were opened by 1962 and were an unqualified success. In the process Queen Alexandra's statue was moved south to stand on what had been the Nurses' Tennis Court and, presumably so that she too could be uplifted by the sight of the new building, she was placed facing north and has been silhouetted against the sun ever since.

Conversion of the West wing followed, though by the time it began it was clear that there could be no Tower block and that the next stages of rebuilding would have to be to the West, the Institute of Pathology and the Dental Institute having blocked the way South. Both were opened in 1965, the UGC grant for the Dental Institute being extended to provide the Clubs Union Building next to it, thus making possible Hugh Laird's brilliant idea of turning the Athenaeum and Students' Dining Room in the main College into the Blizard Club. The modernised West Wing opened the following year.

The Link Block.

The 'Sammy', the Clubs Union and the Dental Institute.

iii

With the new Dental Institute the intake of dental students was doubled, reaching 50 per year but while the dental entry increased the medical entry went down, unlike that of almost every other school in this period of rapid expansion of medical education. It was thought best to keep the pre-clinical intake steady at 80 in view of the fact that there were only 600 beds available for teaching in Whitechapel and the Oxford/Cambridge entry had been running at about 30 per annum. 600 beds of course compared favourably with what most schools had had at their disposal hitherto but it was still 200 less than the College had been used to for so long - and only half the number the Hospital still maintained in its various parts. Besides, general firms were decreasing as the London continued to carry the weight of specialised care: the only other teaching hospital in the Region, St Bartholomew's, having kept its newer specialist departments at Hill End near St Albans for some years after the war.

Arrangements were made to send senior students to Regional Hospitals. St Margaret's Epping and the Chelmsford Hospitals began at this time to take students from the London for regular teaching - a much appreciated contribution to the course which has been continued to the present day. While the available clinical resources were augmented in this way the number of students coming from Oxford and particularly from Cambridge declined over the sixties so that the resulting relatively small school continued to enjoy access to large numbers of patients. The relationship of students to them, however, changed dramatically in the decade between the mid-fifties and the mid-sixties, as it did in every school.

The extent of the change from the kind of clinical experience available to students in the early fifties was clearly revealed by studies made by the Association for the Study of Medical Education of all students in all years in all but three of the schools in 1961 and (in conjunction with the National Foundation for Educational Research) of all first and final year students in 1966 (30). The involvement of students in clinical procedures fell markedly. By 1966 the average number of lumbar punctures performed by students at the end of the course was 1: nearly 60% of all final year students in the country had never performed a lumbar puncture, 78% had never performed an abdominal or pleural paracentesis, 70% had never washed out a stomach, nearly 30% had never passed a catheter, 22% had never given an intramuscular injection and 5% had never stitched a wound. Nearly two thirds of all inal year students were unaware of ever having contributed to a decision which could have affected the course of a patient's illness, and most of those who had, had done so during privately arranged attachments to non-teaching hospitals in their holidays, mostly in the United States.

The experience of students at the London in 1966 in regard to such clinical activities did not differ appreciably from those at other schools, but they had performed routine laboratory tests on patients (e.g. white counts, or haemoglobin estimation) less often than the national average. The Londoners had spent longer in District Hospitals (usually 3 months apart from midwifery) than the students of most schools, and visited more patients at home. Their attitude to the course was similar to that of most students. As everywhere else, the majority found the academic standard of the course neither too high nor too low, while those from Oxford and Cambridge and those who had taken an intercalated BSc found the standard of the clinical course too low. These differed from the majority also in having more regular study-habits, preferring reports of original work to text-books, and finding ward-rounds of less value.

Main common room in the new Union building.

So far as the students themselves were concerned those entering the London in 1966 were as a group younger than those of any other school in the country - their mean age being 18.4 years (the average age of all students on entry to the pre-clinical course had dropped by over one year in the previous decade, making medicals the youngest group entering university). The London, with girls making up only 7% of the class, had the lowest intake of women in the country. Its first year students, living mostly in lodgings or at home, faced a travelling time of over one hour, longer than any others: the final year, with 40% in hostels, had a shorter travelling time than any.

85% of those joining the London in 1966 had put the school as their first choice. About one third of the A level passes they had obtained had been in the D and E grades. Just over a quarter had been to public schools, considerably less than at most London medical schools; one third were drawn from Class 1 of the Registrar General's Social Classes, less than the national average and much less than had been the case in the London itself five years earlier. 23% were the children of doctors, compared with 20% in 1955 and 25% in 1935.

Such changes in the make-up of the student body made no noticeable difference to its enjoyment of life at the London, enhanced by new clubs union and hostel facilities. Clubs and societies continued to flourish, scoring successes in inter-hospital competitions from time to time, though in some sports national changes altered fixture lists, as in Rugby where young hospital sides ceased to be on equal terms with the bigger clubs. Annual events followed the post-war pattern but with few married students, few house officers had children and the Christmas party for them was given up. Staff participation in Clubs Union activities declined, with little attendance at such events as the Clubs Union Dinner, leaving successive presidents with a difficult task in finding guests and speakers. As the Union had been started by hospital staff and its constitution built around them it was necessary once again to change the constitution so as to allow more participation by the slowly growing number of College staff.

College Hall.

With the swinging sixties and the 'permissive society', the appearance of students at the London changed as everywhere else: hair grew longer, ties fewer and bare toes peered out through sandals. The ward sisters of bygone days would have been outraged but their successors were little troubled, students having become observers of medical care rather than participants in it. Patients remained, what patients usually are, very patient and always willing to help disentangle the shining stethoscope of the new clinical student from whatever chain or decoration he or she felt obliged by fashion to hang around the neck. That phenomenon of 'student unrest', however, which haunted so many universities in the late sixties never reared its head at the London though there were difficulties of a different kind at the end of the decade. Medical students at Cambridge suddenly became greatly attached to the East End and some thirty ardent young men and women, distinguishable from each other mainly because the former tied their hair with ribbon at the back, arrived to start the clinical course and solve what they saw as the crisis of medical care in East London. They found the amused tolerance with which they were greeted by their fellow students and especially by patients a little shocking at first.

While medical students in some parts of the world were roused by anger at either gross under-privilege in the population as a whole, or vast numbers of medically indigent, or the unsatisfactory state of medical education, clinical students at the London and the rest of Britain were not. They could see the relatively small extent of poverty and medical indigence for themselves and in 1965 the unsatisfactory state of medical education was acknowledged by the appointment of a Royal Commission.

iv

The sixties brought a totally new attitude to postgraduate medical education. Throughout the fifties the number of graduates seeking postgraduate training had continued to increase, and had been swelled by graduates from other countries, particularly those, such as India and Pakistan, where the standard of undergraduate courses, diluted by the rapid establishment of new medical schools, made postgraduate training essential - but where none was available. All competed for junior hospital posts in which, despite the almost complete absence of training programmes, or any formally organised educational activity, in-service experience could be obtained and from which the examinations for post-graduate diplomas could be taken. On average those aiming at hospital consultan appointments in Britain spent thirteen post-graduat years moving from post to post, often from town t town, overworked and poorly paid and frequentl with little guidance or help.

Anchor Cottage,
the Sailing Club's House at Burnham-on-Crouch.

In 1961 the Christchurch Conference in Oxford mounted by the Nuffield Provincial Hospitals Trust marked a turning point. It brought a clear under standing of the different stages of which medica education had come to be comprised; undergraduate graduate, postgraduate and continuing. Equall important was a change of attitude in the Ministry o Health towards postgraduate training and continuin education, away from a firm belief that they were n concern of the NHS towards an active engagement i them, accepting that the standard of care provided i the NHS depended very largely on doctors acquirin the skills of current practice as postgraduates and o

Tutorial.

their being able to keep up to date. As a result there came better pay for junior hospital doctors, study leave, money for hospital libraries and for vocational training schemes in general practice.

The concept of the Postgraduate Medical Centre was accepted too -an educational complex of library, lecture theatre, seminar rooms and offices run by a Clinical Tutor, to serve the senior and junior staff of a District Hospital and all doctors working within three quarters of an hour's drive from it. With the aid of the Nuffield Provincial Hospitals' Trust, the King Edward's Fund, NHS moneys and especially the appeals from doctors to their local communities, 300 postgraduate medical centres were opened in England and Wales between 1960 and 1970.

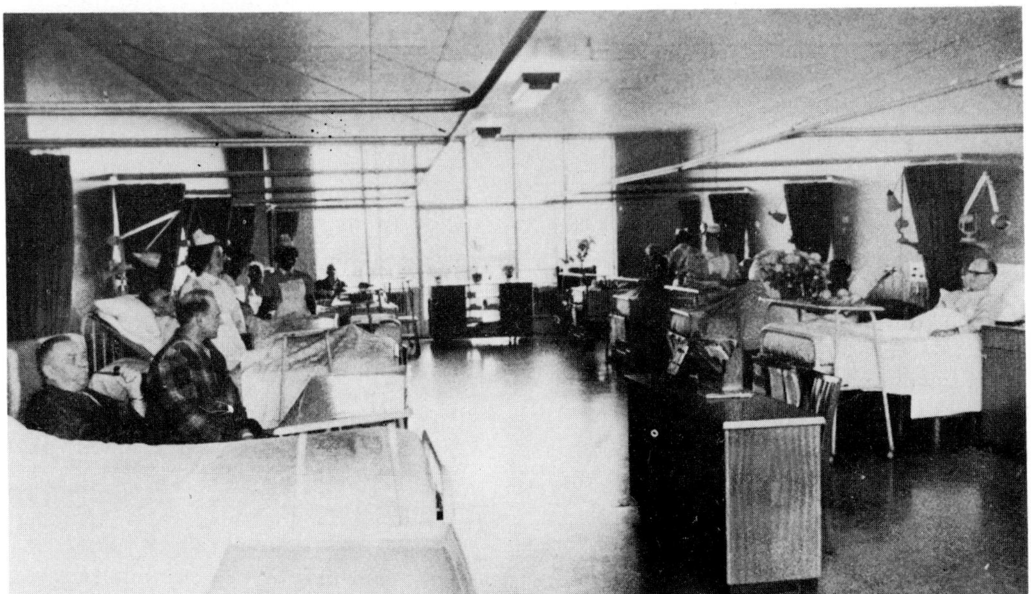

The modernised West Wing, a twelve bed ward.

V

The fact that although much had been done to improve postgraduate medical education there were still few training programmes, no approved posts, no means of ensuring adequate facilities, no method of establishing and maintaining standards and no single body with any statutory responsibility for the standard of postgraduate training or continuing education, was one reason why the University Grants Committee proposed a Royal Commission on Medical Education. The second was that whilst arrangements were in hand for modernising the medical schools outside London, the problem of modernising the 12 schools and the many postgraduate institutes in London still had to be solved. Thirdly the steps that had so far been taken to expand medical education were clearly insufficient, especially bearing in mind the very large number of junior doctor posts held by graduates from overseas, and the extent of emigration.

The Commission, under Lord Todd as chairman, started work in September 1965 and quickly issued an interim report recommending additional ways of immediately increasing the number of student places. It then proceeded to review once more the whole subject of medical education, taking vast amounts of evidence and making numerous enquiries including the surveys of medical students conducted by the Association for the Study of Medical Education. It reported in April 1968 and its main contention, that the preparation of a doctor must be a three stage process (undergraduate, graduate and postgraduate), far from proposing anything new, merely approved the direction in which medical education had been moving since the Goodenough Committee had recommended the same (though without postgraduate training for general practitioners) twenty four years earlier. It confirmed also Goodenough's recommendation of university medical centres comprised of a medical school, one or more teaching hospitals and a range of others. It agreed too with the conclusion reached by the University Grants Committee, ten years earlier, that the optimum size of a medical school had now to be one with an annual entry of between 150 and 200 students.

The Commission made various proposals regarding the organisation of postgraduate medical education, recommending that the General Medical Council be made responsible to the Privy Council for setting and maintaining the standard of it. Even before it reported, the GMC issued new Recommendations as to the Curriculum, defining the stages of medical education but pointing to its lack of authority over the last. The Royal Colleges too proceeded to begin, or increase efforts to assess the value of training posts and the Nuffield Provincial Hospitals Trust made funds available to start a National Council for Postgraduate Medical Education. The Royal College of General Practitioners continued its efforts to establish training schemes. Most of the bodies concerned with this part of the Commission's Report were therefore already moving in the direction it suggested by the time it came out. Parliamentary legislation was required of course to make the GMC responsible for all stages of medical education and this the Government offered in July 1969. The profession, however, was not happy - largely because the recommendations included a further Medical Register which would indicate to the public which doctors had satisfactorily completed postgraduate training in each branch of medicine. The profession asked for time.

The kind of flexible undergraduate course the Commission recommended (with not less than two years of basic medical sciences; not less than two years of clinical work; and the third, fourth or fifth years spent by students studying subjects of their choice in greater depth) was in line with that some universities were already developing. Its adoption by others could not be required by government but government support was needed, and offered, to make the necessary premises, facilities and staffing available. The schools most needing that support were those in London, concerning which the Commission made six recommendations:

1. The number of pre-clinical places in London should be increased from around 800 to 1200 in the first instance - so as to allow maximum educational use to be made of the country's largest single concentration of medical resources.

2. The number of schools should be reduced from 12 to 6 - by pairing them - so as to allow pre-clinical departments of a viable size and each school to have a full range of clinical departments with academic staff.

3. Each paired medical school should come into association with a multifaculty college - so as to enable teachers in medical schools to come in contact with teachers in other university disciplines and vice versa.

4. Postgraduate institutes should come into association with the paired medical schools - so as to end the isolation of the former and provide the latter with academic staff in the specialties.

5. Money should be provided forthwith to start filling the gaps in academic staffing.

6. General responsibility for the implementation of the complete plan for London should be placed in the hands of a Committee with representation of the University, the UGC and the Health Authorities with an independent Chairman and members - and 'should remain in being long enough to ensure that, in future developments, short-term convenience is not allowed to nullify long-term planning' (31).

vi

The University of London concentrated first on the last of the Royal Commission's recommendations about London. It declined to accept an independently chaired committee to oversee the rationalisation of medical education in the capital. It did so very quickly without consulting the schools and a high price has been paid for this hasty decision ever since, despite recurrent efforts to bring University, UGC and the Health Authorities together in numerous different ways at various different times. A Todd Steering Committee was then established by the Senate, which consulted the Schools and Institutes. Before the process could begin however it was decided to rebuild St George's and Charing Cross medical schools alongside the new hospitals at Tooting and Fulham respectively - each as an independent complete school capable of taking up to 160 students per annum. This decision immediately made it impossible to reduce the 12 London schools to six pairs, and ensured that the remaining 10 schools might have to share only 880 pre-clinical places between them. From then on the possibility of one or more London schools having one day to close or be merged became a probability.

The Postgraduate Institutes and the British Postgraduate Medical Federation were unenthusiastic about the Todd proposals concerning them. They argued that they were centres of excellence which was true, because those that were good were very good and those that were not so good were, there being no other centres in their subjects, the best available. They argued that they should be left alone and provided separately, or at least in some kind of groups, with all the money, man-power and buildings on which their future development depended. Even at a time of growth like the late nineteen sixties the chance of that happening was unlikely. It was soon to become impossible.

The undergraduate schools were no more enthusiastic about the Todd proposals than the Institutes, but each looked at them from its own particular view point. The London's view point was somewhat exceptional in

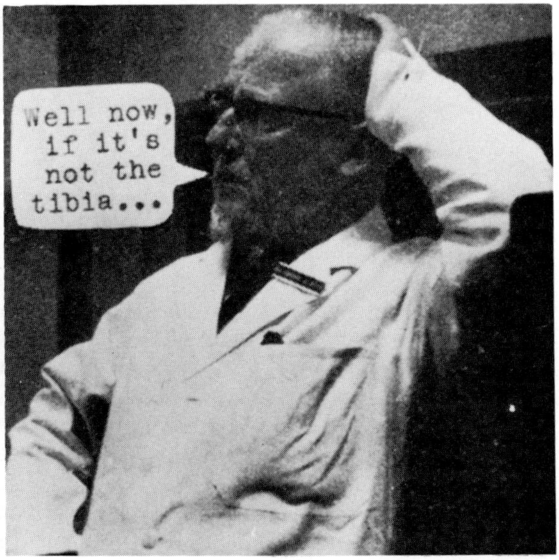

Sir Henry Osmond-Clarke.

Kenneth Cross, Professor of Physiology.

The Gazette had comments of its own to make on medical education.

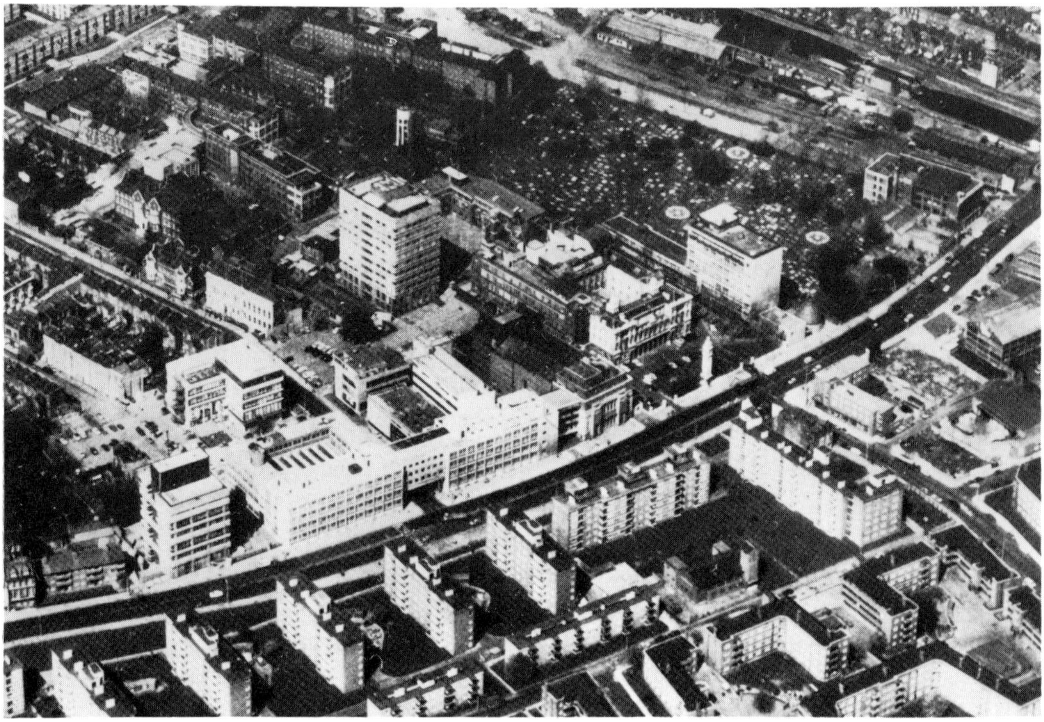

Queen Mary College and Mile End Hospital — the Burial Ground extends from the Mile End Road to the Hospital.

that in 1967, before the Royal Commission had reported, Harry May decided, after 15 years as Dean, not to seek re-election. In the ensuing peculiar Papal-like process of casting about for a new Dean the Academic Board decided to invite back the physician whose promotion from Sub-Dean had been recommended, but vetoed, ten years previously. He had spent those years, while continuing as a physician to the London, in various educational activities including membership of the Medical Sub-Committee of the UGC and the development of postgraduate medical education through a part-time post at the Ministry of Health. He was also a member of the Royal Commission - and knowing what its report was likely to say and how much its recommendations on London were likely to be resisted, made the task of attempting to implement them both unappealing and yet difficult to decline.

In 1967 I became Vice-Dean preparatory to becoming Dean the following October. The Royal Commission reported in April 1968 and the Sub-Committee of the Academic Board which began at once to consider those recommendations which applied to the London, did so with one of those who had proposed them as its chairman. A statement of the College's views was agreed, nearly unanimously, by the Academic Board and approved by the Governors, and sent to the University in October 1968. In it the College expressed its agreement with the Commission's recommendation that medical education should consist of a more flexible undergraduate course (with considerable opportunity for the student to concentrate upon a subject or subjects of his own choosing) followed by a postgraduate course in which further education is blended with in-service training.

The College stated its own educational priorities as: 1. To establish new and strengthen existing academic units in the clinical and pathological fields. 2. To secure adequate provision for teaching the behavioural sciences and the application of science to clinical medicine. 3. To provide better accommodation in which the established pre-clinical departments can teach a larger number of students for a course of two years.

It stated its wish to play a greater part in the care of its graduates during internship and later training; to collaborate with the London and St Bartholomew's

Hospitals and the Region in providing postgraduate training and continuing education; and to accommodate one or more Postgraduate Institutes in Whitechapel.

With regard to St Bartholomew's and Queen Mary Colleges it pledged itself to a 'policy of maximal collaboration,' drawing attention to the Commission's own statement that such proposals would not be realisable unless money was provided for the purpose, over and above that required for normal rebuilding and expansion, together with 'ear-marked' funds for academic development. Collaboration with St Bartholomew's should be such as 'to provide between the two Schools the widest range of academic units in the quickest possible time - without prejudice to the question of formal union of the two schools. Collaboration may well proceed more quickly and easily without union, whilst also indicating the best lines on which to unite, should this prove desirable.'

The University's Todd Steering Committee considered the written views of the schools and interviewed representatives of each. The University Grants Committee did the same. Then, in the summer of 1969, University and UGC issued a joint statement approving the principle of pairing medical schools and of linking them to multifaculty colleges. The statement included: 'The pre-clinical departments of St Bartholomew's Hospital Medical College and the London Hospital Medical College will become part of the enlarged biological sciences complex at Queen Mary College... the acquisition of a site close to the College will be urgently pursued.'

The three Colleges had already established a Tripartite Committee which was now reconstituted as a Joint Policy Committee with terms of reference laid down by the University, covering all new developments including the filling of vacancies among university and hospital consultant staff.

The London Hospital Medical College which had entered the sixties unsure, for the first time in its long history, of the direction it should take, reluctant to go forward but unable to go back, ended the decade with a policy which was as clear and challenging as any in the past, capable of creating a university medical development more exciting than any in the country, but dependent for its fulfillment not on the College alone but on its new partners, St Bartholomew's and Queen Mary College, also.

Before the sixties ended another decision brought still further hope for the future. In 1968 it was agreed that the Brentwood Annexe would be closed and that Mile End and St Clement's Hospitals would become part of the London. The hospital would still have to function on more than one site but the sites would be only a mile apart.

The London from the air in the sixties.

A succession of Deans covering 71 years.
William Wright (1910-1937) centre above,
A E Clark-Kennedy (1937-1953) centre below,
H B May (1953-1968) left,
J R Ellis (1968-1981) right.

Chapter 11.

The Nineteen Seventies

i

The College entered the nineteen seventies in the fortunate position of having clear policies already debated, agreed and documented. The Dental School's new team of departmental heads was developing its own new undergraduate course in its new buildings. The Medical School was ready to fill the gaps in its academic staffing in pathology and the clinical subjects, create the necessary facilities and ensure a student entry nearer to the optimum size. To achieve these aims it needed a substantial increase in its income, new buildings and the cooperation of the hospital and health service authorities.

In clinical subjects priority had to be given to those of major importance in the undergraduate course such as Therapeutics, Child Health, Obstetrics and Gynaecology and Community Medicine: all requiring adequate clinical facilities as well as accommodation for teaching and research. In pathology the needs of Microbiology, Haematology, Chemical Pathology, Immunology and Virology were particularly urgent and as important to the hospital as to the school. At a conservative estimate an additional 30,000 square feet of usable space was required to provide reasonable working conditions for the necessary staff.

At the same time the pre-clinical departments, housed in the old College building opened in 1887, urgently needed (despite the modernisation that had been achieved) more and better facilities even for an annual intake of 80 students let alone the greater number which would bring the school into line with others. The students also, both dental and medical and those taking an intercalated BSc, needed room in which to study, receive tutorials or small group teaching, over and above that provided by the library and museum. In brief the College needed the rebuilding, modernisation and expansion still being completed in the medical schools outside London but which in London would now clearly wait, except for St George's and Charing Cross, on the outcome of rationalisation.

While permanent preclinical facilities for the London and St Bartholomew's at Queen Mary College were being planned and built, arrangements would have to be made temporarily to improve conditions at the London. Meanwhile, however, decisions could be taken regarding permanent facilities for the clinical medical school in Whitechapel, in conjunction with the hospital and in collaboration with Barts so as to ensure the provision of all that would be necessary on each site without unnecessary reduplication. The Tower Block scheme for rebuilding the London Hospital having been abandoned, and there being no alternative to a move westwards, it had been decided that Phase I of the rebuilding programme would consist of a new block on the site of the Alexandra Wing spreading south between Turner Street and the modernised west wing down across the residents' tennis court, the Cardiac Department and the Bearsted Theatre, to the pre-clinical laboratories along the north front of the main College building.

The new block would contain a new Bearsted and a postgraduate lecture theatre in the basement together with the Central Sterile Supply Department. On the ground floor an Accident and Emergency Department would provide proper accommodation for those services which had originally been given in the purpose-built Receiving Room but which, since its conversion to a fracture clinic at the end of the war, had ever since been squeezed into what had been designed as the Matron's Office. The remainder of the new building would include operating theatres, those built by Knutsford being beyond further conversion, a radiodiagnostic department hitherto housed like so many in basements, and two floors for university clinical departments.

To make this plan possible it was necessary to provide alternative accommodation for the maternity wards, the hospital administration, the facilities for house-officers and all the other activities housed in the Alexandra Wing. The first priority therefore was the building of a 'decanting' block on the east side of the main hospital where the Bernhard Baron Institute of

Pathology had stood bordering Bedstead Square and the one-time home of the Elephant Man. This new Holland Wing included a top floor for the Medical and Surgical Units provided by the UGC It included too a new Cardiac Department and Maternity Ward, a new boardroom and administrative offices, and a common room for the residents. The old Residents' Dining Room had found a new home in a temporary building called the Garden Restaurant situated on what were once the tennis courts between Queen Alexandra's statue and Stepney Way - with a Nurses' Dining Room on one side and a Lay Staff Restaurant on the other and (because Consultants had become accustomed to lunching alone in state in the old Board Room) a Consultants' Dining Room above.

All this considerable and complicated redevelopment across the site proceeded apace while Phase I of the rebuilding programme, the new Alexandra Wing, passed through the various planning stages. Then, early in the seventies, it was realised that staff and students working in the preclinical laboratories immediately adjoining the proposed new block would be well situated to learn all about the erection of a five story building but quite unable to do anything else. So the land on which the laboratories stood, bought from the hospital after the war, was sold back to the NHS which, together with the UGC provided a new building further south. This was designed to provide the College with an animal house, which until the move to Queen Mary College could be used by the pre-clinical departments. Its rather austere appearance reflecting its ultimate purpose, immediately earned it the name of Colditz.

None of these plans however did anything to provide the urgent needs of the various departments of Pathology. Clearly these could only be met by temporary buildings wherever room for them could be found. Over the seventies the necessary space was provided - the Walden building close to Colditz, Medical Microbiology in Ashfield Street alongside an attractive brick building erected by the Arthritis and Rheumatism Council to house the Bone and Joint Research Unit, and eventually teaching laboratories in Turner Street, south of Gwynne House and the Good Samaritan. The whole area between Turner Street and New Road, from Newark Street to the north and Ashfield Street to the south, was cleared. Learning and teaching space for students was provided in the Newark building on the western side balancing the Turner building to the east and leaving a car park between the two.

The Holland Wing.

Thus throughout the seventies the Whitechapel campus continued in a constant state of demolition and reconstruction. Criss-crossed still by the many streets, crowded always with public as well as hospital and college traffic, not to mention builders' lorries, its appearance was always changing. In addition to the developments described above and to others like the new Princess Alexandra School of Nursing, the Ellicott and Hill computer buildings, and the Three Feathers Club, already completed or completing, further blocks of flats for nurses were built out of endowment funds close to John Harrison House in the south. One new building, the Turner Street Laboratories, was completed, totally destroyed by fire the same night, and promptly rebuilt. The area was not the quietest or cleanest situation for a medical centre but it was never dull, and those concerned with finding the funds and preparing the plans for new buildings (like Hugh Laird and John Davies, the college's Domestic Bursar) would have been kept busy even if nothing else had to be done.

But there was much more to be done, even so far as accommodation was concerned. Moving into Mile End meant that facilities had to be provided there for teaching and for students: as also in the hospitals in New Ham to which, with that District's assistance, students were moved from hospitals further afield so as to bring them nearer to the medical school. All the time, however, the central feature of all this reconstruction remained Phase I, the new Alexandra Wing, to make way for which so many changes had to be made and on the completion of which the final outcome of the main plan depended. Delays of one kind or another held up both planning and funding. Then when the old Alexandra Wing had been evacuated and was about to be pulled down, a preservation order was placed on it and it remained empty, its roof part gone and exposed to the elements, while ambulances learned to use a temporary entrance up a ramp beside the Holland Wing.

Then this forlorn relic of where generations of governors and house governors had governed, generations of house officers had played billiards, successive Matrons had lived and generations of Old Londoners' children had been born, was demolished and replaced by a vast hole in the ground. Then the nation's financial collapse postponed building indefinitely even though the project had gone out to tender. By 1976 when the College had succeeded in filling the 'gaps' in its clinical academic staff and increased its student intake it had, instead of the accommodation it had expected, a hole in the ground

The Hostel, the 'Pill-box'. (The Basil Samuel lecture theatre of the Princess Alexandra School of Nursing) and John Harrison House, first of the new Nurses' Homes.

to the north and another in the garden next to the library ready for a new Radio-Isotope laboratory. Work on Phase I eventually began in January 1978 and the building itself was completed in 1981.

ii

Back in 1970 of course there was no sign of a financial collapse. A time of growth and full employment continued. The National Health Service had on the whole been remarkably successful in providing more and better care, despite the fact that it had been designed to offer a very different kind of medicine and had been based in the main on antiquated hospitals suffering the effects of war. Medical advances which but a few years before had been exciting new examples of 'high technology' had come to be accepted as routine procedures by the public, largely unaware of the demands they made on money, manpower and equipment. 'Supporting services' of medical science, pathology, anaesthetics and the like expanded rapidly and yet remained shortage specialities. Public satisfaction with medicine's increasing capacity to diagnose and treat was accompanied by the hope and expectation that it would increase still further, but not accompanied by any lessening of public desire for the comforting which previously had so often been all that medicine had to offer.

People wanted care and attention from a familiar family doctor, ready to make house calls at any time, and prompt admission when required to a hospital close by equipped for all manner of care, but not too big and certainly without the disregard for privacy and comfort which characterised hospitals in most other European countries at the time. While growing waiting lists, the reluctance of GPs to join Health Centres and the increasing use of deputising services evidenced a gap between what was wanted and what was available, there was nonetheless a widespread confidence that given time, and more money, then before long more doctors, nurses and every other kind of health worker, would result in public expectations being met. What doctors lacked most in 1970, it seemed, was time.

Even so many agreed that perhaps the administration of the Service left something to be desired, especially in regard to integration between hospitals on the one hand and the general medical services on the other. The profession itself had drawn attention to this in the report of its Medical Services Review Committee in the sixties, and had advocated some kind of integrated Area Health Authority. Attention had been drawn also to the fact that teaching hospitals were not only important to medical education but were essential to the Service as referral centres, and yet were not always getting what they needed and were sometimes lacking any clear policy.

Philpot Street looking North: the Hostel and the Institute of Pathology.

So reorganisation of the Health Service was planned and came into force in 1974, creating District and Area as well as Regional Health Authorities - with teaching hospitals in England coming under Districts. It was soon to prove as unsatisfactory as the reorganisation of nursing services which had preceded it, but unlike the latter was to be subjected to further alterations in the hope of making good at least some of the mistakes. Unhappily no alteration, however unsettling to those trying to run the Service, could integrate the general medical services with the hospitals while GPs remained separately funded outside the service as independent contractors.

Scarcely, however, had the various Health Authorities been appointed and gone through the arduous task of interviewing all the administrators (lay, medical, nursing and other) in the country and appointing them either to their previous or to some different post or made them supernumerary to establishment, than the price of oil went up, the national economy went down and every Health Authority was in dire financial trouble. To many a brand new Authority (made up largely of lay members with no earlier experience of health services) and most newly created District Management Teams, the challenge of how to keep things going in such a crisis seemed big enough. They were then confronted with a problem called 'R A W P.'

No 53 Philpot Street, for 10 years the headquarters of the Association for the Study of Medical Education, now the Tower Hamlets District Health Authority.

Understandably the originator of this problem has never been named and as its precise purpose has never been clear it remains known only by the initials of a working party - the Reallocation of Resources Working Party which worked out a formula for curtailing the funding of Regions which had hitherto been in receipt of higher incomes so as to increase the funding of those previously receiving less. This greatly increased the

Building progress as seen by the Gazette.

difficulties of those Regions whose higher incomes reflected greater needs (without in fact meeting rising costs), helped others more easily to make both ends meet than would otherwise have been possible, and effectively brought further development virtually to a standstill in all. Surprisingly this process of achieving equality by levelling down did not reduce the 10% difference between the funding of the Health Service in Scotland and that in England and Wales. Equally surprising some of those Regions whose funds were being curtailed hit on the idea of buffering those Areas, particularly the more rural, which had previously been receiving less, by reducing the funding of those previously receiving more.

Whatever virtues such a reallocation might have had if made in a time of growth, its application in a period of recession was bound to have the most serious consequences for the teaching hospitals in London. The best administration in the world could not possibly cope effectively at one and the same time with a financial crisis, inter-regional RAWP, intra-regional RAWP, the unknown implications of as yet undecided rationalisation of medical schools and post-graduate institutes, and the necessary but inevitably slow phasing out of dilapidated hospitals made redundant by medical and demographic change but still locally loved and trusted. Unfortunately any attempt to achieve administrative miracles was further frustrated at District level by the requirement to manage by consensus. The difficulty of achieving a consensus between people of totally different training and experience, on issues which few fully understood, led all too often to slow decision, or worse still to none other than how to express next year's plans in time for the 'planning cycle'.

The University Grants Committee and the University of London (showing a degree of cohesion never previously achieved by the faculty of medicine) made valiant efforts to contain this threat to the seed corn by defining the minimum clinical resources necessary to a medical school. They succeeded to some extent in slowing down the speed of application of a misguided policy which nonetheless continued and the effects of which were then compounded by pressure to divert resources from the already underfunded care of the acute sick, in order to try to improve that of the old and the handicapped and to increase that given in the community.

Seen in retrospect the sadness of the seventies, so far as the Health Service was concerned, is enhanced by the fact that many of the aims pursued were laudable in themselves. The damage was done by attempting to achieve them at the wrong time and by ways which ignored inescapable features of modern medicine. As medical care includes more that is complex and costly, concentration of medical resources is irresistible and proceeds inexorably in every country, fastest in those attempting to maintain standards in times of recession. Every year hospitals become fewer but larger, so that the interdependent specialities can share supporting services and free money and manpower for the community, the aged, and the handicapped. But not even the most affluent countries can equip every district hospital to provide every service and the more district hospitals there are the greater the demand they create for referral centres which depend on the extra facilities provided by Universities.

Intra-regional reallocation, at the right time and carefully controlled, might be justified, but the essentially centrifugal policy of intra-regional RAWP was precisely the opposite of that demanded by the circumstances. Tragically the damage done by it was to be greater and longer-lasting because it was not immediately apparent. At the very time Health Service policy was bleeding the teaching hospitals in London they received from the medical schools a transfusion which allowed the establishment of academic clinical units and pathological departments, thus creating the university medical centres essential to the efficient functioning of a national health service. The process was expedited as every teaching hospital gladly looked to university staff to plug the gaps in its ranks, so that expansion proceeded everywhere without regard to the rationalisation of schools which had yet to come, but which in the seventies was still being resisted. So the worst effects of a misguided policy were temporarily buffered and were not to become fully apparent until later when rationalisation of schools became inevitable and university funding was itself cut to the bone.

Even so posterity will no doubt record that the most serious damage to the NHS and British medicine in the seventies came not from lack of money or managerial foolishness (crippling though both were at the time) but from political interference of a different kind. The arbitrary decision to separate private beds from NHS hospitals did more than reduce the latter's access to an important source of income at a time it was sorely needed. It meant that the increase in private hospital care, which was bound to come, developed outside the NHS to its continuing and increasing detriment. Perhaps more serious still was the introduction of payment for overtime by hospital doctors which did more than anything else to change, probably for ever, those professional attitudes which had done so much to keep the service going and build it up despite all difficulties.

F W Webb, Academic Registrar and William Wright's 'motto' variously translated as 'Temper bitter things with a gentle smile' or 'Grin and bear it'.

Thus weakened in both body and spirit it was not surprising that the country's largest employer of manpower found one of its other great assets, the loyalty of ancillary staff to hospitals dependent on them, gravely undermined by industrial action. A service increasingly hard put to meet rising demands was forced for the first time to reduce the amount of care it could offer.

Throughout this difficult period the London had some particular disadvantages but also some important advantages. The North East Metropolitan Region, which in 1974 became the North East Thames, entered the Health Service with less well-developed hospitals than almost any. It needed more money than most and could not in 25 years make good its initial deficiencies sufficiently to provide its growing population with a hospital service which was both better and more economical. Nevertheless it became a 'donor' Region scheduled for a minimal increase in annual funding. Of all its Areas, that of the City and East London faced the most peculiar set of circumstances. It contained a total population of around half-a-million, inhabiting the City and three boroughs which had been badly damaged in the war, were experiencing inner-city decay, and suffering more deprivation than almost any in the country. It catered also for a very large influx of daily commuters and its two teaching hospitals, Barts and the London, provided specialised and referral care for much of the Region's total population of over 3 million.

The Area's other hospitals were many and for the most part old, dilapidated, ill-sited, small and poorly-equipped. Newham alone had eight hospitals, unco-ordinated and none able to provide long-stay care for the Borough's mentally ill, handicapped or aged. General medical services were equally unusual. Newham had approximately 100 GPs working from almost as many different premises though by the mid-seventies it could boast one or two health centres. Tower Hamlets had none but its population of around 150,000 was served by some 90 GPs with an average list of under 2,000. Few lived within the Borough, many were singlehanded, a high proportion were elderly and by no means all had premises equipped with running water.

Whitechapel was no longer a predominantly Jewish quarter but Tower Hamlets remained a multi-racial community with immigrants from many lands, especially East Africa, Bangladesh and Pakistan. Its many hostels were full and it continued to be a focus point for people, young and old, drifting with no fixed abode and drawn from all over the British Isles. Some old tenement buildings like Fieldgate Mansions were

The Arthritis & Rheumatism Council Building, housing the Bone & Joint Research Unit with part of Medical Microbiology beyond.

deemed unsuitable for permanent residents and provided cheap accommodation for students. Others were as crowded as at any time in the past. Many of the little streets of terraced houses, on the other hand, had been replaced by blocks of flats and high-rise buildings which proved exceptionally unsuitable for a population increasingly composed of elderly people previously accustomed to all the support the vibrant, cheerful and friendly community of the East End was renowned for providing. The elderly saw the Receiving Room of the London not only as their primary source of medical advice, as their predecessors had done for two centuries, but also as a means of escape from an isolation their forbears had never known.

Admission to local hospitals other than to the London and Barts remained easy up to the early seventies, the total number of beds not having fallen at the same rate as the population. Doctors and patients had grown accustomed to a faster admission and longer stay than had ever been possible in pre-war days leaving them unprepared for the changes which they could not foresee but which were sure to come. The Area Health Authority, however, was aware of this situation from the moment it took office. From 1968 Hospital Services Committees in Tower Hamlets and Hackney had been making detailed studies of both Boroughs. Each committee consisted of lay and medical representatives of all the hospitals in its district. They were chaired by the Deans of the two Medical Colleges and shared a common secretariat headed by Sotiris Argyrou who, in 1974, became the Area administrator. The new Health Authority therefore began with much of its preparatory work already done and its lay members had from the outset the advantage of being better informed of needs and current provision than their counterparts elsewhere. A degree of District consciousness had developed in two out of its three Districts.

Thus despite the enormity of the task confronting it the City and East London Area Health Authority got away to a good start under Francis Cumberlege as chairman. Members had an intimate knowledge of as well as concern for the Districts from which they were drawn and quickly appreciated the peculiar nature of its health care problems. The Authority also became quickly aware of its responsibilities to medical education and remained so, consistently supportive of the two Medical Colleges which collaborated closely with it and with each other. The Authority did much, or at least all it could, to point out the dangers of RAWP within the North East Thames Region and to minimise its ill effects.

It was not however in its power totally to prevent strikes and in the Gazette of 1977 the Dean's Report recorded: 'As the fanfares (for the Queen's Jubilee) sounded in St Paul's, and the bells pealed and the cheers of the crowd could be heard in the distance, the front hall of the London carried the information -The Hospital is closed to admissions and patients will be discharged as quickly as possible. Thus industrial action achieved what nothing else, not even the blitz, had been able to do in all the years since 1740. While reaction to this evidence of undoubted social change ranged from horror and numb disbelief to that of the visiting administrator who hoped we would be in for only a few weeks of "inconvenience", it is a safe bet that noone, including those taking industrial action over what seemed to them at least to be a just cause, ever wanted it to happen. In that lies perhaps the saddest irony - but perhaps also hope for the future. As life flows slowly back into the hospital and we learn once again the lesson of the last war that you can empty a hospital overnight but it takes many weeks to fill one, perhaps everyone connected with the London in 1977 will go forward determined that never again if they can prevent it will there be another notice in the front hall like that which was posted this June.'

iii

While the sufferings of the Health Service grew worse throughout the seventies (except for a new outlook in general practice which created interest in group practices and health centres) medical education fared considerably better. Progress was made in various ways in many places in the first half of the decade and it was only in the last years that financial stringency began to take its toll. Postgraduate medical education improved even though the Act making the General Medical Council responsible for the standard of it did not come into force until 1978. Defining the requirements for accreditation in the main specialties made better training programmes possible, despite a tendency to rigidity which was neither intended nor desirable. Inspection of posts by joint committees from the Royal Colleges and Universities ensured more adequate facilities and raised the quality of training. Postgraduate medical centres continued to prove their worth.

In the field of general practice the MRCGP examination was launched and much was done to prepare GPs as trainers pending the time when vocational training would become mandatory for all wishing to become principals. The number of training programmes increased steadily though the physical state of general practice premises was a difficult barrier to overcome in some areas. At first no practices were considered suitable for training in Tower Hamlets but eventually the Medical College was instrumental in starting a scheme based on the London Hospital and GPs in Newham and Tower Hamlets.

Pre-registration training also came under scrutiny. It had begun in 1953 with neither trainers nor trainees having much idea what was expected of them and most of the former assumed that house officers were ready to function efficiently as such and did not see themselves as trainers at all. As far back as 1964 an ASME Survey had revealed that supervision was often inadequate and that many house officers were working a 100 hour week (31). Efforts were made to improve the selection of posts and lessen the work load but the situation in general remained unsatisfactory and the establishment by the GMC in 1973 of a code of good practice came not a day too soon.

So far as the London was concerned action began in 1968 with the appointment of A D M Jackson, consultant paediatrician, as Postgraduate Sub-Dean to the College. By travelling the country and gaining the collaboration of consultants he built up a sufficient number of suitable posts to meet the needs of the school and obtained the agreement of all to appointments being made by a computerised matching plan, in which the preferences of applicants are matched to those of consultants. Even more important, and more difficult, he established a system of adequately reporting on the performance of the trainees. In this most sensitive and important area of medical education Tony Jackson's contribution to the London was outstanding. He also succeeded in achieving much needed improvement in the accommodation provided for house officers in Whitechapel.

As vocational training for general practice did not become mandatory until the end of the decade it could still be argued throughout the seventies that the undergraduate course ought to include everything with which a general practitioner might be confronted. Nonetheless some schools made substantial innovations, notably the two new schools at Southampton and Nottingham which set aside one year of the five year course for projects in subjects chosen, with guidance, by students themselves. The new clinical school at Cambridge followed the same line allowing those who stayed on at Cambridge after two years of basic medical science and a third year studying any of a wide range of subjects, to take the final MB after a two year clinical course.

Tony Jackson, first Postgraduate Sub-Dean.

In London, however, the schools were still suffering from the fact that, as the Royal Commission had pointed out, they had not for many years had 'financial support comparable with that made available to medical schools in other British centres' (31). Over that vital period when medical education was being modernised, at great expense, the London schools had 'suffered increasingly from too little spread too thinly over too many centres' (33). There was not at first much that most could do even though the University revised* the regulations for the MB BS degrees giving

* The Working Party which drafted the revision included three Londoners: Clifford Wilson, now Dean of the Faculty, H B May and myself.

schools the choice betweeen designing their own course (to be submitted for approval to the faculty of medicine) or following one laid down in broad terms by the University consisting of 2 years of basic medical sciences (with examinations at the end of each year) and a clinical course three months shorter than in the past with a once per year clinical entry. The regulations for the latter were, in fact, so devised as to allow schools considerable freedom to go their own way, especially if they opted for internal examinations in the clinical subjects, to which the University had agreed in the sixties after a long campaign headed by Clifford Wilson of the London.

Israel ('Sonny') Doniach, Professor of Morbid Anatomy.

Thus the London schools found themselves required to change their curricula but still lacked the wide range of academic staff, in pathology and the clinical subjects, necessary for the university-based student-orientated type of course recommended by the GMC and possible elsewhere. In this state they wrestled unhappily with the Todd proposals for reshaping medical education in London and in particular with the twinning of schools which had been approved both by the University and the University Grants Committee but was regarded with little enthusiasm by most pairs of twins.

So far as the London and Barts were concerned twinning had a clear and agreed purpose: 'to provide between the two schools the widest range of academic units in the quickest possible time.' One of their immediate needs was in the field of Child Health. Not only did they lack academic staff but the declining number of children admitted to hospital had greatly reduced the experience of paediatrics available to students at Barts and the London, because the second largest childrens' hospital in the metropolis was situated midway betweeen them. A survey of paediatric teaching across the country had demonstrated this weakness (34) and the Todd Report had specifically recommended that the Queen Elizabeth's Hospital Hackney (recently transferred to Great Ormond Street) should become part of the hospital group associated with the St Bartholomew's and the London Hospital Medical Colleges.

Thus began the first of many complex and protracted negotiations between the two colleges on the one hand and Postgraduate Institutes and hospitals on the other. Agreement was finally reached that the Queen Elizabeth would remain part of the Great Ormond Street Group but would provide beds, outpatient facilities, accommodation and research facilities for a joint Barts/London academic unit of Child Health. Arrangements were made to ensure the necessary liason between the many university and hospital entities involved, the University Grants Committee provided additional funds with which to start the unit and Professor Christopher Wood was appointed to this first Joint Chair.

Attention turned next to preparing development policies for the quinquennium which would begin in 1972. Again the London and Barts worked closely together identifying those departments which were necessary in each school (and had either to be provided or strengthened) and those which might be shared. Each school had gaps which clearly had to be made good on its own site - the London, for example, had an academic unit of Morbid Anatomy (in which Sonny Doniach had succeeded Dorothy Russell) and of Bacteriology (in which Claude Barwell had succeeded Sir Samuel Bedson) but badly needed staff in Haematology, Chemical Pathology, Virology and Immunology. At Barts, on the other hand, endowment funds had been used to establish academic units in some of those subjects.

The Todd Report had argued that 'every modern

medical school worthy of that description should have academic departments, with professorial heads, in all the main subjects of the undergraduate clinical course: such departments exist in nearly every medical school outside London.' Accepting this as a long-term aim the London and Barts Medical Colleges proposed to appoint academic staff in the specialties as and when opportunity offered in either of the main hospitals, to be supported by the main Medical and Surgical Units until such time as independent specialist academic units were possible. They identified however certain areas, in which they proposed to make good existing deficiencies by joint action. These included, besides Paediatrics, Obstetrics and Gynaecology, the whole field of Social Medicine and General Practice. Plans were made too in regard to Forensic Medicine and Anaesthetics in which there were already academic staff at the London, and Oncology and Radiotherapy where academic appointments had been made at Barts.

As the joint development plan was prepared to enable the two schools to make good the academic development which universities outside London had enjoyed over the past twenty years, the University Grants Committee announced that medical schools might expect around 3% growth in the 1972-77 quinquennium. Enquiries at the Conference of Metropolitan Deans revealed that this would scarcely allow the London schools to maintain their present position. It was proposed therefore by the London that the time had come for the Deans to seek the implementation of the Royal Commission's recommendation that additional funds, over and above those needed for normal rebuilding and expansion, should be provided forthwith to enable the London schools to make good the deficiencies in academic staffing to which it had drawn attention. A memorandum to this effect was eventually sent to the Senate Steering Committee dealing with the implementation of the Todd Report and, although signed only by the Dean of the London, all the Deans of the undergraduate schools attended the subsequent meeting and vigorously supported the proposal. The University decided to ask the University Grants Committee, which agreed to provide additional funds.

All schools in London then laboriously redrafted their development policies to include those gaps in academic staffing in pathology and clinical subjects they considered most serious. They were rewarded with additional funds to make good about half of what they asked for. In the case of the London Hospital Medical College this resulted in agreement to increase its grant by rather more than £750,000 over the five years from 1972 to 1977 - and the process of implementing its joint development plan began.

In consequence the London was able in the next few

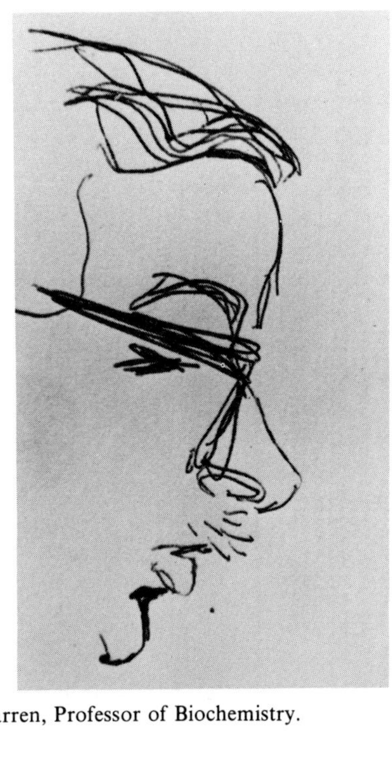

F D Warren, Professor of Biochemistry.

F R Johnson, Professor of Anatomy (Pre-clinical Sub-Dean).

E S Watkins, Professor of Neurosurgery.

years to establish an academic element, ranging from an individual to an academic unit, in Haematology, Chemical Pathology, Therapeutics, Endocrinology and Metabolism, Rheumatology, Cardiology, Gastroenterology, Urology and Neurosurgery. In some cases these were linked to corresponding developments in Barts and in addition joint appointments were made in Virology, Immunology and Sociology. The schools combined also to create a Joint Chair of Obstetrics and Gynaecology, sited at the London end, and a Joint Chair of Reproductive Physiology at Barts; similarly a Joint Chair of Environmental and Preventative Medicine was established at Barts and one of Clinical Epidemiology at the London.

These many new academic appointments helped of course to provide medical services and the old College department of Bacteriology which had hitherto engaged mainly in research was converted into one of Microbiology which took over responsibility for service in Tower Hamlets and, like the other departments in Pathology, increasingly provided help for Newham. Microbiology, Haematology and Immunology provided staff or services for the postgraduate Urological Hospitals. Similarly clinical units spread staff out to help with the care of patients and teaching in other hospitals in the Area, in addition of course to Mile End. The Medical Unit (in which Clifford Wilson had been succeeded by Jack Ledingham) spread to Bethnal Green, joined by the Therapeutics Unit under Duncan Vere; the Surgical Unit (in which Victor Dix had been succeeded first by William Irvine and then by David Ritchie) spread to Queen Mary's Stratford, St Mary's Plaistow, and East Ham Memorial Hospital; Peter Huntingford (first joint Professor of Obstetrics) gave assistance to the maternity services in Newham; the Psychiatric unit moved to St Clements and the Anaesthetics Unit provided staff for Forest Gate and later for St Andrews. A similar process saw academic staff from St Bartholomew's contributing to hospitals in Hackney.

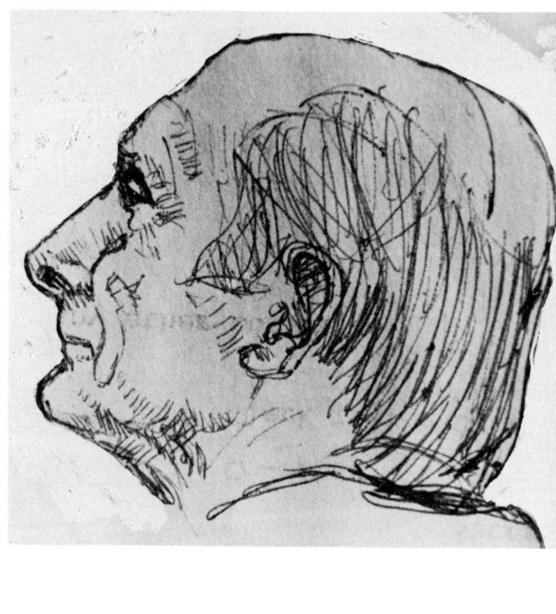

J M Ledingham, Professor of Medicine.

At the start of the process of building up a range of academic staff needed for medical education, hospitals showed the same reluctance to collaborate which had characterised their attitude to university 'infiltration' in the past. As soon, however, as the Health Service began to feel the effects of financial cuts and RAWP the situation changed. Not only were the necessary clinical facilities made available for university appointed staff but hospitals actively sought university assistance to maintain and if possible develop services. Joint appointments of widely different kinds were devised between the two Medical Colleges, the Area Health Authority and other bodies. The Royal College of Surgeons, for example, agreed to share its British Oxygen Chair of Anaesthesia with the London and the holder, J P Payne, was appointed Professor of Anaesthetics at the London when Roy Simpson emigrated to the United States.

In 1976 the Dean was able to report: 'These developments, not of isolated academic entities but of closely interwoven University and National Health Service Collaboration, have resulted in the creation of something new but essential to modern medicine and medical care, a university medical centre - based not on a single teaching hospital nor even on a single medical school, financed both by University and National Health service funds, and meeting the referral needs of millions while providing comprehensive care for the local population. Clinical departments, comprising both NHS and academic staff, are clustered sufficiently closely together to allow that interdisciplinary approach to patient care, teaching, training and research, which the fragmentation of medicine has made necessary; and all are backed by University departments in the basic medical sciences.'

University backing came also from further afield - in Physics and Geography for example from Queen Mary College, in Bioengineering from links between Michael Freeman and Imperial College and in Cardiology through links between Alastair McDonald and Chelsea College.

By 1978 the London Hospital Medical College was relating to 12 hospitals, providing the medical manpower for some 350 beds and some 35 outpatient clinics per week, together with most Pathological services for two Districts and one group of Postgraduate Hospitals. Most of its new clinical academic staff, however, shared one great disability. The accommodation which it had been expected would be ready for them, was not. Only in January 1978 did the building of Phase I, the Alexandra Wing, begin. In their first years they shared, with remarkably good grace, what little space could be found and began research under the same difficulties as those faced by the Medical and Surgical Units in the early fifties.

Meanwhile the development of the rehoused and refashioned Dental School continued to proceed apace. The new team of senior lecturers appointed in the sixties, with Geoffrey Slack as Professor of Dental Surgery and Loma Miles as Professor of Oral Pathology and Oral Medicine, was built up step by step into a range of departments, with professorial heads, in Oral and Maxillo-facial Surgery (Seward), Conservative Dentistry (Allred), Prosthetic Dentistry (Fish), Oral Pathology (Miles) and Oral Medicine and Periodontology (Duckworth). Mike Braden was appointed to the first chair of Dental Materials in the country and brought a new scientific strength to the College as a whole. Slack's own chair of Dental Surgery was converted to one of Community Dental Health and Dennis Berman appointed to a new chair of Child Dental Health. A department of Oral Microbiology was developed under Jeremy Hardie and Dental Biochemistry incorporated in the College Biochemistry Department.

G R Seward, Professor of Oral Surgery (Dean of Dental Studies, 1975-1979).

Coincidentally with these changes in the staffing of the College came changes in the students. The annual entry of dental students was increased steadily up to the fifty for which the new school was designed. From the end of the sixties also the London enjoyed great popularity at Oxford and Cambridge. Students at both universities were encouraged to study the different clinical courses available and the custom began of visiting different schools. Many chose to visit the London and were taken round the Hospital and College by London students. Most liked what they found and the number of applications for the clinical course soon rose to well over a hundred per year. The process of choosing between thirty and forty of them added a new burden to selection as most applicants had many and varied achievements to their credit at the end of the second year at university.

Immediately it was constituted the Joint Policy Committee of Barts, London and Queen Mary College began the task of designing the proposed new pre-clinical facilities. The Jewish Burial Ground stretching along the eastern border of Queen Mary College from the Mile End Road to Mile End Hospital offered a perfect site, contiguous with both the multifaculty college and the hospital. The purchase of land in London is seldom easy but the difficulties are magnified many times when that desired has provided over centuries the last resting place of thousands of members of a faith which holds its forbears in great respect. Yet the quiet perseverance of Queen Mary College's Principal, Sir Harry Melville, and its Registrar, Colonel Robert Tong, aided by the helpful and understanding collaboration of the Jewish Community, backed up by efficient action from the University of London and the University Grants Committee resulted in the purchase of the site, the passing of the necessary Act of Parliament and the reinterment of all but the most recent graves in a new site in the Essex countryside. The old adage that it is easier to move a cemetary than change the medical curriculum was proved right. What might well have proved to be the greatest stumbling block to the BLQ project was overcome so quietly and quickly that the only body to draw regular attention to it has been the Public Accounts Committee which from time voices its anxiety that the expenditure of public money has not been followed up by more rapid action.

London Hospital Mile End, foreground, and Queen Mary College. The burial ground is clear for the Medical Sciences building and library. The land adjoining the Regent's Canal (extreme left) will be used for Student Residencies and Sports Centre.

The Royal Commission's proposal implied that the new facilities for basic medical sciences should accommodate two hundred medical students for a two year course, fifty dentals for at least one year, facilities for students taking an intercalated BSc, facilities for clinical students taking optional courses or a Bachelor of Medical Sciences degree, and preferably some students studying for a degree in Natural Sciences. The Joint Policy Committee's first task was obviously to check whether the clinical facilities available in the Area would remain adequate to provide for a three year clinical course for two hundred students together with whatever number might be expected to come from Oxford and Cambridge after the latter had developed its own clinical school. Detailed studies revealed that an Area of approximately 600,000 inhabitants together with a further 500,000 made up of patients referred from elsewhere and commuters, would continue to provide adequate clinical resources for an annual entry of 300 clinical students.

The consequent BLQ proposal that the combined Barts/London school should be planned to take an entry of up to 300 medical students reached the University just as it became clear that the medical schools outside London, including the new schools of Nottingham, Southampton and Leicester, could not after all provide sufficient places to allow the country a total entry of 3,500 (exclusive of students from overseas) by 1975 - the target the Royal Commission had proposed on the understanding that future requirements should then be reestimated. The proposal was considered first by the Joint Medical Advisory Committee, a new and much needed body which brought together for the first time the heads of the medical schools with the representatives of the Boards of Studies in the many different medical subjects. It noted the Todd recommendations that the number of pre-clinical places in London should be raised by 400 to 1200, and that 200 of the new places should be found as soon as possible. It agreed that schools should be asked what increases they could take immediately. Barts and the London were among those willing and able to increase their intake and their offers were agreed both by the University and the UGC on the understanding that BLQ would eventually take at least 200 medicals per annum, 100 from the London and 100 from Barts. In consequence the number of pre-clinical students admitted to the London was increased by 25% from 80 to 100 beginning in 1974.

Meanwhile it had been agreed to change the College's admission policy in a number of respects. Female applicants would be considered on equal terms with male, and all would be required (in conformity with the University's minimal requirements for entry) to have passes at A level in Chemistry or Physical Science, and in two other subjects, one of which should be a science. O and A level grades would be considered in the light of educational and other circumstances and passes at C grade at A level indicated a sufficient command of basic science. Students would not normally be admitted at less than 18 or over 30 years of age and wherever possible should be encouraged to have a break between leaving school and entering university. Applicants from local schools should be interviewed even if their academic attainments at the time of application were not encouraging.

By the mid-seventies the proportion of women had risen from 7% to 33% though the number of applicants remained somewhat smaller than at other schools, perhaps because few girls had been admitted in the past and possibly because some parents and some teachers imagined the East End of London to be a less than ideal environment for young ladies. By the mid-seventies approximately half the entering class had enjoyed upwards of one year between school and university in which to complement whatever experience life had so far provided for them. At the same time applications from older students increased as many with first degrees in other subjects or with experience in some other walk of life began to seek admission to medicine. Many of course faced formidable financial difficulties but like the ex-service students of the post-war years they made a welcome addition to the student body as a whole. From time to time also the College had the advantage of little groups of students coming as refugees from other lands to finish studies begun elsewhere by taking, as the only qualification available to them, the Conjoint or LMSSA. Over the years such students came in succession from Hungary, Czechoslovakia, Kenya, Uganda, Malta and South America.

V

The coming together of a group of young active teachers, whether in an old school or a new, is frequently the occasion for serious reappraisal not merely of its courses but of the whole philosophy of its education. Just such an occasion was provided by the appointment of dental teachers to the London in the sixties and they began to consider the future of dental education even before the new Dental Institute was opened. The design of the Institute itself reflected the

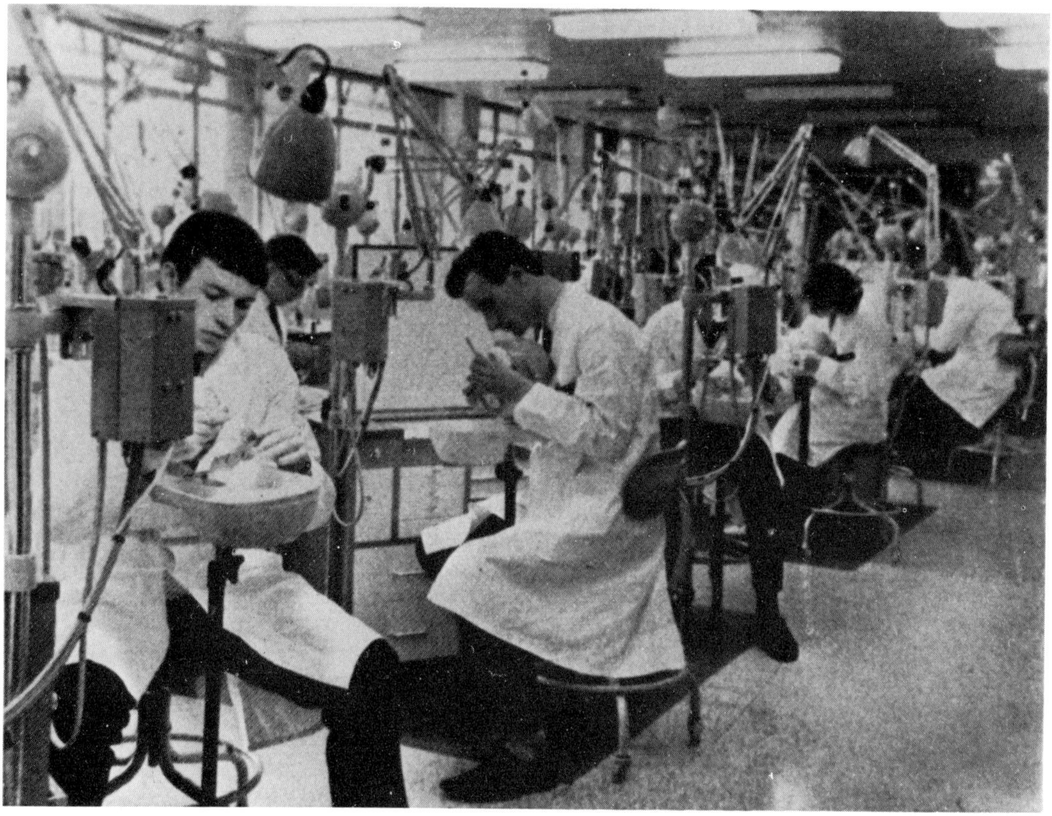

Dental practice gives way to dental care

outcome of their initial thoughts, particularly in regard to the relatively large proportion of space allocated for research and the care taken to ensure that so far as possible clinical facilities were provided for common use and not fragmented into small insulated clinics ear-marked for individual departments.

From these early deliberations by heads of departments, most of them senior lecturers, there developed a carefully organised intensive in-depth study of dental education involving the whole school. Its eventual report, entitled 'The Future of Dental Education' has had a major influence on the development of the subject both in Britain and overseas. Its importance to the London was even greater for it provided what dental and medical schools seldom have - a strategy, based on detailed study, fully thought through, its principles defined and agreed, and the whole committed to writing. In consequence this Dental School has been able to pursue a known educational policy, which has been taken into account in all new developments, in the creation of posts and the filling of vacancies. As a result the school has remained remarkably cohesive, knowing where it wants to go, and how far it has got. At any one time its curriculum has been based, of course, on its existing resources, but as they have changed in accord with agreed aims so the curriculum has been adapted to bring it nearer to the ideal that has remained clearly in view. Thus the school has been in a very different situation to the common one in which periodically the curriculum is reviewed by a tactical exercise consisting of the redeployment of existing resources, but in which the resources are changed between reviews in reponse to influences which do not include an agreed educational policy.

The training of dentists, like that of doctors, must necessarily take note of what their future functions are likely to be and from the sixties the London's vision of future dentistry has included increasing collaboration between dentists and other professionals. It has also included changes in the kind of dental care likely to be needed. Its educational policy therefore has been based on the belief that dentists should be prepared to face a changing future and to be leaders in a dental team while at the same time trained to the highest level of performance in current practice. With these aims in mind the school set out to introduce students to clinical experience even in the first pre-clinical year. It has pursued the concept of students providing whole care for patients and of accumulating their practices so as to learn from the beginning how to manage a general dental practice. The different dental disciplines have been taught concurrently rather than consecutively as in the past, departmental boundaries have been broken down and interdepartmental collaboration fostered.

A general dental practice was established within the London and by the end of the seventies a second set up in a Health centre, created out of the old East End Maternity Hospital, thus allowing students to work in the community as well as in hospital. The establishment of a Dental Auxiliary School, training Dental Surgery Assistants, Hygienists, Therapists and Technicians, enabled dental students not merely to come into contact with other members of the team but to work and learn with them in a training unit specifically designed and equipped for team training.

in which students sit and patients take it lying down.

The change in facilities altered the nature of dental training as much as did the changes made in the course itself. But equally important was the change made in the climate of the school by its engagement in research. Though not without distinguished researchers in the past it had depended largely on teaching (mainly by example of high quality) from practitioners who could give only part-time to the school. In its reconstituted form all its different departments became actively engaged in research thereby imparting a new emphasis to teaching leading to a less empirical and more enquiring approach. Equally important research activities attracted very considerable financial support in areas as diverse as the Medical Research Council's Dental Epidemiology Unit under Geoffrey Slack, Professor Braden's department of Materials Science and Harry Allred's Experimental Dental Care Project funded by the Department of Health.

The story of the new Dental School is very much a success story, full of activity in education, research and the care of patients. Even a brief account of its development under four successive Deans of Dental Studies (Slack, Duckworth, Seward and Allred) can give the impression of a separate entity, distinct from the Medical College as a whole. In reality the Dental School in the seventies, notwithstanding a necessary degree of autonomy, was very much a part of the College - with dental and medical students more closely integrating than previously, dental teachers contributing to College management, much collaborative research, and a major part in the development of the Dental School being played not only by specialised pre-clinical teachers such as Ron Fearnhead (Professor of Dental Anatomy) but by all pre-clinical departments, and especially by Hugh Laird, the College Secretary.

The Medical School's opportunity to adapt its curriculum to the changing nature of medicine, and to the even more rapidly changing conditions of medical care, came with the University's revision of the regulations for the MB,BS degrees in the early seventies following the Todd report. It was not, however, preceded by new buildings as was the case with the Dental School and decisions had to be made while new academic staff were being recruited, not after they had taken post. In addition the curriculum had to be such as to allow up to 40 students to join from Oxford or Cambridge after studying the basic medical sciences which would be difficult to achieve in a 'horizontally integrated' course with clinical and preclinical subjects taught together from the start. There was little support anyway for such integration in the pre-clinical departments and the service committments of the clinical staff would have made it difficult for many to arrange to teach at times dictated solely by the curriculum. There was little hesitation therefore in deciding to follow the 'University-Sponsored' course consisting of two years devoted mainly to basic medical sciences followed by a clinical course of nearly three years. 'School-based' examinations (set and held in the school but with additional external examiners) were chosen in preference to those provided centrally by the University but the timing of them had of course to conform with the regulations of the London MB: Part I at the end of the first year, Parts II and III at the end of the second, Part IV (Pathology) after no less than three years, and clinical examinations at the end of the course.

The new regulations required the inclusion in the first two years of Psychology and Sociology 'as applied to Medicine' and the principles of Biometry and Medical Statistics with examinations in them at the end of the second year. In consequence although the preclinical course was extended from five terms to six it remained crowded with the addition of the new subjects to Anatomy, Physiology, Biochemistry and Pharmacology. It says much for staff and students that the great majority of the latter succeeded in mastering this multiplicity of subjects at least to the extent of passing examinations. Of necessity information gathering took priority over any other kind of intellectual development but projects remained a part of the course in Pharmacology and were included in Sociology and to some extent in other subjects. Students for the most part were remarkably happy and many found time for activities other than study.

In designing the new clinical course account had to be taken of the fact that it was over three months shorter than before, that there would be only one entry each year instead of two, that the number of students would increase and that opportunities had to be provided in the later part of it for students to integrate for themselves all they had previously learned in different parts of the course. The programme finally decided upon consisted of three Phases of approximately equal duration. The first was designed to enable the student to acquire basic clinical method, basic knowledge of Pathology and Clinical Medicine, an understanding of the common disorders of function and structure, the development of symptoms and signs and the objects and principles of treatment. Individual firms in Whitechapel and Mile End each provided a short introductory course for a small number of students. A foundation course followed based on pathology, medicine and surgery, with firms in Newham as well as Tower Hamlets. The phase was then completed with a second medical and surgical firm and a short Pathology course.

The second phase of some ten months was designed to give students an awareness of the special problems, skills and scope of the major specialities. The third provided opportunities for integration through experience in Child Health, General Practice, Outpatients, a District Hospital outside London, a short medical and surgical firm at the London - with a final period for revision and two months elective sometime during the phase.

R Duckworth, Professor of Oral Medicine (Dean of Dental Studies, 1969 to 1975, Dean of the College from 1986).

H Allred, Professor of Conservative Dentistry (Dean of Dental Studies, 1979 to 1985).

A committee of staff elected from the various groups involved in teaching and of students elected from each of the years in the school, was established to monitor the curriculum, through an annual review conducted mainly by students. Through this "Education Committee" students became aware of those constraints which in different ways at different times affect all schools, and staff became aware of what students actually experienced in each part of the course. The need for continuing modification became clearly apparent - with students contributing greatly not only to the motivation for change but to ways and means of achieving it.

In its general arrangement and structure the London's medical curriculum in the seventies remained a modified version of that which had evolved in the late fifties and the sixties, responding to changes in medical care and hospital organisation rather than reflecting any new philosophy of education. Outwardly still traditional, at least in its subdivision into pre-clinical and clinical parts, it nevertheless differed profoundly from the kind of vocational training which had originated in and been so well developed at the London itself. Students of the London in the seventies were able perhaps to see a wider range of people and conditions than ever before, in a wider range of hospitals, and other situations (including the home except in regard to midwifery) and to see even more through illustrations included in teaching or provided in slides and videos for study in their own time. They met perhaps fewer children and young adults as patients but more with chronic disorders and far more old people - fewer with florid easily diagnosed acute organic disease (except on electives spent in third world countries) and many more with complex problems and psychological and social difficulties. Comparison of the notes written by students and house officers in the seventies with those written by their predecessors of forty years earlier reveals infinitely more recorded about the patient as a person.

On the other hand this wide range of experience came mainly from observation of, rather than from participation in, the care of patients - even in subjects such as midwifery. Final year firms, with only one or two senior students attached to each firm, provided opportunities for sharing in all its business activities and most enjoyed one or more periods of two weeks each acting as 'locum' or student assistant in lieu of house officers on leave. Even so, at the London as elsewhere, students could no longer function as doctors in the way their predecessors had done in the past, mainly because patients no longer needed the kinds of treatment which had at one time been given by students. Throughout almost the whole clinical course a doctor-patient relationship had by the seventies been replaced by a student-patient relationship, making it more difficult to acquire a high degree of competence in those clinical skills such as gaining information from, or imparting information to, patients and relatives. Similarly that knowledge of people and of their reactions to illness and doctors, which is acquired most easily by sharing responsibility for their care, was

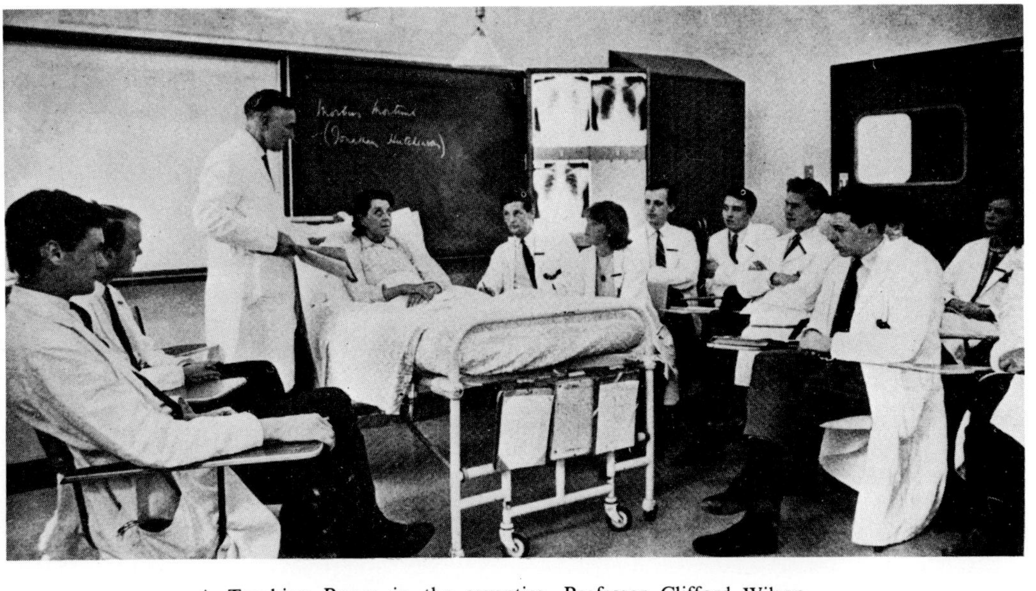

A Teaching Room in the seventies, Professor Clifford Wilson.

now outwith the reach of students and had become another of the objectives to be achieved in the next stage of training.

By the seventies too the range of teaching methods in use at the London, as in most medical schools, was greater than ever before. On general firms some physicians and surgeons continued the time-honoured practice of passing from bed to bed accompanied by students and junior staff, confirming diagnoses, discussing treatment, making decisions or approving those already taken. Others used the privacy of teaching rooms both for teaching students and for discussion of each patient's problems by the firm as a whole (including nursing and other staff) and for deciding policy in regard to them. In special departments even greater diversity prevailed - some clinging to bedside teaching of a traditional kind, others endeavouring in different ways and to differing degrees to offer a more systematised introduction to the specialty, making increasing use of educational technology in the process.

The most striking contrast with the past, however, was in the number and variety of staff with whom students came in contact. Whereas in the 1870s less than fifty teachers provided the entire course for an annual entry of between 60 and 100 students, in the 1970s each entry of 100 received the attentions of almost fifty teachers in the pre-clinical course alone. Each clinical student in every entry of 140 would come into contact with well over 100 teachers, and still have no occasion to meet another fifty - many teachers meeting only a proportio of the whole student body. Staff-student relationship were less close, not only because students shared less i the work of clinical units (no longer responsible to th 'chief' for his patients so much as attached to one o more consultants or to a department) but also becaus all attachments were for relatively short periods. Fo most students therefore the closest and longest lastin influence in the clinical course was the clinical tutor more than half of whom by the seventies were senio members of staff making in spare-time and for little o no financial recompense a major contribution t education.

There are of course advantages to students in bein able to observe a wide variety of doctors, eac demonstrating different attitudes as well as differen skills, duties and interests. The problem, however, o maintaining communications and a cohesive teachin team is considerable when several hundred teacher are contributing to a College in many differen subjects, disciplines and specialities in a wide variety o hospitals, clinics and general practices - especiall when a vital part of the team is comprised of junio hospital staff who themselves are in training an constantly changing. The administration of time tables and the deployment of teaching space an equipment alone constitutes a formidable admin istrative challenge, faced at the London by the sam General Office which Mr Osman as Registrar ha bequeathed to Fred Webb. With little more space an a relatively modest increase in personnel it coped in a

'Self teaching facilities' — tapes, slides and videos in the Museum.

near miraculous way with the ever-increasing paperwork and the complex network of communications on which a modern medical school depends.

The best educational ideas, the best teachers and students, the most excellent resources of every kind including patients, come to nought if the administration is unable to maintain that final common path through which must pass every communication from the school, staff and students - and back again. Information on the reactions to the course and of the progress of individual students during it is as vital a part of communication as the timetable, the allocation of students to it and the objectives it is intended to achieve. Examinations, themselves a considerable administrative undertaking, provide valuable information but reports on students at every stage are more important and the nature of the information sought serves as a reminder to teachers of the objectives of each stage.

Back in the 1860s it was the need to know how each student performed as a clerk, dresser or house-officer, so as to ensure that those appointed to more responsible posts were ready for them which led Walter Rivington to propose better administration in the form of a Dean and Vice-Dean and led later to the appointment of a Secretary and an administrative structure. In the 1970s the College again faced a need to reconsider its administration, which led to a reorganisation of its governance as a whole but which did not on this occasion produce any crisis in regard to the enormous task of administering the curriculum because of the presence of a small number of highly experienced individuals totally dedicated to it. No medical school can ever have been better served than the London was at this time by Hugh Laird, the College Secretary, Pamela Wise his Assistant, and Kay Reynolds whose title of Assistant to the Dean gave no indication of the vast number of functions she fulfilled with quiet and tireless efficiency. No medical students can ever have been given better personal attention than that given to those of the London by Doris Sadler, Assistant Registrar.

So communication with teachers increased and students received guidance on how to make best use of the course by all the means possible. Information from students was provided, most effectively, regularly and systematically by them. Information on their progress was sought from all teachers, provided by most and in greatest detail by their tutors. It served to identify the best and the relatively small number facing difficulties but had little to say about the many in between. It provided the majority of students with little indication of their progress beyond the fact that it was satisfactory but it enabled the Dean and the three Senior Tutors reading reports on every student every few months in the first clinical year and therafter almost every month, to keep the state of the school and the progress of each year continually under review.

It is normally difficult to compare one school with another but at the end of the seventies the University of London made comparative studies of the 12 schools. These showed that the London had been considerably less demanding than all but one of the schools in the Advanced level grades required of entrants but over the decade had scored more first time passes in the MB than almost any other, and by far the highest proportion of First Class Honours in those of its students taking an intercalated BSc. Examination results are only one, and not necessarily the best, criterion by which to judge the outcome of an education. They tell more of the knowledge and perhaps the skills attained than of the degree of intellectual development achieved or the attitudes acquired. They tell nothing of career aims but annual national studies of house officers showed that throughout this period Londoners were attracted to most branches of medicine and that when schools were graded according to the number of graduates aiming at a career in general practice the London came consistently in the top half.

In the early seventies the school was unusual in not requiring every student to spend time in general practice. Instead it encouraged and enabled those interested to do so, with the result that up to three quarters of each entry were attached for varying periods to selected practices, many being attached at different times to both a practice in the East End and to an Old Londoner in some other, contrasting, part of the country. When the new clinical curriculum came into operation in 1976 and University regulations required all students to spend a period in general practice, the experience of many students of the London became less than it would otherwise have been. Objectives for this attachment were drawn up by a committee of staff and students and approved by the Academic Board. Most of the GPs who had previously contributed agreed to continue to do so and the attachment of students to them could be made effective by Doris Sadler's close knowledge of both students and teachers.

Most students however ceased to seek extra time in this

The Clubs Union Bar

field and preferred to use their two or more months Elective in some other way. Similarly few chose to use their Elective for further and deeper experience of the wide range of excellent specialist departments at the London so that, as so often happens, insistence on students seeing as much as possible of everything resulted in all seeing a little more than they could easily profit from in quick succession and few having the deeper experience which most specialities can make so valuable for some students. The desire to have as much as possible of every student's time naturally slows progress towards enabling special departments to make the full contribution to the undergraduate course of which they are capable.

Leaving aside the use of special departments, however, the medical curriculum of the London in the seventies probably took as much advantage as possible of the wide range of resources available. Though not likely to stretch the intellects of the many very able students, and offering too few opportunities designed specifically for intellectual development, it nonetheless appeared to be enjoyed by most. All the available evidence suggested that students applied themselves effectively to the course, though lacking the incentives provided in the past by responsibility to patients and with little opportunity to learn by doing. With a pass rate of around 90% in finals fear of examinations was noticeably reduced and presumably students were motivated largely by their own interest in the content of the course and to some extent by the interest taken in them by their teachers - which is usually enhanced when students are keen, caring, and (in both senses) smart, as those of the seventies undoubtedly were.

vi

Enthusiasm and energy characterised most aspects of student life in the 1970s. The larger number of students, the total number of undergraduates rising in excess of 800, stretched facilities at Hale End to the limit despite the considerable extension of them which had been made by taking over the adjoining playing fields. The larger number of women brought new successes in womens hockey and rowing without affecting other sports, the College enjoying one golden period in which it won all the major competitions. Societies had their ups and downs, only the oldest, the Medical Society, disappearing (like the Boxing Club) seemingly for ever - perhaps because its function of creating a forum for the discussion of topical, particularly ethical, issues could be fulfilled by the London Medical Group providing a central organisation serving all the schools. By contrast the Dramatic Society became increasingly active, its productions surpassing those of earlier periods in both number and quality.

The Clubs Union building, subject like all the Whitechapel campus, to repeated break-ins, caught fire and the Athenaeum and Bar were gutted. In 1976 the Clubs Union or the College Secretary to be precise, faced the Inland Revenue over the liability of part of its income to Income Tax. In the High Court the Attorney General found Hugh Laird to be a witness of unusual vigour and clarity, and that the Union's Constitution proved it to be still firmly tied to those purposes of student welfare for which it had been founded. There being no question of the Union being used for educational, political, religious or other activities, the case was won. On the other hand the Clubs Union dinner died for want of interest, neither staff nor students finding much satisfaction in speeches from the lesser ranks of show business or minor media personalities, despite the opportunities for throwing as well as eating food. Its demise was followed by a different kind of dinner subsidised by the Union and the College, attended by those students and staff who had served the Clubs and Societies over the year, and enabling the Union to entertain guests from the University and other Colleges, the Health Service and those in many walks of life who in one way or another help its members. The change from its members being entertained to the Union entertaining others continued to fulfill the original function of staff and students dining together, whilst at the same time enabling both to make social contact with a variety of others - ranging from Vice-Chancellors, heads of Colleges and Health Authorities to representatives of the local community, including the Local Authority, the clergy, police, the local Banks and the many others on whose goodwill much in a medical school depends.

Autumn Balls in the College Hall continued to follow Summer Balls somewhere up West - both increasingly popular and sometimes including a quiet period or even a room in which the older generation could cut their voices down to a loud shout and actually converse with each other. Christmas became a time at which all the College and much of the Hospital closed down after a week or two of anticipatory celebration by numerous departmental parties and a Christmas Show of great ingenuity, much enjoyment and an interesting monitoring system comprised of past producers and performers. New events included an Old Peoples' Party involving students in as much work collecting and returning the guests as in entertaining them. A summer festival and participation with other colleges in a rag week were other innovations. Sports day continued most years - fun and games of various kinds replacing many of the more serious athletic contests of former days but some time-honoured events retaining popularity as witness the Dean's Report in 1977 describing the victory of Willie Evans in what had been the Chiefs' but had become the Consultants' Race.

'A combination of handicap, a good get-away, gathering momentum and less than excellent hearing resulted in his failing to heed the recall for a false start necessitated by Mike Floyer's still youthful eagerness. The sight of Willie breasting the tape alone was an inspiration to the young and a relief to at least one of his old students who had visions of bending over a prostate body repeating to himself as taught long ago "Can I hear the first sound?"'

Thus the range of student activities grew greater than ever before, involving perhaps a greater proportion of students, and including a very efficient Accommodation Committee handling rooms and flats in East London much needed by students despite a bigger Hostel and a share, with Barts and Queen Mary College, in a new Hall of Residence in Woodford, provided for the three Colleges by an anonymous donor. Inevitably however staff became less aware of student activities than in the past when the numbers of both were smaller, the activities fewer and the Clubs Union itself was situated in the main College building. Seeing less of each other and leading increasingly different lives students had difficulty in realising that staff needed considerable notice and frequent reminders of even the most attractive events. Conversely students knew less than in the past of hospital activities and consequently could no longer produce a Gazette with coverage of the London as a whole, equally interesting to students, staff, and Old Londoners.

The last issue of the old Gazette came out in 1975 but happily coincided with fresh efforts by the Medical Club to revive its original function of serving the Alumni. Until the first world war its Council, made up partly of Hospital and College Staff, and partly of Londoners from elsewhere, had maintained the Old Londoners' Dinner, reunions and all the various activities relating to past students. During the first war these ceased and after it they were restarted by the Medical Council of the Hospital, leaving the Club to run the Benevolent Fund and the Agency which provided locums and assistants for Old Londoners in general practice. After the second world war, the Council of the Club, led by George Neligan, Alan Brews and Will Tegner, was anxious to resume its original functions but the Medical Council was happy to continue with them and did. By the seventies however the Dinner was failing to attract and it was clear that a more determined effort was necessary to maintain communications between the London and Londoners.

The end of the Gazette not only broke the last connecting link but provided the opportunity for a new one. The Club devised a new form of subscribing membership, produced a new Gazette and with a subsidy from the College sent it to all Old Londoners of known address and to several hundred who were no longer known at the address they had left behind them. Nonetheless enough were reached to achieve enthusiastic support for the new arrangements and the Medical Club became once again the body responsible for the medical Alumni. The Dental Club, which, though younger, had from its start been an extremely successful and efficient guardian of the affairs of dental Old Londoners, joined with the Medical Club to produce a Gazette which is designed to keep all Londoners in touch with the London and reaches all subscribing members of either Club providing only that they pay their subscription and keep the Editor informed of their correct address.

vii

By 1970 previous systems of communication were breaking down in many, if not most, walks of life. The Health Service was no exception even before its reorganisation in 1974 created the four tiers of District, Area, Region and Department of Health and Social Security. In the London Hospital itself the medical advisory system had begun in the 1830s when the House Committee requested their medical officers to hold regular meetings and appoint one of their number as a spokesman with whom it could communicate. This had to all intents and purposes been absorbed into the London Hospital College Council in 1855 but when Hospital and College amalgamated in 1879 and the College Board took over management of the College, the Council soon became mainly concerned with Hospital matters. After the separation of Hospital and College in 1948 it concerned itself again with the

The Gazette's first cover by Professor Henry Tonks of the Slade School of Art, one-time Lecturer in Anatomy LHMC.

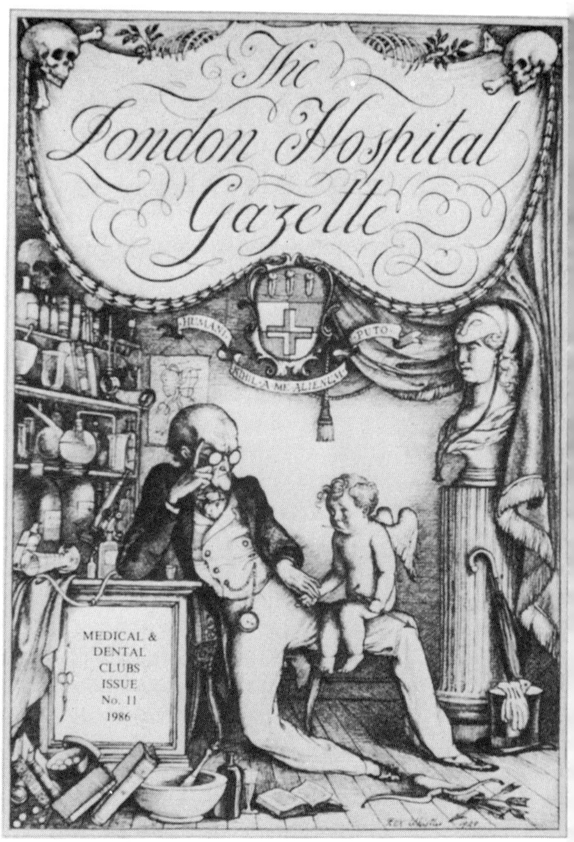

The cover by Rex Whistler in use since 1929

affairs of the school but the Academic Board grew gradually in strength and by 1970 had begun to appoint its own chairman (Clifford Wilson being the first) and become the body to which the College Governors looked for advice - while the Hospital Governors looked to the Council.

By that time, however, the Medical Council (though consisting only of consultants, clinical professors and readers) had grown to such a size that the old hospital Board Room could accommodate little more than a third of its members. Had the same third attended regularly every month the Council could have provided the Board of Governors with more consistent advice but, human nature being what it is, attendance tended to depend upon the agenda - with the inevitable consequence that motions passed by those attending one meeting were not infrequently rescinded by those attending the next. It was decided therefore to establish Departments (in the clinical as well as the pathological subjects) enabling the consultants in each to collaborate in defining a policy for the practice and development of it which they would loyally support. It was decided also to group like Departments into Divisions. Departmental problems and aspirations could then be considered in a wider forum and, provided Departments functioned efficiently, Divisions could effectively feed an executive or Final committee of the Council or the Council itself.

After 1974 this system was extended to include all hospitals in the Tower Hamlets District. It was capable of effectively channelling medical advice to the District Management Team and of enabling the latter to communicate with all medical staff to whatever extent it felt inclined - which, initially, was less than was necessary and on occasion achieved by direct contact with individuals thus by-passing the advisory system and undermining confidence in it. The District Management Team likewise had difficulty in maintaining communications between hospital staff and the Area Health Authority. The Regional Health Authority, despite a variety of somewhat tenuous links, remained largely out of reach of medical advice from the consultants providing medical care in its hospitals.

The College also faced problems of communication. Like most educational institutions the efficiency of its courses depended on maintaining contact with an ever increasing number of teachers; the financing of most of its 800 undergraduates and growing number of postgraduate students depended on regular reports of progress to innumerable grant-giving bodies. Similarly the improvement of pre-registration training required another whole system of communications with both trainers and trainees. At the same time, like all medical schools, but unlike schools in any other university faculty, it had to relate in the most intimate way (ranging from payment of cleaners to matters of high policy) with a government health service, at the level of the London and other hospitals, the Districts of Tower Hamlets and Newham, the Area Health Authority, various Postgraduate Authorities, and the Region. To most of these it had to relate both directly and also through the federal University of London, necessitating the creation of new mechanisms for bringing together for example all the schools in each Region.

Meanwhile the College itself had outgrown the system of governance created when it separated from the London Hospital in 1948. In 1946 it had employed 30 academic and 22 other staff and had received an income of £67,000. In 1969 its staff had risen to 165 academics and 195 others and its income was nearly 1.25 million. By 1978 it had 263 academic and 221 other staff and an income of around 4 million. The Academic Board which in 1948 had 22 members (of whom 10 were part-time hospital physicians or surgeons) had grown by the inclusion of every new professor but still had only slight representation of readers and almost no other staff save for cooption of the Medical and Dental Sub-Deans. Moreoever its proceedings, inheriting past tradition in such matters, were officially secret: papers being delivered to members by hand in envelopes marked Stictly Private and Confidential. Academic Staff below professorial rank sought solace in a Staff Association.

In the early seventies a Working Party was set up to consider ways and means of improving the system of governance. Its recommendations aimed to achieve better communications throughout the College, more effective participation in governance by staff of all levels and by students, more effective representation of staff involved in inter-departmental and extra-departmental activities, and better liason between the College and other bodies. It proposed a system of academic departments and academic clinical units relating to Academic Divisions of Basic Medical Science, Pathology, Medicine, Surgery and Dentistry. It suggested a broadly based Academic Board, representing all levels of staff (through Divisions), containing all appointed teachers (professors and readers) and a small number of students.

Divisions were established in 1975, their functions, composition and procedure being laid down by the Governors on the advice of the Academic Board. The recommendation that there should be a Standing or Executive Committee of the latter did not find favour, but events soon proved that when the Board needed to refer functions to a smaller body (as for example the review of staffing in the light of its economic resources) it could be created by election from the five Divisions. The latter provided a simple means also of constituting boards or committees for the day to day management of various facilities - such as the Library, Audio-visual communications, Computers, Museums, Teaching and Research Space. While responsibility for defining the College's educational policy remained with the Academic Board, and curriculum committees maintained to implement it, the Medical and Dental staff-student committees (with joint staff and student chairmen) were made responsible to the Board for keeping each course under review, ensuring feed-back, and identifying areas where change might be needed.

Thus the College tried to find a governance structure which would enable it to function effectively as a much larger organisation in a new and uncertain world. The changes made were considerable even though initially proposed by the oldest rather than the youngest serving members. Students showed the most reluctance to being incorporated into 'management' but once involved contributed conscientiously. Some staff, on the other hand, found it easier to define the responsibilities of their respective posts than to fulfill them. But those who found the changes most difficult were of course the 'administration' who carried the main burden of implementing a new system of management after many years spent applying that which was being replaced.

In 1978, describing the previous ten years, the Dean wrote: 'Such a period would have severely tested a school already fully developed, housed and equipped - with its organisation already adapted to new conditions. That the London has not merely come through, but so far has come through successfully, emerging stronger and more cohesive than 10 years ago, is because it has been able to count on Hugh Laird working ceaselessly and with a single-minded dedication to the College as a whole, accepting change, making change, never losing sight of the strength of the past, and combining consideration for those now in the College with care for those who will come after. Few people are confronted with such a situation in the last third of a working life spent in one place, and fewer still rise to the occasion' (35).

H P Laird

J W Walmsley

College Secretaries:

The new organisation was in action but still novel and untried when Hugh Laird retired in 1978 and the College had to search for a successor. From a large field, containing applicants with experience of university and medical administration, it chose a young Lieutenant-Colonel still serving in the Royal Marines. James Walmsley joined in the autumn of 1978, having characteristically prepared himself by reading everything written about the College, past, present and future, beginning with Clark-Kennedy's history of the London. Taking office 102 years after the first of his five predecessors - Dr Kershaw, Dr Chevers the Principal, Munro Scott the Warden, Burdon and Laird - he was confronted with a more formidable task than any of them and immediately proved equal to every aspect of it.

In 1978 also the Gazette recorded the departure of other familiar figures: 'Few Old Londoners of the past thirty years or so will have difficulty in remembering John Entract, librarian, military historian, firm believer in the traditional English virtues and occasional accordion player...At the end of March Fred Webb retired after completing fitfy years in the service of the College, but will continue as Clerk to the London Hospital Medical Club and Technical Editor of the Gazette. It is impossible to overestimate the value of such a contribution to the College, but a measure of the respect and affection in which he is held by Old Londoners was shown by the hundreds of letters from all over the world which arrived - with cheques totalling £1,500' (36).

Webb's successor as Registrar, Jim Butter, found a different academic administration from that which Fred had inherited. The Dental Sub-Dean had been replaced by a Dean of Dental Studies (Harry Allred) a Postgraduate Dental Tutor (Roy Duckworth) and a Senior Clinical Tutor (Dental) (F C Smales). In place of a Medical Sub Dean there were a Postgraduate Sub Dean (A D M Jackson), three Senior Clinical Tutors (F J Goodwin, A H McDonald and F P Marsh), a Senior Tutor for Medicine (M A Floyer), a Senior Tutor for Surgery (A D W Maclean) with Rea Johnson as Pre-Clinical Sub Dean and the chairmen of Divisions and various Sub-committees. The College had thus a considerable number of staff, drawn partly but not mainly from its 36 Professors, sharing the burden of administration with the Dean - carrying responsibility for different extradepartmental activities in addition to departmental functions and well informed about the College as a whole.

viii

The changes made during the seventies by the College in its size, staffing, organisation, buildings and courses, would have been easier had they been started earlier and proceeded gradually in calmer conditions. As it was they had of necessity to be made quickly and the opportunity for development which was present in the early seventies was all too soon overtaken by national economic collapse. While the Health Service struggled with rising demands and falling income, coincidental reorganisation and the unhappy attempt to equalise diminishing resources across the country by re-allocation, severe cuts in university funding combined with inflation and the abandonment of the quinquennial system to make the financing of every medical school a perilous process of moving precariously from crisis to crisis. All too often schools remained in ignorance of their annual income until the end of the financial year, with problems of cash flow solved by last minute unheralded additional payments.

Throughout these difficulties the London and Barts maintained their close collaboration, warmly supported by Queen Mary College, (under its new Principal Sir James Menter), combining in a joint approach to Area, Region and University, all of which grew accustomed to their speaking with one voice. As Reggie Shooter, Dean of Barts, rightly claimed at the London's Clubs Union Dinner, 'twinning' enabled Deans to share not only their problems but the daunting task of representing their schools. Yet twinning was little favoured elsewhere. The University's new Joint Medical Advisory Committee reviewed the Todd recommendations yet again without evoking enthusiasm for them. Only 'BLQ', after being referred back to the University by the BLQ Joint Policy Committee itself at the instigation of representatives of the London, was reaffirmed as University policy after detailed review.

The Postgraduate Institutes in particular had the greatest difficulty in agreeing on any policy for their individual or collective future. At the London alone hours of thought and effort were devoted to long drawn out negotiations with Great Ormond Street and the Institute of Child Health, the St Peter's Hospitals and the Institute of Urology, Moorfields and the Institute of Ophthalmology, St Mark's, and the London School of Hygiene and Tropical Medicine. Important agreements were reached with some and joint appointments made with others. Successive

R M M Pryor,
Chairman of the Council of Governors, 1956-1986.

tripartite committees of NHS, UGC and University wrestled with the same problems, instigated reviews and established working parties to go over ground already surveyed by the same authorities independently. Meanwhile the various postgraduate university medical institutions in London continued, like the undergraduate schools, to appoint the academic staff each needed, the proportion of the total University Court resources made available to medicine rose from 30.6% in 1969/70 to 35.5% in 1978/79, and the University's total financial provision went down in real terms, with promise of worse to come.

So ten years after the Todd Report had recommended additional money (to enable 6 paired London schools to enjoy the same academic development in medicine as other universities), one pair of schools, 10 single schools and numerous postgraduate institutions had undergone varying degrees of development which could no longer be maintained in the face of a collapsing national economy and the rationalisation of London Hospitals. A working group established by the Conference of Metropolitan Deans had already concluded that if a state were reached when the total revenue available to Medicine in the University was insufficient to enable all schools and institutes to continue as viable units, it would be necessary to consider closing one or more of them. It had also suggested that two major capital projects - BLQ and the University College Royal Free project, were so large and expensive that the possibility of achieving them was remote. It came as no great surprise when the Vice-Chancellor, Lord Annan, decided to set up a Working Party to undertake a major review of resources for medical and dental education in London.

The Working Party began its enquiry in March 1979 under the Chairmanship of Lord Flowers, Rector of Imperial College. It was told to assume that the current number of undergraduate and postgraduate students would be maintained and that the total funding of medical and dental education in London would not be reduced as a direct consequence of its recommendations. It was requested to recommend what redeployment of resources should be adopted to maintain present standards; to recommend which if any schools or institutes should be closed; how to achieve any closure or redeployment with minimal upset to staff, students teaching and research; and to report on completion of its task in 1980. These ominous terms of reference reflected the extent to which the problems which Todd had set out to solve in 1965 had been magnified by both action and inaction while the country moved from a time of growth to one of deep recession.

This return to the situation of a decade earlier was particularly hard for the London and Barts who, virtually alone among the 30 medical university institutions in London, had together loyally followed for 10 years the course laid down for them in 1969. Instead of moving forward to BLQ, on the anticipation of which their joint development had been based throughout, they found themselves required, like everywhere else, to go through yet another process of reappraisal with all the uncertainty and suspension of progress such a process always brings. Both Deans had intended to retire in 1978 but had agreed to stay on, in the interest of continuity while College Secretaries changed, until 1980. Both were now asked to stay on until 1981. The Dean of Barts agreed. I thought that after 12 years as Dean, one as Vice Dean, and an earlier 10 years as Sub-Dean, both the College and I deserved a change. I felt that the next two years would be crucial to the future of the London but in the

the Summer of 1979 I also knew that I could not hope to maintain the same tempo of work and effectively fulfill the same, let alone greater, responsibilities until 1981. I could not, in fairness to the College and all concerned, agree to continue as Dean for two more difficult years without some reduction in the duties of Dean and unless someone else were appointed forthwith to share the remainder.

One of the more arduous tasks carried by the Dean and the Dean's Secretary at the London, but by other staff in most other schools, was the management of the selection and admissions to the medical school, with oversight of the same in the dental school. In recent years David Maclean had given increasing help with this and in 1979 (an office and secretarial staff having been provided) generously accepted appointment as Sub-Dean for Admissions notwithstanding the demands of general surgery in two hospitals.

In September 1979 the Academic Board recommended to the Governors that David Ritchie, Professor of Surgery, should be appointed Dean-Elect to share the remaining duties of Dean and me until September 1981. This was agreed.

The Rowing Club returns to the River Lea.

Chapter 12.

The End of the Beginning

i

The last five of the first two hundred years of the College are not yet far enough away to be presented other than as a picture painted in broad strokes, highlighting what seem from a personal viewpoint to be important features, outlining figures departing from the scene but leaving all others grouped together as a mass in the foregound without any attempt to pick out those, whoever they may be, who are even now shaping the future.

The background, the context in which the College stands at the end of two centuries, is for the most part sombre, with brighter patches here and there. Ignorance of the origins of many major causes of disease and death still limits prevention in countries like Britain. But medicine's ability to help by more accurate diagnosis and more effective treatment continues to grow - along with its potential for harm unless practised under good conditions after both education and training, and with the benefit of continuing education. So costs continue to rise and, coupled with inflation and ever-expanding demand, ensure that an NHS provided with more money than ever before is hard put to maintain the quantity and quality of service previously provided, let alone extend and improve care in fields hitherto covered only in a rudimentary fashion.

The price that has to be paid for increasing the provision made for the old and the handicapped by limiting that for the acute sick is now apparent. The cost of providing more care in the community is becoming clear. District hospitals upgraded by re-allocated funds lead to more referrals than can be coped with by university medical centres whose growth has been cut back. In order to improve the situation created by the reorganisation of 1974 the Service has been reorganised again in 1982 and 1985 requiring all senior administrative staff, (lay, medical, nursing or other) on each occasion, to be interviewed and appointed to their own or some other posts, made supernumerary or prematurely retired.

Yet the Service has been maintained and its basic strength compares favourably with what is available in other countries. Such facts, however, tend to be obscured by political argument from a public which hears more about shortage of money than the increase in service which has been achieved in many areas. So widespread public dissatisfaction exists and is exacerbated by the concentration of resources, (especially the closure of small, unsuitable, expensive hospitals,) on which not only improvement but the maintenance of current standards depends. Inevitable expansion of the private sector does little to lessen the dissatisfaction of those who pay for it, or those who do not but benefit from it none the less. Hope and expectation of improvement have been replaced by fear of collapse.

Apprehension about the state of medical care is enhanced by the increasing fear of ill health which naturally accompanies a rising standard of living, which itself brings a concern for the handicapped seldom manifested in the past when the quality of life for the unhandicapped left so much to be desired. At the same time greater longevity brings more rather than less fear of death, and certainly more fear of ageing. Paradoxically, better health has increased apprehension about the medical care which helped to create it. As a result medicine and medical services provide a welcome target for mass media desperately seeking an additional means of capturing the attention of customers sated with a daily diet of sex, violence, crime, corruption and terrorism.

News of medical failings can be made more sensational than the news of progress or possible break-throughs - but is handled selectively. The state of hospital kitchens, hidden from public view, is newsworthy and can be attributed to inadequate inspection. Dirty wards and corridors are commonplace and cleaners are members of unions whose sole function is to protect them. Medicine is a different matter. Doctors, as a profession, have been accustomed to submitting to a corporate discipline which exists not for the good of the members but of the public in contact, the patients. There is therefore no organisation which can speak for the profession as a whole on clinical issues. Grey areas, in which much depends on medical judgement are highly news-worthy, even if highlighting them inevitably leads to more confusion than illumination. Any hospital can be impugned in the certainty that neither it nor any other can respond.

So dissatisfaction with medical services is accompanied by loss of confidence in doctors, from whom so much is expected partly because of an inflated belief in their powers and partly because of a decline of faith in most other sources of help and support. Loss of confidence brings a natural desire to limit the doctors' powers by legislation for every eventuality, and a wish for more participation by the public in the management of services, and by the patient in the management of his own problems - the desire being inversely proportional to the understanding of how complex the problems may be. The need for better communications between the public and medicine, and the patient and his doctor, grows daily - ironically accompanied by preparedness to trust to treatments which, especially if labelled unorthodox, are thought to require no rational explanation. Recourse is sought to what is called 'Alternative Medicine' though 'Additional' might be a more appropriate term in the absence of any decline in the demand for 'Orthodox Medicine'.

Not surprisingly morale of those who work in the Health Service generally is not high, though bolstered by the fact that those who provide care are more aware than others of the extent to which they are succeeding in overcoming the difficulties with which they have been confronted. Morale is lowest perhaps among doctors, particularly those in hospitals which have been hardest hit. They include the teaching hospitals in London, some of which have suffered more than others from the reorganisation of 1982 when Area Health Authorities were abolished. The City and East London Area, for example, was serving a population of half a million in a few square miles, together with an equal number of referrals and commuters. Its continuation as a District would have allowed the continued development of an effective service. Its fragmentation into three Districts, the smallest (Tower Hamlets) having a population of 140,000, was a serious set back which will not be quickly or easily overcome.

Morale in teaching centres is suffering also from cut backs in university funding. Huge reductions have been withstood only where full use has been made of the £153 million set aside by Government to achieve early retirement and enable the retired to continue teaching for a period of three years at no cost to the institution. The additional clinical academic staff appointed by London medical schools in the seventies, who succeeded in buffering the teaching hospitals against the reallocation of their funds elsewhere, have been whittled down or are forced to limit their academic functions of teaching and research in order to try and maintain service. Rationalisation of schools and hospitals still further taxes energy and enthusiasm.

Public sympathy for institutions and people caught in such a difficult and dangerous situation tends to be muted. There is some awareness that over forty years British medical education has moved from the 19th century concept of medical schools producing safe general practitioners to a three stage preparation of medical school, general training and specialised training. This is not perceived however as a necessary effort to ensure that doctors are adequately prepared to tackle the complexities of a new and rapidly changing medicine - and able to understand and thereby control the application of its new powerful and potentially dangerous scientific content. The British public has difficulty in distinguishing between scientific knowledge and the scientific method of thought which allows that knowledge to be used in the right way in the right amount at the right time.

The heavy involvement doctors are believed to have in 'high technology' leads not to the hope that they are intelligent enough and sufficiently well educated to control their machines, but rather to the suggestion that an interest in machines should be discouraged at an early age - despite the fact that the most technical specialities (on which so much else depends) have more difficulty in recruitment than others. Fears are expressed that medical schools are admitting students who are clever - which is seen both as a break with tradition and a sure way of excluding a warm human approach. These apprehensions are encouraged by an increase in 'academic' staff at a time when the image of a professor, in England at least, still lies somewhere between an absent-minded backroom boffin unable to take good care even of himself, and a latter-day research-crazed Dracula.

ii

Medical students of the 1980s certainly do differ from

those who have gone before them though the greater lack of homogeneity, itself a difference from fifty years ago, makes collective description difficult. The range of home and educational background of those entering some schools, particularly in London, is wider than it once was. The great majority have chosen medicine as a means of helping other people. A few visualise it as a way of putting the whole world to rights, but such ambitions are so often accompanied by difficulty with the basic sciences that some fail to gain admission, while others abandon the course on discovering that medicine is not after all well positioned to cure all the ills of mankind.

All applicants believe prevention to be more important than cure but almost all seek entry in order to make sick people better. Whereas in the past most wished to do so by physical means, using their own hands, the majority now favour a wider range of methods and see themselves restoring Mrs Brown or Mr Robinson to health by the judicious use of drugs and careful attention to the psyche. The change presumably reflects no more than the fact that surgery is no longer seen as the only or even the major means of successfully intervening in the course of disease. Some still want only to be surgeons and other early deciders wish to be general practitioners - a few have psychiatry in mind and almost none seek a life-time in research. Most have made no firm choice of career within medicine - but of those who enter as dental students more have firmly chosen dentistry as a career than in the past when perhaps too many turned to dentistry having failed to enter medicine.

Students at the London in the 1980s, medical and dental, can be fairly described as keen, able and interested in both people and medicine or dentistry. Most approach their studies more conscientiously than students in the past, without losing touch with life even in the first two years grotesquely crowded with subjects and examinations. Relatively few alternate lengthy stretches of blissfully avoiding teaching and learning with short periods of desperately attempting to memorise meaningless facts. The majority are keen to have more responsibility. A few begin increasingly to fear facing the reponsibilities from which they are kept for so long. Feelings of frustration and uselessness are more stressful than overwork or academic

The monastic existence is over.

difficulties.

Life in the Medical College is in many ways less restricted and isolated than it was. Students work in many different environments. Even apart from electives which are often spent in the most distant parts of the world, most are well-travelled. Contact with students of other health professions is usual, at least at the social level - necessitating yet another revision of the constitution of the Clubs Union in 1981 so as to enable more students of other health professions to enjoy the facilities of Clubs and Societies. The traditional monastic existence has long since gone, ended not only by the admission of women to medicine and dentistry, but also by the abandonment of those barriers to social contact between students and nurses the surmounting of which such required feats of ingenuity and daring. The widening of horizons and greater opportunities for a fuller life have not led to any lessening of interest in the College itself.

'Those who criticise the young in medicine today for being too clever, too technological, cold and narrow would be reassured by a few visits to the Union Building. They would find the range of social, cultural and athletic activities being pursued quite remarkable and any idea that this betokens merely the careless rapture of a world-within-a-world would soon be dispelled by the sight of students, oblivious of time and at their own expense, preparing themselves for the future by intensive practice in repelling space invaders' (37).

Traditional activities are pursued with as much energy and enthusiasm as in the past and the banner 'The London for the Cup' strung across the Marble Arch betokened more enterprise than sticking the same message all over the walls and windows of a rival school. New activities like Final Year Dinners to celebrate the end of the course in company with tutors, and Year Books containing portraits of all the class, indicate a desire to perpetuate happy memories. A Clubs Union Dinner with Princess Anne, Chancellor of the University, as Guest of Honour, natural enough in the eighties, would not have been contemplated by hosts or guests in earlier times.

While students have changed much, staff have not stood still. In fact one of the major differences between those of the 1980s and their predecessors is the extent to which they are on the move. One or two conferences, one period of examining at home and another overseas, together with participation in postgraduate and

continuing education, or the affairs of a specialist association or Royal College, (not to mention those of a federal University and the NHS) make demands which some meet out of holidays but which otherwise can result in being away for upwards of three months in the year. Relationships with students are more tenuous and many other factors, in medicine more than dentistry, (especially the fact that staff and students no longer work together to the same extent on the care of patients) have combined to change the nature of their contact with each other. Students, though not necessarily more critical of teaching than in the past, are more critical of teachers - though less well situated to evaluate the latters' responsibilities, aims or clinical performance. The relationship between consultant and students is not as close as was that between chief and dressers or clerks. It is less likely to lead to adulation and is sometimes a source of tension.

Dental students qualifying from the London in the 1980s are as ready to begin practice as their predecessors were. Newly qualified doctors of course are not. Their knowledge of medicine is more extensive than that of their predecessors but much of it has been little used since it was acquired and so is not easily accessible - that which was learned first being the most difficult to retrieve. In the past much less was learned about medicine but most of it was continually used in the diagnosis and treatment of patients for whom students were responsible, and in the process much was learned about people and their reactions to illness, adversity, medical care and doctors. The newly qualified of the 1980s have still to acquire that knowledge of people which comes only from participating in the care of different kinds of people suffering from different kinds of problems.

Those who have taken an intercalated BSc or had some similar learning experience during the five year course have had the opportunity to develop an enquiring, analytical approach, independent judgement and critical awareness. Others may have developed the same without the same specific experience. Most are well aware that learning is a process which must continue throughout professional life. All however have yet to develop most clinical skills.

Few have yet had much experience of giving information to patients and all have practised the skills of obtaining information from them only under the restricted conditions imposed by a student-patient relationship. The process tends to become one of history taking, with the emphasis on taking. Enthusiastic students, responding to enthusiastic teachers, are in danger of becoming trained to conduct an enquiry in a routine way, concentrating on the questions, and carefully recording the answers in a given sequence. What question should be asked next becomes of more importance than what the las answer might imply. Interpretation may be left unti 'all the evidence' has been obtained and written down by which time many cues have been missed and some clues obscured. Not surprisingly, when students become doctors and history-taking is replaced by interviewing patients, some find that the intuitive processes which were working overtime at the start of clinical studies are scarcely working at all at the end.

So the pre-registration year provides not only the chance to develop competence in clinical procedures but the first real opportunity to practice basic clinical method in the context of a doctor-patient relationship - using knowledge, skill and intuition in pursuit of a frequently changing hypothesis as to what the problems may be, and every now and then, ceasing to enquire in order to reassure or merely listen. Developing such technique can be a slow process for those who have fallen into the habit of 'taking the history' with what Sydenham called a mind empty of any hypothesis

Princess Anne, Chancellor and the Vice-Chancellor (Sir Randolph Quirk) attend the Clubs Union Dinner.

whatsoever.

For most the pre-registration year passes quickly and happily, caring for patients as a working member of a professional team. It usually creates a desire to learn more about many aspects of medicine which were covered in the undergraduate course but had little meaning in the absence of clinical experience. Most young doctors are anxious therefore to have a period of general professional training in which to get wider clinical experience, learn more about people, learn more about those subjects which have become more understandable and relevant, and find out which branch of medicine they are best suited for. Many however are even more anxious about career prospects than career choice and feel obliged to get started as quickly as possible on postgraduate training for a specialty or vocational training for general practice.

The temptation to forgo an important stage of medical education is all the greater because as yet it is neither officially required nor effectively organised. So more graduates avoid it and medical schools feel obliged to continue to give teaching that is premature because no later opportunity for it exists. Coverage remains a dominant factor in deciding the curriculum, which remains overcrowded even when integration is used to save time, by making the content more easily understandable and by cutting out unnnecessary repetition.

iii

In 1979 the College, its academic staff built up in conjunction with Barts, was ready to develop an educational strategy for the medical school as had been done for the dental school in the late sixties and early seventies. A working party was set up to consider the kind of school-based degree courses in medicine which could start when the new buildings became available. But long before the spring of 1982 when the Queen stood in the new Bearsted Theatre and declared the Alexandra Wing open, the attention of the College, and that of all other London Schools, had been diverted from completing the adaptation of medical education to modern medicine, and rivetted instead on

The Drama Society at the Edinburgh Fringe Festival.

the rationalisation of university medicine in London, and on how to make both ends meet in a time of financial crisis.

In February 1980 the report of the Flowers Working Party recommended that the Westminster Medical School should be closed, that the Institute of Basic Medical Science at the Royal College of Surgeons should cease to be part of the university, and that the remaining 32 separate establishments should be grouped into six Schools of Medicine and Dentistry. It proposed that one of these, to be called the Harvey School, should consist of the London Hospital Medical College and Dental School, St Bartholomew's Hospital Medical School, and the Institutes of Urology and Ophthalmology in association with Queen Mary College. It proposed an entry of 50 dental and 250 medical preclinical students, with an additional 10 clinicals from Oxford and Cambridge. Combined preclinical departments were seen to be necessary. New ones at Queen Mary College were thought to be ideal, but unlikely to come about in the near future and so it was recommended that they should be housed in extensions to the buildings erected by Barts in the 1930s in Charterhouse Square in the City.

Sir Alan Parks, PRCS.

Sir Desmond Pond, PRCPsych.

This new 'framework for medical education in London' created as hostile a reaction as that of the six schools proposed by the Royal Commission in 1968 - and considerably more panic as it became clear that the problems had not gone away in the intervening years, but were now more urgent and had been made worse by the decisions to rebuild Charing Cross and St George's Medical Schools to a considerably larger size in defiance of the Todd recommendations. Much debate, much publicised agonising and many negotiations took place before the Flowers Report and a modification of it prepared by the Medical Faculty reached the University Senate in the Autumn of 1980, only to be turned down by one vote.

Subsequent events, as they affected the London, were recorded by the Dean in the Gazette of 1981. 'The Senate's decision not to go ahead provided, of course, a wonderful opportunity to declare null and void the BLQ plan to build pre-clinical departments for the London and St Bartholomew's on the land at Queen

Mary College bought for the purpose 10 years ago. For a couple of days it looked as though all was lost, but the University's Joint Planning Committee was persuaded to ask the UGC if it still had capital for BLQ. The reply in effect was yes, but none immediately available to expand the St Bartholomew's preclinical departments in Charterhouse Square so as to accommodate ours. So BLQ stayed in the picture while a new profile for the reorganistion of medical education in London gradually took shape in the Senate House, without consultation with the schools but with reference to the outcome of a costing exercise (studying the staffing and annual costs of all the schools in the greatest possible detail.)

'The first hints of what kind of profile the Senate would be invited to consider reached the schools in mid-March 1981 via the press - including a proposal to reduce the St Bartholomew's/London entry from its present 250 preclinical medicals to 200, presumably so as to accommodate them all in Charterhouse Square, with the dental pre-clinicals going to Kings College in the Strand. This proposal was described in a number of newspapers as a recommendation 'to close the London'. It created a feeling of gloom and despondency, considerably deepened by the simultaneous announcement of Government cuts in University funding over the next three years which, taken in conjunction with new arrangements for overseas students, will necessitate a very serious alteration in staff-student ratios and inevitable redundancies in university staff.

By the evening of Friday 13th March, the London was experiencing in full measure what several other schools had experienced earlier in this long game of musical chairs - the discomfort of finding that the music had stopped and that we were left sharing a rather small seat in the wrong place, aggravated by uncertainty as to whether the music would start again. However by the following Monday the Governors had agreed a very factual statement of reasons why the BLQ concept was still immensely worth-while and this, thanks to a superhuman effort by the administrative staff of the College, was soon disseminated far and wide in time for the Senate's seminar discussion of the new profile, at which the need to look more closely into the pre-clinical possibilities in East London was accepted. A week later the Senate agreed that a separate enquiry should be made into the comparative running costs of a joint St Bartholomew's/London preclinical school for about 200 medicals at Queen Mary College (which it described as academically the most desirable situation) or Charterhouse Square.'

iv

The enquiry was conducted by a Working Party chaired by Professor L C B Gower, former Vice-Chancellor of Southampton. It consisted of Sir Kenneth Berrill, former chairman of the UGC, Sir John Butterfield, Regius Professor of Physic at Cambridge, Sir James Menter, Principal of QMC, Professor R W Sykes, Vice-Principal, the Deans and Deans-Elect of the two medical colleges. Peat, Marwick, Mitchell & Co were employed as accountants and Messrs Cluttons as chartered surveyors. The report was published in June 1981 and showed that the running costs of a single new preclinical building at QMC would be approximately the same as those of the several separate buildings in Charterhouse Square when extended to take 200 medical and 50 dental students. Both would be some £150,000 per annum cheaper than maintaining the existing two pre-clinical schools.

Meanwhile as the enquiry was being made and another Working Party was considering the future of Dentistry (eventually concluding that the Royal Dental School should be closed but the London's Dental School maintained in its entirety) the University decided that the future framework of medical and dental education in London should consist of eight, not six schools: University College and the Middlesex, the London and Barts, a reunion of St Thomas's and Guy's, the merging of Charing Cross and the Westminster, King's College and Hospital, St George's, the Royal Free and St Mary's.

In November 1980 the Senate decided that each pair of schools destined to form one of the four new large institutions should begin by establishing a Consortium with an independent Chairman and two members of Senate. Each Consortium would then proceed towards a single budget and academic board at whatever speed it found appropriate. So far as the London and Barts were concerned this meant replacing the Joint Policy Committee under which they and Queen Mary had worked together for 10 years with a looser kind of consortium lacking QMC.

The London's official response not only stated its plea for continuing the old system but accurately forecast what the abandonment of it would bring: 'We feel very strongly that arbitrary abandonment of the existing mechanism for joint development would inevitably seriously undermine the credibility of any new one. It would be different if we had not been engaged in "twinning", but we have, and we have loyally abided by the required mechanism for it, and in doing so the Colleges have built up that trust in each other on which not only past but all future success in joint development must depend. Unfortunately St Bartholomew's have declined to attend the Joint Policy Committee and consequently our agreed system of collaboration, which has hitherto worked so well, has ceased to function at the very time the University is asking us to consider changes in it. It is a sad irony that the only two medical schools who have consistently and successfully responded to the University's policy of rationalisation since 1968, have now been halted by the Senate's decision to leave that process to whatever willingness may at this time motivate individual schools.'

The other schools involved in pairing showed unexpected willingness to proceed at speed. Charing Cross and the Westminster merged, University College and the Middlesex got together to plan a combined school, and St Thomas's and Guy's recreated the United School they had previously been. But the London and Barts, which in the seventies had developed so much together (not only in Joint Academic Units, but in joint appointments in subjects like Clinical Pharmacology and Psychiatry, in which each had separate chairs, and by collaborative teaching and research without joint appointments of any kind in fields such as Haematology and Rheumatology) now became separated by the issue of where the future teaching of preclinical subjects should take place.

V

The change in relationships was quickly followed by changes in personnel. In September 1981 the Deans of both Colleges retired. At the London the description of the Dean's departure recorded in the Gazette by Martin Goodman, Student President, shows that no matter what the 1980s might bring, the students remained in good heart and equal to every occasion:

'The College building was resplendent with palm trees, ornamental fountains and coloured lighting; the library was festooned with blue and white streamers. After the formal farewells from the College the students had an hour and a half to say their own special goodbye. Beginning with a slightly fanciful interpretation of the hospital's history and Sir John's part in it (had he really clerked in the Elephant Man ?), it progressed with the Rowing Club's version of the Eton Boating Song and ended with a spirited performance of the

The Can-Can Girls of 1981 bid farewell to the Dean.

Can-Can. To be precise, three performances of the Can-Can. It was a most happy evening ending with the presentation of an engraved decanter and a greenhouse' (38). The retiring Dean was told it was up to him to choose in which to keep the gin.

Professor David Ritchie was seen into office by Miss Reynolds, staying on in the interest of continuity until her own retirement after 37 years as Assistant to the Dean. The four Deans with whom she had worked attended the farewell party of one 'who has nearly always been first in and last out of the College every day, who now sometimes says "if you don't mind I don't think I'll come in on Sunday..." who can convince anyone that it is considerably easier to make a lasting peace in Northern Ireland than it is find the Dean, and who with a single glance can quell anyone from a revolting student, or a protesting professor, to Hugh Laird under way with a full head of steam' (37). An outstanding example of a most gentle person maintaining and exacting the highest standard of service to an institution.

Another equally devoted and efficient servant of the College, Miss Wise, Assistant to the College Secretary, retired soon after, and at the end of a year Professor

H D Ritchie, Professor of Surgery, Dean 1981-1983.

Ritchie asked for three months leave and then resigned. The chairman of the Academic Board, Professor Michael Floyer, took over as Acting Dean until appointed to the post in April 1983 with all its many problems soon compounded by the resignation of James Walmsley, the Secretary who had so ably filled he gap left by Hugh Laird and wrestled so effectively with all the enquiries and negotiations concerning BLQ. David Edwards came from the RAF to find a College preparing to celebrate its Bicentenary and at he same time striving to secure its future. Other changes included the retirement of Tony Jackson after 3 years as Postgraduate Sub-Dean and the succession of Professors R D Cohen, W Keatinge, S I Cohen and Gedis Grudzinskas to the chairs of Medicine, Physiology, Psychiatry and Obstetrics respectively.

A reduction of some 7% of its total staff over three years enabled the College to keep in line with its falling income and achieve a reasonably balanced budget. But or many months in 1982 industrial action reduced the Hospital's bed occupancy to 80%. Nonetheless, Michael Floyer was able to report in the Gazette of 983:

The Arthritis and Rheumatism Council has given us nearly half a million pounds to endow permanently a Chair of Rheumatology. Thanks to John Blandy, Grand Metropolitan have given us a similar sum to endow a Readership in Oncology in memory of Sir Maxwell Joseph... a grant from the Regional Health Authority has enabled us to appoint two local GPs as part-time Senior Lecturer and Lecturer. In addition Barts and ourselves have succeeded in obtaining one of two UGC £80,000 per annum awards to enable us to set up a Joint Department of General Practice.'

At the same time research was flourishing as never before in academic units at long last properly accommodated in the new Alexandra Wing and in the newly opened Gastroenterological Research Building provided by a donation of a million pounds from the Wingate Hyams Trust at the suggestion of David Ritchie. Further development in research came with the appointment of Newell Johnson, Professor of Oral Pathology, to be Director of an MRC Dental Research Unit in Whitechapel and Professor of Dental Sciences at the Royal College of Surgeons. The new accommodation for academic units also freed space for the research activites of hospital staff, many of whom, like Sir Alan Parks PRCS, had hitherto been conducting their research under great difficulties.

The Dean was able to report also: 'The fifteen year old

Professor M A Floyer, Dean 1983-1986.

dances, the pas de deux with Barts and the pas de trois with BLQ continue as before, but the tempo of the music increases, with occasional trumpet blasts from UGC and from London University. In December 1982 the Colleges applied to the UGC for a grant to enable them to build a pre-clinical school at QMC to house the medical and dental departments from the London and Barts together with a few Joint Clinical Departments. A committee from the three Colleges has been set up under Sir Frederick Dainton in order to plan the project. It is called the City and East London Medical Education Group or CELMEG (a good name for a breakfast cereal?) for short. Although the London and Queen Mary remain wholehearted about the venture, Barts are still uncertain.'

By 1984 it was possible to report that detailed plans had gone to the University for transmission to the UGC (as indeed they had done in 1974) and that CELMEG had formed a 'Working Party to discuss the complicated question of governance of the combined London/Barts medical school and its relationship to Queen Mary College. The Chairman is Professor Allott, representative on CELMEG of the Barts Council of Governors. He is Professor of African Law in the University Department of African and Oriental Studies; many have commented on the aptness of such an appointment to harness the tribal loyalties of two medical schools with long traditions.'

Of the different options put to it, including conversion of existing parts of QMC, the UGC finally chose that which had first been put in the early seventies, a new building on the boundary of Mile End Hospital and Queen Mary College.

'Much time,' reported the Dean in the Gazette of 1985, 'has been spent in drawing up a project definition for this. In addition we have had to make an investment appraisal showing the revenue savings to be made by the use of this building in place of the pre-clinical schools here and at Barts. These have recently been submitted to the UGC by the University and we still await a decision by the UGC and the Treasury in allowing us the capital to start building.'

It took longer, however, for the Gazette to be printed than for the UGC and the Treasury to reach a decision. In June 1985 the University was informed that the UGC was able and willing to pay for a new pre-clinical building between Queen Mary Hospital and the Mile End branch of the London Hospital to accommodate 200 medical and 50 dental students. It would include facilities for academic clinical units in conjunction with a post-graduate medical centre to be built by the NHS. (The units originally suggested by the Colleges were General Practice, Gerontology, Clinical Epidemiology and Obstetrics). There would be money also for associated developments in Queen Mary College.

So almost at the end of its first 200 years the London Hospital Medical College learned that it could go forward into the future as well situated for medical and dental education in the 21st century and beyond, as it had been when it opened in 1785 or at any time since. Eighteen years and two months had passed since the Royal Commission had first recommended that Barts, the London and Queen Mary College should join forces to create a medical school of a size and kind appropriate to the 21st century, with facilities for basic medical sciences in a multifaculty college next to a hospital at the centre of an area containing a resident population of more than adequate size and immense variety.

In the seventeen years since the University and the UGC had jointly approved the proposal it had been studied again in depth not only by the Flowers Working Party but, both before and after, by the Colleges, the Medical Faculty, the Joint Planning Committee and the Senate - and on every occasion approved as academically ideal. Every possible variant of the necessary building had been painstakingly explored and costed in capital and revenue terms before finally an option had been put forward by the three Colleges and approved by the University which could fulfill the academic ideal and create revenue savings at a capital cost the country was willing and able to meet. Few developments of its kind can ever have been subjected to such scrutiny by so many for so long as BLQ. No concept that was not inherently right could have survived such testing.

vi

Probably no better opportunity than BLQ for providing a medical and dental school with all it will require in the future is to be found in London, or anywhere. The population of the three East End Boroughs requires a network of hospitals which also serve an equal number from further afield. Hospital and community services together necessitate a full range of departments which, supported by academic staff, can meet not only all the needs of basic medical and dental education but also hose opportunities for students to study subjects of heir own choice in greater depth on which the levelopment of independent judgement and critical awareness depends. At the centre of this network providing services and teaching facilities is a large multifaculty College.

The relative merits of teaching basic medical science in he context of a medical as opposed to multifaculty nstitution can be debated endlessly but there is no lenying that the ideal situation is where departments of basic medical science adjoin both those of other aculties and a hospital - and the least satisfactory rrangement is where a preclinical school is separated rom both. The issue is not merely one of the need for medical and dental students to mix with others, nor ven of the need (great though it is) for contact between medical and other staff at the teaching and esearch level. It is that if doctors and dentists are to be ducated as well as trained then undergraduate medical and dental) education must be fundamentally a university function rather than a vocational training with a degree at the end of it. It is immensely helpful therefore if it can begin in a university.

The situation at Queen Mary College is unusual. It has oom for a basic medical science building (big enough o house departments large enough to maintain excellence) adjoining both the College and a hospital. It will enable students to begin their studies in a university atmosphere but with the opportunity for contact from the first day onwards with the kind of patients who can help them most. The days have long since gone when patients needed the help of first year students and it is to be hoped they will never return. The acutely ill of today are no longer so numerous as they were. They are most helpful to and can be helped by senior students but few can be expected or allowed to contribute to those just starting. Students in their first year or two will be helped most by, and can give most help to, patients with the chronic disorders so common today and those in geriatric wards who welcome interest, have a plethora of abnormal physical signs, long and instructive histories to relate and too much time on their hands. The Mile End branch of the London Hospital (in addition to other functions) cares and will continue to care, for large numbers of such patients.

But the teaching of basic medical science and its relationship to clinical teaching is but one part of medical and dental education. Other aspects raise problems that are equally important and sometimes more difficult to solve. One is that no single curriculum can now prove equally satisfactory for all students so that after a common core a variety of options and

St Katherine's Dock in the 1980's.

alternatives is needed, especially in those parts of the course aimed at intellectual development. Granted a wide range of staff such opportunities can be provided without much difficulty but effective use of them depends on an efficient tutorial system whereby students become known as individuals, their varying needs are assessed and they are helped to take those courses most appropriate to them.

The larger the school the wider the range of staff and the more varied the options - but the more difficult it is to care adequately for as many as 200 students per annum as individuals. Years ago, however, St Bartholomew's showed, by its Collegiate Establishment under Sir James Paget, how to apply in London the system by which Colleges at Oxford and Cambridge monitor the progress of their students and enable them to make best use of the various courses provided by the University. Precisely the same educational function can be provided in London now by the old Hospital Medical Schools, each already equipped with the necessary educational and recreational facilities. Originally providing the entire course, they now provide a home base for students whose courses take them to many other places. All that is needed is to appoint some of the many teachers as Fellows. Each School or College will then have tutors who can not only fulfill a vital educational function (in addition to whatever duties they have in a university or NHS department) but in the process preserve the School's identity for the annual entry of a hundred or so students for which it is responsible, and pass on that tradition of service which has continued unbroken in the hospitals for centuries and is so important to the upbringing of doctors and dentists. The larger London schools can gain all the advantages of size without becoming impersonal.

Medical and dental students, however, have to do more than learn about medicine or dentistry and how to use their minds effectively. Their long university course coincides with a most formative period of personal development. But the more they lack responsibilities to patients, the more they are cut off from the working world around them and live in a world of their own. This can be fun but preparing for a lifetime of responsibility to a community is not helped by isolation from the one in which their undergraduate course is given. They need and usually want to be part of it, belong to it and learn from it those aspects of life which cannot be learned by residence in a hostel, valuable though some experience of that can be. Some communities, however, are easier to join than others

Other docks offer other pleasures.

and some have less than others to give. The suprem
good fortune of the Colleges of East London is th
their students can so easily join one of the most, if n
the most, stimulating and exciting communities in th
country. Maybe the City of London will be prett
much the same in 2050 as it was in 1950 - infarcted b
day and silent by night - and no doubt it is in th
national interest that it should. But Tower Hamlet
Hackney and Newham are always changing, vibran
full of vitality and enterprise, each successive infusio
of new blood successfully surmounting whatev
adversities it finds, perpetuating the irrepressible spir
of the East End.

vi

To the London Hospital Medical College the new
that a new basic medical science building for BL
could and would be provided at Queen Mary's came a
a fitting climax to the end of its first 200 years. Suc
opposition to it as some preclinical teachers had felt i
1968 had long since faded as they saw that, apart fro
its intrinsic merits, it was the only way to maintai

Queen Mary College seen from Mile End Park. The Regent's Canal runs in front of the Lock-keeper's cottage.

strong preclinical departments - other than by combining those of Barts and the London in Charterhouse Square, sequestrated from both clinicians and other university departments. Through the seventies BLQ was for the London the light at the end of the tunnel. In the eighties it was a beacon of hope shining amidst the encircling gloom.

Queen Mary College (celebrating its first centenary) looked forward eagerly to the advantages of closer contact between medicine and its other Faculties. At St Bartholomew's, however, conflict between a vision of promise for the 21st century on the one hand and contentment with current conditions on the other, had always led many, including some of those cloistered in Charterhouse Square, to regard BLQ as good men often see good things - Lord give me chastity, but not just yet. The brighter the light at the end of the tunnel the less welcoming it seemed. The news that the end of the tunnel had been reached brought more reaction than rejoicing and in October 1985 the College announced that while prepared still to combine its clinical school with the London it did not wish to move its pre-clinical departments to Queen Mary's.

Two possibilities remain: either the three Colleges will combine as planned despite the current reluctance of one of them or, alternatively, the London and Queen Mary College alone will combine to provide preclinical teaching for an entry of 200 medical and 50 dental students who will go to clinical courses provided by the London, or by the London and Barts. The first alternative is that which the London and Queen Mary's much prefer but they have been asked if they are willing to implement the second and have formally stated that they are.

Either way therefore the London Hospital Medical College is assured of going forward true to its tradition and still on the same course laid down by Blizard when he appealed for funds with which to build a school in which 'proper and effectual methods' could be adopted 'for the education of young persons who are to practice Physic and Surgery' so as to 'contribute to the good and happyness of mankind'. The College was started to improve medical education. In 1785 the best way of doing so was to create a hospital medical school but its tradition has been to search always for more effectual methods or to adapt the old to changes in society and the advance of medicine to which it has itself contributed so much. The hospital school was a means to an end, not an end in itself. The College has never stood still and seldom if ever been satisfied for long with what it had to offer. It has been shaped and reshaped over the years by successive generations of teachers devoted not merely to the College but to Blizard's ideal of service, the advance of medicine and the improvement of education.

The story of the College is the story of the same tradition being maintained over two centuries but translated time after time into terms more appropriate to the present. Blizard's 'let your search be after truth' and his example of service and humanity; Billing initiating clinical teaching and Davies introducing the stethoscope and the elicitation of physical signs; Pereira bringing order to Pharmacology: John Little defining the College in 1854 as 'a complete medical school in connection with a hospital upon the model of the medical faculty of an University': Walter Rivington in 1879 deploring 'the diffusion of the teaching function' in London, pleading for a teaching University which could establish up to three strong schools of basic medical science, and arguing the need for salaried posts in which professors could concentrate on patient care, teaching and research because 'by concentration alone can excellence be obtained': Jonathan Hutchinson developing postgraduate medical education and asking to be described on his tombstone as 'a man of hope and forward-looking mind': Hughlings Jackson forwarding Neurology and James Mackenzie Cardiology, ushering in an age of serving physicians and surgeons advancing one speciality after another: Souttar's innovative Surgery and Turnbull's rigorous insistence on absolute accuracy in every pathological investigation: Arthur Ellis using the Medical Unit to bring on a generation of academic physicians imbued with a sense of service: Dawson pioneering the Health Service: Donald Hunter, the beloved physician, bringing preventive medicine to life: Clark-Kennedy teaching and practising holistic medicine and advocating the closer union of the London and Queen Mary College: Clifford Wilson indomitably keeping the university ideal alive in the 1950s and 1960s when for the first time the hospital was tempted to look backwards instead of forwards: Geoffrey Slack and his colleagues changing a school of empirical Dentistry into one in which students are trained while receiving a university education.

All at their different times sought 'proper and effectual methods' to educate young persons to practice Physic and Surgery so as to contribute 'to the good and happyness of mankind.' The ideal fired each with the personal magnetism that enabled them to succeed. None left the College as he found it and each step forward moved it closer to that union of hospital and

The Alexandra Wing from the Whitechapel Road.

The College in 1985, Alexandra Wing beyond.

university, in a community served by both, which the next step will at last complete.

All faced great difficulties, in finding the necessary funds, in getting the buildings and facilities essential in their time, and in achieving the right balance between service and education, and the research and development indispensable to both. The future will be no easier. Less money and fewer academic posts will increase the temptation to place research before service and education in selecting teachers. Ending the total reliance on state funds which has impeded progress in the recent past will see a return to the days when the College set out to get for itself that which a hard-pressed state cannot provide. Yet the greater ease with which funds can be found for research than for education or service may, as has happened in other countries, threaten the delicate balance that has to be maintained between the three elements of that essential trinity.

Fortunately the College has had the wisdom to mark its Bicentenary not with an appeal to support one or other of the three but for a library to support them all. Nothing could be more appropriate and nothing is needed more. The library opened by the Prince of Wales 100 years ago cannot meet the needs of all the undergraduate and postgraduate students of medicine, dentistry and the other health professions, nor those of their teachers, nor of the medical and other staff on whose care and research the 'good and happyness' of those they serve depends. Conversion of St Augustine's Church, standing empty and deconsecrated next door, provides an ideal answer to the most pressing need of the College as it starts its third century.

Further additions to the Whitechapel Road.

The church and the crypt below it will make an unusually fine as well as a very beautiful library, and in addition will preserve for posterity more than an exceptional building. Every bay, shelf, journal stand, table and chair can commemorate some individual or event from the College's past, the thanks of those grateful to it, or the support of those who wish to forward its functions of service to patients, research and education. Fitting out a new library offers unlimited opportunities to contribute to any activity in medicine, to provide permanent reminders of the links forged between the College and the countries from which its students came or to which they went, and even to record the names of those who enjoyed winning the rugby cup.

So the College ended its first two hundred years, as it had begun them, with an appeal for a building in which to improve medical education - but this time not in the green fields of Whitechapel, nor as on later occasions in the seething squalor of overcrowded dockland, nor in the midst of inner city decay, but in a new Tower Hamlets alive with new industries and business ventures, new housing developments of every kind and new systems of transport and communications, but still with the same vigour, enterprise and irrepressible spirit. The College too was both different and yet the same - old and new buildings on a campus in which gardens and terraces have replaced some but not all of the little streets which open on to the Whitechapel Road thronged as always with people of every race, creed and colour - crowding the market stalls and checking the time by the Hospital Clock. To show that its spirit remained unchanged students celebrated Bicentenary Year by bringing home, for the second year running, the University Gold Medal and by winning the rugby cup, the interhospitals cricket, hockey, judo and waterpolo cups, and the University association football cup.

The new Library.

The Whitechapel Road thronged as always with people of every race, creed and colour — crowding the market stalls, and checking the time by the Hospital Clock.

Celebrating Bicentenary Year.

The first to respond to the Appeal was Archie Clark-Kennedy. He wrote also to **Anthea McEwan,** splendid organiser of the Bicentenary Dinner of the Medical and Dental Clubs: 'You wont remember me but I was once the Dean and I want a ticket'. He wrote too to the Gazette:

'One last word before I say my goodbye. May I in my extreme old age venture to appeal to everybody, both old and new Londoners, to rally to the London in our Bicentenary week, not only to honour our history and meet one another, but in a concerted effort to enhance our public image in order to gain benefactors in these hard and difficult times.'

When the Bicentenary came in October 1985 Archie Clark-Kennedy was not present because in September, as he had himself written of William Blizard: 'death came to him quietly in the ninety-third year of his age'. But from all around the world Londoners rallied to the College, filled St Paul's for a service of thanksgiving and rededication and attended the Bicentenary Dinner at Grosvenor House to 'hail the return of the auspicious day' on which England's first medical school was opened. Samuel Arnold's music for Blizard's Ode, performed at the Albion in 1785, could not be found but Rule Brittania and Land of Hope and Glory were sung to the band of the Royal Marines by two thousand seven hundred Londoners in honour of a College handed down to them by a long line of predecessors and held in trust for the future.

The toast is — "the immortal memory of William Blizard, our founders and benefactors".

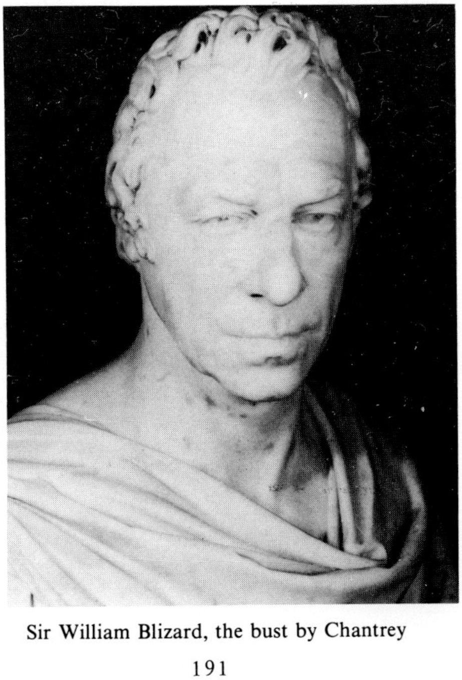
Sir William Blizard, the bust by Chantrey

ACKNOWLEDGEMENTS

With the exception of those listed below the illustrations in this book are from London Hospital or LHMC sources. Most grateful thanks are due to the Photographic Departments of the Hospital and College, especially to Ray Ruddick, Patricia Burgess and Ian Berle who completed the arduous tasks of reproducing documents, drawings and photographs, many of which have been taken from past issues of the London Hospital Gazette. Most of the illustrations of the College in the nineteen-fifties are from a photographic record of every event in the College year, which I commissioned when Sub-Dean and which was superbly made by Tony Hicklin and friends. A selection of pictures from it now hangs on the staircase of the Clubs Union Building.

The Blandy drawings of the early fifties were made when he was a student. Those of members of the College staff in the seventies and eighties have been gleaned from his agenda papers of the Academic Board and other committees. Regrettably it has been possible to include only a token few of the rich store of remarkable and revealing likenesses which may well prove to be the most rewarding outcome of many lengthy meetings.

The excerpt from the Appeal by Blizard and Maddocks, and William Clift's drawing of Blizard are reproduced by permission of the Trustees of the British Museum — and 'The Doctor' by permission of the Trustees of the Tate Gallery. Queen Victoria's arrival at the London in 1876 and the drawings of the College and the Library in 1887 are reproduced with permission from the Illustrated London News. The portraits of Maddocks, Pereira, Little, Andrew Clark, Hughlings Jackson, Robert Hutchison and Bertrand Dawson are included by courtesy of the Royal College of Physicians of London. The drawing of Bethnal Green in 1773 is reproduced by permission of the Borough of Tower Hamlets and the pictures of Queen Mary College with permission of the College from its centenary publication 'From Palace to College' by G P Moss and M V Saville.

The extracts from the memoirs of Redcliffe Nathan Salaman are reproduced by kind permission of his executors, Myer and Raphael Salaman.

Kitty Blandy drew the Bicentenary version of the College crest which appears on the front cover.

BIBLIOGRAPHY

The most important sources of detailed information on the London Hospital Medical College are the minutes of the Body of Associated Teachers and its successors the Medical Council of the London Medical School. These cover the period 1846 to 1876. The College Board minutes run from 1876 to 1948 and the minutes of the Council of Governors, its Standing Committee and the Academic Board cover the period 1948 to 1985.

Hospital records, the minutes of the House Committee and Court of the Governors of the London Hospital exist from 1740 onwards up to the start of the Board of Governors in 1948, followed by the District Health Authority from 1974. References to the school however are limited until the Hospital's official recognition of its existence in 1837.

The College Prospectus provides much information from 1894 onwards. A prospectus was published prior to 1868 but copies have not survived.

No one, of course, can read or write of the College without reference to A E Clark-Kennedy's two volume history of 'The London' or the abbreviated version 'London Pride'.

1. Newman, Charles (1957) The Evolution of Medical Education in the Nineteenth Century. Oxford University Press.
2. O'Malley, C D (1970) The History of Medical Education. University of California Press. Los Angeles.
3. Davies, Richard (1759) The General state of the Universities. Bath.
4. Gillman, J (1838) The life of Samuel Taylor Coleridge.
5. Bulloch, W (1933) Roll of the members of the Staff of the London Hospital from its foundation. In possession of the London Hospital Medical College Library.
6. Cooke, J (1835) A Brief Memoir of Sir William Blizard. Longman, Rees, Orme, Browne.
7. Clark-Kennedy, A E (1962) The London. Vol 1., Pitman Medical Publishing Co Ltd.
8. Munk, William (1878) The Roll of the Royal College of Physicians of London. London.
9. Hutchinson, Jonathan Jr. (1895) Sir William Blizard. London Hospital Gazette 1, 85.
10. Clippendale, S D (1912) Some early members of the Hospital Staff. London Hospital Gazette 19, 168.
11. Medical Circular (1852) i, 243.
12. Humble, J G & Hansell, P (1974) Westminster Hospital 1716-1974. Pitman Medical.
13. Hunter, W (1914) Historical Account of Charing Cross Hospital and Medical School. John Murray. London.
14. Medvei, V C & Thornton, J L (1974) The Royal Hospital of St Bartholomew 1123-1973. London.
15. Paget, Stephen (1903) Memoirs and Letters of Sir James Paget. London.
16. Rivington, W (1879) The Medical Profession. Dublin.
17. Byers, John (1913) Obituary of Jonathan Hutchinson. British Medical Journal, June 28, 1401.
18. Treves, Frederick (1913) Sir Jonathan Hutchinson as a teacher. London Hospital Gazette 20,
19. Treves, Frederick (1923) The Elephant Man and other reminiscences. Cassell, London.
20. Salaman, Redcliffe Nathan (0000) Personal Memoirs.
21. King, Ambrose J (1975) Fifty years at the London. London Hospital Gazette 77, (5) 13
22. May, H B (1975) Phoenix. London Hospital Gazette 77, (5) 4
23. Report of Interdepartmental Committee on Medical Schools (1944) (Goodenough Report). HM Stationery Office, London.
24. Percival, R C (1975) Sport within the Clubs Union. London Hospital Gazette 77, (5) 21
25. Bomford, R R (1978) Students and Housemen in the Thirties. London Hospital Gazette, (Medical Club Issue) 3, 29.
26. Clark-Kennedy, A E (1939) Dean's Report: Prize-Giving. London Hospital Gazette 42,

27. Broadley, Margaret (1980) Patients come first. The London Hospital Special Trustees.
28. The Dragon (1913) London Hospital Gazette 19, (4).
29. University Grants Committee (1967) University Development 1962-1967. HM Stationery Office Cmnd 3820.
30. Survey of Medical Students in 1966 (1968) Report of Royal Commission on Medical Education, Appendix 19. HM Stationery Office, London Cmnd 3569.
31. Report of Royal Commission on Medical Education (Todd Report). HM Stationery Office, London Cmnd 3569.
32. Hutton, P W; Williams, P O; Graves, J C & Graves, V (1964) The Pre-registration house appointment. Lancet 1,38.
33. Editorial, 'London' (1969). British Journal o Medical Education 3,2.
34. Jackson, A D M (1966) A survey of paediatri teaching in the undergraduate schools of th United Kingdom. British Journal of Medica Education 1, 25.
35. Ellis, J R (1978) Hugh Laird. Londo Hospital Gazette (Medical Club Issue) 3, 11
36. The year at the London (1978) Londo Hospital Gazette (Medical Club Issue) 3, 9.
37. The year at the London (1981) Londo Hospital Gazette (Medical & Dental Club Issue) 6, 4.
38. Goodman, M (1982) The Clubs Union 1981/ London Hospital Gazette (Medical & Denta Clubs Issue) 7, 12.

The seal made by John Ellicott for the London Hospital and adopted as the crest of the Medical College

INDEX